LANCHESTER LIBRARY

3 8001 00243 3930

£1750

S T E P P I N G L E F T

D1609761

Ellen Graff

STEPPING

Dance and Politics in New York City, 1928–1942

LEFT

DUKE UNIVERSITY PRESS *Durham and London 1997*

P0 02017
9/7/98

© 1997 Duke University Press
All rights reserved
Printed in the United States of America on acid-free paper
Typeset in Berkeley Medium by Tseng Information Systems, Inc.
Library of Congress Cataloging-in-Publication Data appear
on the last printed page of this book.

Coventry University

For my parents
Virginia Ackerley Graff
and Sherman Graff

C O N T E N T S

Acknowledgments

Perhaps any act of writing involves a dance with one's past. My mother Virginia A. Graff had a keen sense of moral justice. The socialist vision which she embraced was increasingly unpopular during the era in which I grew up, but nevertheless influenced me. My father, who shared this political vision, believed firmly that things of the spirit could be set into words. Fé Alf, the German modern dancer who lived next door to me as I was growing up, taught me to dance and led me to an understanding of what movement could mean. How, I now ask myself, could I have written on any other subject but dance and politics.

I owe my gratitude to many. First, and most important, the dancers themselves, whose efforts and talents and passions are the subject of this book. Edith Segal, Edna Ocko, Sophie Maslow, and Jane Dudley gave generously of their time and memories in interviews with me. Dancers Fanya Geltman, Nadia Chilkovsky, Paula Bass, Mura Dehn, Sue Remos Nadel, Lili Mann Laub, Anne Lief Barlin, and other WPA workers shared their histories with Karen Wickre as part of the Research Center for the Federal Theatre Project, and I am indebted to them and to Karen Wickre who conducted the interviews. Pauline Bubrick Tish, a dancer in the original *How Long Brethren?*, generously shared her own research with me. My memory of performances by dancers Muriel Manings, Donald McKayle, Pearl Primus, and other members of the New Dance Group in fluenced the writing of this book and to them I also owe thanks.

Colleagues and relatives of the dancers represented in this book were generous in sharing information and in helping me to obtain personal records; Shari Segel Goldberg gave me access to files and photographs of Edith Segal, and Daniel and Zachery Sklar contributed photographs and memories of the work of their mother, Miriam Blecher. I owe thanks to Frances Sosnoff and Emanuel Geltman, who encouraged my first research efforts by showing me how widespread involvement with the left-ist community had been, and how many of the lives that surrounded me in my Upper West Side community had been touched by the movement of the thirties. I happened to speak with Frances one day while waiting for a bus on the Upper West Side. She kindly asked me about my work and I shared with her my obsession with what I believed to be an obscure area in dance history. Oh, she said, you should talk to my sister-in-law. She was part of the WPA project. Her sister-in-law is Fanya Geltman, a principal in these pages. Manny Geltman was a founding editor of the political journal *Dissent*.

The influence of my dance teachers, first Fé Alf, later Gertrude Shurr, May O'Donnell, and Martha Graham, is written on my body as well as on my soul. They taught me that movement is a spiritual commitment and I believe this still. To colleagues who first showed me how dance and scholarship could be combined, most especially Cynthia Novack and Deborah Jowitt (who also read this manuscript in its earliest form and offered invaluable comments), I am deeply indebted. Janet Soares always provided a supportive and critical ear as well as endless ideas and a willingness to share her myriad connections. I probably can never thank Marcia B. Siegel, my adviser, enough; she read the very first drafts, provided generous commentary, and believed in me and this project long before I did. Thanks to Rachel Toor, of Duke University Press, for her encouragement, and to all the editors who have helped guide this project to fruition, including Pam Morrison, Bob Mirandon, and Barbara Palfy.

Barnard College provided me with a special leave to finish this project, for which I am deeply grateful. To Sandra Genter and the Barnard College Dance Department I owe thanks for creating an atmosphere in which dance and scholarship could flourish. I am likewise grateful to those students who listened to my lectures about the thirties and asked pointed questions, always sending me back to the drawing board, including Rachel Feinerman, Dillon Paul, Rachel Ebling, and Peter Von Ehrenkrook. Thanks to colleagues at the Department of Performance Studies at New York University, where, as graduate students in dance, we struggled to bridge the seemingly impossible gap between body and intellect, between performance and academe, especially those members of the Fem Grrrr (Feminist Group): Ann Cooper Albright, Judy Burns, Ann Daly, Leslie Satin, and Carol Martin.

Friends and associates have read and commented on portions of this manuscript at various times; I am most especially indebted to Susan Manning. Thanks also to Judith Bennahum, Lynn Garafola, and the editors of *Studies in Dance History* for their support and also to all those who made possible the June 1993 conference in New York City, "Dancing Of, By, and For the People." The scholarship of others working in the field, including John Perpener, Russell Gold, and Barbara Stratyner, was both informative and stimulating. I particularly thank Stacey Prickett for generously sharing her writing and research with me.

Librarians at the Dance Collection of the New York Public Library for the Performing Arts were always helpful, especially Monica Moseley and Rita Waldron. I am grateful to Karen Powell, Walter Zvonchenko, and Vicky Wolff at the Library of Congress for their help and to the staff of the Tamiment Library. Tim Wheeler of the *People's World Weekly* was generous in providing access to the photographic archives of the *Daily Worker.*

Thanks to Nancy Stevens for invaluable advice about the photographs, and to her parents Nat and Irene, who like my own family were fellow travelers in the world I grew up in, and whose vision helped shape my own.

Finally, and most important, thanks to Frederic Kimball, who read and commented on various drafts, contributing his keen writer's ear and his understanding of American history, to a project which was otherwise unfamiliar to him, and to my children Harry and Camila for their patience and understanding.

Portions of chapters 1, 2, and 5 appeared in "Dancing Red," *Of, By, and For the People: Dancing on the Left in the 1930s, Studies in Dance History,* 5, no. 1 (1994).

O N E

The Dance Is a Weapon

Prologue

When I was cleaning out my mother's apartment I came across a program she had saved from the Inwood chapter of the Peoples Culture Union of America. It was one of my first public appearances. Staged in 1949, just before the full force of McCarthyism compelled all the old-line Communists and fellow travelers to drop out of sight and keep their politics to themselves, this "cooperative" was almost certainly a remnant of the Communist Party's cultural program that had flourished in New York City during the 1930s.

The community of Inwood lies at the northern tip of Manhattan, beyond the Cloisters and the gardens of Fort Tryon Park, in an area bounded by the Harlem River to the north and east and by Dyckman Street on the south. In those days it was a working-class community—half Irish Catholic and half German Jewish immigrants, with the occasional bohemian family thrown in. Mr. and Mrs. Kamarck, who lived just down the street from us, ran the Inwood chapter of the Peoples Culture Union. Mrs. Kamarck was overweight and gave piano lessons in her cramped three-room apartment. On warm spring days she used to take neighborhood children across the street to the park to make crepe-paper flowers. In the wildness of Inwood Hill Park I played make-believe games with her daughter, who was a year or so younger than me. Mr. Kamarck was a printer. He and his wife probably were Communists.

My father was also a printer. He belonged to the International Typographical Union, a militant trade union that was home to many radicals, and he was a member of the Communist-sponsored writers' club Pen and Hammer. Among other memorabilia I encountered as I went through my mother's file cabinet were some articles my father wrote for the *News-*

1. Breadlines in New York City. "Unemployed at the New York Municipal Lodging House during the depression in 1930." (UPI/Bettmann)

paper of the Printing Trades Union and for the *New Masses*. A piece he wrote about the International Typographical Union was published under his pseudonym, George Sherman, since the Party wanted to create a cloud of mystery around those involved in its activities. My mother had a pseudonym as well; Virginia Ackerley (her maiden name) became Alice Vaughn when she was taking part in Party activities. I remember seeing copies of the Communist newspaper the *Daily Worker* in our home, and I would not be surprised to learn that my family sold copies.

I do not think that my parents actually joined the Communist Party, although perhaps in the 1950s, when I was growing up, they would not have told me even if they had. Instead, they were fellow travelers, sympathetic to the Party's goals. Looking around the streets of New York in the 1930s, they would have seen breadlines, Hoovervilles, "Hard Luck" towns, and squatters living in Central Park (figures 1–3). The Party promised social and economic justice, and the Soviet Union, which they visited in 1930 for their honeymoon, was the bold new state lighting the way. "From each according to his ability, to each according to his needs" was a refrain that echoed throughout my childhood.

Idealism and deeply held convictions animated efforts by my parents and many others during the turbulent thirties. They wanted to make a better world, and for some years, I think, they felt that they could help bring that about. The choreographic efforts of a group of New York City dancers who shared the same vision are the subject of this book. While some of them were Communists and some were not, each was driven by a kind of moral fervor to respond to the complex social and political issues surrounding them.

In the midst of the Great Depression the United States underwent a period of economic and political upheaval. President Franklin D. Roosevelt spoke movingly about "the forgotten man" and introduced New Deal legislation to ease economic hardship, while demagogues such as Huey P. Long called for plans to "soak the rich." The Communist Party, USA, enjoyed its most influential decade during the 1930s.

In New York City on March 6, 1930, the Party led a crowd of between 35,000 and 100,000 workers—depending on which press accounts you believed—in a demonstration for "International Unemployment Day."[1] They marched from Union Square to City Hall, and the ensuing confrontation with New York's finest left about a hundred civilians injured. A second demonstration for unemployment relief on October 16, 1930, disrupted the proceedings of the Board of Estimate. It must have been

2. Food for the poor. "Police assist in distributing food from trucks to the needy men and women of New York," 1931. (UPI/Bettmann)

3. "Hardluck Town" on East 10th Street, 1932. (UPI/Bettmann)

4. May Day celebrations were accompanied by workers' choirs, pageantry, and brass bands. Parade of New York City Communists at Union Square, 1930. Offices of the *Daily Worker* are above the Cooperative Cafeteria, directly across the street from the photographer. (UPI/Bettmann)

effective, because the next day the board designated $1 million for unemployment relief.[2]

John Reed Clubs, named after the radical American journalist whose body is interred in the Kremlin wall, were organized in 1929 with the goal of creating a proletarian culture; in 1931 a Workers Cultural Federation was formed after a delegation of American artists returned from the Soviet Union with directives for attracting proletarians, intellectuals, and blacks to their ranks, as well as for organizing agitprop theatrical troupes. In New York City 265 delegates, claiming to represent some 20,000 members from 130 different groups, met to endorse the proposition that "culture is a weapon." As the cultural arm of the Communist Party, the federation was expected to faithfully follow the Party line.[3]

Cultural activities were an important part of many Communist demonstrations. May Day celebrations to honor workers were accompanied by workers' choirs, pageantry, and brass bands (figures 4 and 5). On May Day 1930, for example, a demonstration at Union Square was followed by a celebration at Coney Island, which included performances by several workers' cultural groups. Admission was 25 and 50 cents—free to the unemployed.[4] Crowds attending May Day festivities like this one proved an appreciative audience for working-class performing groups.[5]

5. The dragon of capitalism in the Red Parade on May Day 1932.
Note the banner of the John Reed Club in the background. (UPI/Bettmann)

Meeting places for the union groups taking part in these celebrations were designated in the blocks surrounding Union Square, with the Workers Cultural Federation assigning each group to a different section. A parade route was published. In 1932 demonstrators marched south from Union Square along Fourth Avenue to 14th Street. Turning east on 14th Street to Avenue A, the marchers proceeded south to Houston Street, along Houston to the corner of Ridge and Montgomery Streets, south again to East Broadway, and then west to Rutgers Square, their destination.[6]

Union Square at 14th Street and Fifth Avenue was the hub of radical activity dominated by the Communist Party during those years (figure 6). In 1930 CP headquarters overlooked the square. The offices of the *Daily Worker* were located on Union Square East, right next to the Workers Book Shop and above the Cooperative Cafeteria.

Not far away, within easy walking distance, another kind of revolution was brewing. The nascent modern dance movement was making its home in and around Greenwich Village. Martha Graham had a studio, first on West 10th Street, then on East 9th Street, and after 1934 at 66 Fifth Avenue, near 12th Street. Doris Humphrey and Charles Weidman taught classes on West 18th Street. In 1934 Helen Tamiris moved from Lafayette Street to a studio on West 8th Street. A brief walk would take a dancer from a class at one or another of their studios to the political hurly-burly of Union Square.

This geographic intimacy was convenient for socially conscious dancers, and the collision of the two revolutionary worlds sparked an explosion of choreographic activity. The antiacademy and antielitist basis of modern dance fit nicely within the mission of proletarian culture, just as the proletarian worker proved an eager student and enthusiastic audience for an emergent art. Workers' dance groups sprang up in unions such as the Needle Trades Workers Industrial Union, in recreational clubs such as the German hiking group Nature Friends, and in association with workers' theater groups such as the Theatre Union. A collective known as the New Dance Group delivered affordable dance classes to working-class amateurs.

"Dance Is a Weapon in the Revolutionary Class Struggle" was the slogan of the Workers Dance League, an umbrella organization formed to develop and organize efforts of the various workers' dance groups (figure 7). The idea for the Workers Dance League seems to have been

6. Union Square at East 14th Street and Fifth Avenue in New York was the hub of radical activity dominated by the Communist Party. Demonstration there, 1932. (UPI/Bettmann)

7. "The Dance Is a Weapon." Cover of the souvenir program for the New Dance Group's first annual recital, 1933.

born at a May Day celebration held at the Bronx Coliseum in 1932 in which eleven of the newly formed workers' dance groups participated. According to the *Daily Worker,* dancers Anna Sokolow, Edith Segal, Miriam Blecher, and Nadia Chilkovsky were responsible for its formation.[7]

The League sponsored concerts and contests among workers' dance groups called Spartakiades and facilitated the exchange of ideas and dance scenarios through *New Theatre,* the workers' theater and dance publication. (*New Theatre* actually replaced an earlier journal called *Workers Theatre,* a collection of mimeographed sheets reporting on issues and events in workers' culture.) Workers reported to the League from Philadelphia, Boston, and Chicago, asking advice and sharing ideas, but New York City was the thriving center of activity. After seeing the First Workers' Dance Spartakiade in 1933, one delegate responded enthusiastically, determined to improve the performance of a group in Boston:

> I want to tell you that I was very inspired and also ashamed after seeing the wonderful work the dance groups are doing in New York.

I told as best I could to the group all I learned from watching and listening especially at the council and we have all resolved to work harder and with more purpose hereafter. I feel that my instructing the group will be better because of my trip to New York.[8]

The extent to which social and political ideology could be integrated or could contribute to the aesthetic framework of a dance was debated in periodicals such as *New Theatre* and in *Dance Observer,* a magazine founded in 1934 to promote American dance as an art form. While significant subject matter was the primary issue for revolutionary dancers, other articles examined various formal concerns and urged collaborative methods of dance-making in keeping with the communal ideal. In general, dancers such as Martha Graham and Mary Wigman, the leader of the German Ausdruckstanz movement, were criticized by the leftist press for subject matter that was too personal, too mystical, and too divorced from contemporary social issues as well as too abstract and difficult to understand. The revolutionaries, in contrast, were faulted for lack of professionalism and for the simplicity of their message. The agitprop techniques and heavy symbolism they favored were inconsistent with the goals of modernism.

The history of American modern dance blurred distinctions between revolutionary and "bourgeois" dance in interesting ways. In music and in theater, classical and traditional methods of training and composition were labeled "bourgeois" by the leftist press. In dance, paradoxically, it was the struggling new experiments of people like Martha Graham that came to be considered as the ancien régime. Perhaps if ballet had been an established form in the United States, the new modern dance forms might have been considered revolutionary; they were after all based on an antiacademy and, in that sense, antibourgeois sentiment. Instead, it was the schools of Graham, Humphrey, Tamiris, and the German Hanya Holm (who headed the Wigman School in New York City) that came to be considered as established and traditional training methods, although their techniques predated working-class dance activity by only a few years.

Revolutionary writers and dancers argued over the relative merits of a "revolutionary" technique. Should it be based on communal and folk forms? Or could dancers appropriate "bourgeois" techniques? Grace Wylie, administrator and dancer for the New Dance Group, was one who argued for appropriating technical skills. "[Do] we completely discard their technique and suddenly build our own? We derive whatever is of value to us from the dance as it stands and reject the rest. If the bourgeois dance has anything of value to give us we use it."[9] But Michael Gold, writing in the *Daily Worker*, chastised dancers for being revolutionary in name only. "Do you think you can keep this up forever, this labelling a grey standardized sterile dance by Martha Graham by a hundred different titles—Scottsboro, Anti-fascism, etc., and make us accept the product as revolutionary?"[10]

Other writers argued for an evolutionary approach, suggesting that as revolutionary dancers developed, they would discard the old "bourgeois" technique and create bold new revolutionary forms. They pleaded for critics like Gold to give the dancers a chance.[11]

Debates over technique receded when the Communist Party adopted a new policy called socialist realism, which urged collaboration with bourgeois artists.[12] Dancers in the Workers Dance League were now encouraged to seize bourgeois techniques to make their message more acceptable to audiences. The level of technical expertise may have improved, but the underlying issue—the place of politics in the new art—continued to be controversial.

John Martin of the prestigious *New York Times* set out to define the relationship between art and politics in American modern dance. In October 1933 the nation's first dance critic had gently chided revolutionary dancers by paraphrasing a folk tale about making hare pie—first you had to catch the hare. To the revolutionary dancers he said, "To use art as a weapon, it is essential to see that first of all you have caught your art."[13] In subsequent columns he alternately praised the dancers for making artistic progress and complained that they did not belong on the stage. For example, a solo concert sponsored by the Workers Dance League in 1934 impressed Martin, and he noted the vigor of movement and intensity of feeling that marked the young dancers' efforts.[14] But a program of group dances presented a few weeks later was met with biting criticism—for the manner of presentation as well as for the quality of many of the dances: "Starting half an hour behind schedule, interrupted by two speeches from the stage, badly stage-managed and lacking in general theater discipline, the recital placed itself pretty definitely in the category of the amateur."[15]

By June 1935 Martin launched a full-scale attack on the Workers Dance League, which had recently changed its name to the New Dance League in an attempt to broaden its appeal. Martin could not deny the audience's enthusiasm or the fervency of the dancers' beliefs, but he lashed out at the superficial thinking and danced generalizations that he felt characterized their performances. In what he called an open letter to the group, Martin pulled no punches. He accused it of soapbox electioneering in the middle of a performance and compared the whole thing to a medicine show.[16]

Martin was not exactly a disinterested observer. As one of the earliest advocates of modern dance, he played an important role as a proselytizer and visionary in its development. His writings aimed at educating a new audience as well as educating all dancers to standards of professionalism. In his columns and in the series of lectures that he arranged at the New School for Social Research on West 12th Street in Manhattan, Martin was defining standards for a new American art form, separating the workers' dance movement from what would become the mainstream of modern dance. *The Modern Dance,* four of his New School lectures given in 1931–1932, was published in 1933 and revealed his concerns with form and technique. But content, the hallmark of any revolutionary art, was not discussed. Nadia Chilkovsky and the Workers Dance League were included on the New School series in 1934, but she was dropped the following year despite the fact that an estimated 34,000 people had seen performances by workers' dance groups that season, according to accounts in *New Masses.*[17]

Reports such as these may have been exaggerated. Still, a lot of workers were exposed to new movement ideas during the early 1930s. The audience for American dance was growing, and critics—revolutionary and otherwise—vied for its allegiance. Even balletomane Lincoln Kirstein joined the ideological fray with an article in *New Theatre,* "Revolutionary Ballet Forms." In it, Kirstein lobbied for the European classicist George Balanchine's inclusion in a new socially conscious art form:

> He knows ballet as ballet is dead. . . . Ballet as innocent amusement is far too little to demand of it . . . the greater participation of the audience as a contributory factor in heightening the spectacular tension, the destruction of the proscenium arch as an obstructive fallacy, the use of negros in conjunction with white dancers, the replacement of an audience of snobs by a wide popular support are all a part of Balanchine's articulate program.[18]

When I began researching this book I imagined my subjects as a radical core of propagandists, not to be confused with the creative dancers who were developing what would come to be called modern dance, but which was then known simply as "new" dance. In my thinking, one group, the revolutionary or radical dancers,[19] was clearly dedicated to a socialist vision that could be embodied in staged actions, while the other group, dubbed arty and "bourgeois" by the leftist press, was com-

8. Soloists of the Workers Dance League. Clockwise, starting above Miriam Blecher in *Woman* (center), Anna Sokolow in *Histrionics,* Jane Dudley in *The Dream Ends,* Lillian Mehlman in *Defiance,* Sophie Maslow in *Themes from a Slavic People,* Sokolow, Maslow, and Mehlman in *Challenge* (*Death of Tradition*), Nadia Chilkovsky in *Parasite,* and Edith Segal in *Tom Mooney.* (Photographs by Nat Messik. Chilkovsky photograph by Matyas Caldy. Reproduced from *New Theatre,* January 1935.)

mitted to an aesthetic vision that would be experienced as dance. One was movement, the other art. The working title for my book was "Proletarian Steps: Radical Dance in New York City, 1928–1942." As I began to write, however, it was clear that distinctions between the two camps were considerably less rigid than I initially thought.

Despite the debate surrounding "bourgeois" dance among leftists, most of the leaders of the revolutionary dance movement continued to study and perform with one or another of the established quartet. The cast for a Workers Dance League solo concert in 1934 included Nadia Chilkovsky and Miriam Blecher, former students of Hanya Holm at the Wigman School, as well as Anna Sokolow, Lily Mehlman, and Sophie Maslow of the Martha Graham company, and Jane Dudley who would join the Graham company the following year (figure 8). In 1935 Marie Marchowsky from the Graham company and José Limón and Letitia Ide from the Humphrey-Weidman company joined the performers in the League (figure 9).

The radical propagandists, it seems, willingly made themselves into instruments for the fledgling modern choreographers at the same time that they marched in May Day parades, danced in Communist pageants, and struggled to make a place for themselves as independent choreographers in concerts sponsored by the Workers Dance League. More, the populist audience attending revolutionary dance concerts was introduced to modernist concepts of choreography while they soaked up Marxist ideology. Far from being antagonists, the two movements creatively coexisted, exchanging audiences, bodies, and ideas. It was not a question of dance *or* politics; it was dance *and* politics. The revolutionary fervor of dancing modern—using power and force in a fight for freedom and egalitarianism in movement—was joined with the revolutionary vision promised by the Soviet Union. Throughout a critical period in the development of American dance, writers and dancers were engaged in passionate dialogues concerning the relationship of art and politics.

The terms revolutionary and bourgeois most accurately describe ideological divisions existing between American dancers before 1934. Put simply, revolutionary dancers were those responding to Marxist doctrines, while bourgeois dancers were independent of specific political ideology. But while many radical dancers expressed commitment to socialist ideals and sympathy for the new Soviet state, they were not necessarily or always acting on directives issued by the Comintern (the Communist International). They simply set out to change society. In these pages I have not attempted to discriminate among socialist, communist, and left-wing ideologies of the 1930s, except when internecine

9. The New Dance League solo recital, December 22, 1935. Clockwise, starting above Bill Matons (center), Jane Dudley, José Limón and Letitia Ide, Anna Sokolow, Marie Marchowsky, Sophie Maslow, Lily Mehlman, Rose Crystal, Merle Hirsch. (Reproduced from *New Theatre*, February 1936.)

warfare broke out in the leftist press, but I have focused on broader principles of social justice, readily located in Marxist thought, that united
revolutionary dancers.[20]

After 1934 the distinction between revolutionary and bourgeois groups
became muddy, partly because the Soviet policy of socialist realism
influenced revolutionaries to adapt bourgeois techniques and partly because Roosevelt's New Deal and the growth of the Popular Front col-
lapsed some ideological barriers between communism and "Americanism." (Communist leader Earl Browder actually declared in 1935 that
communism was twentieth-century Americanism.)[21] Still, performances
after that date were clearly influenced by the backgrounds and political commitments that choreographers made earlier. In this respect, the
terms remain useful for distinguishing each group's trajectory throughout the 1930s.

In the late 1920s and early 1930s revolutionary dance was characterized by an ideology of participation; workers became actively involved in
dancing out their issues. Compositions by choreographers such as Edith
Segal, who worked with lay dancers as well as with professionals, enjoyed a ready-made audience generated by the Communist Party. Revolutionary dance was workers' dance—in unions, at summer camps, and
on legitimate stages such as the Center Theatre at Rockefeller Center.

While the primarily working-class audience enthusiastically applauded most efforts by revolutionary dance groups, in proscenium theaters critical attention was drawn to the lack of professionalism and
technique of some; on the concert stage, reviewed by the mainstream as
well as the radical press, many dances and dancers were found aesthetically wanting. "New" dance by this time was gathering its own band of
advocates, and only two of the revolutionary groups managed to negoti-
ate the tricky meeting of art and politics. In works produced by the New
Dance Group and by Anna Sokolow's Dance Unit, choreographers made
dances about working-class causes, but the proletariat was no longer on
stage to represent itself.

Beginning in 1936, a populist tradition continued, however, in the
work of the Federal Theatre and Federal Dance Projects that employed
many revolutionary dancers. Helen Tamiris, always an advocate of
dancers' rights and liberal social policies, was the most important figure
here, although many other choreographers worked for the project, including Doris Humphrey, Charles Weidman, and Anna Sokolow. The
collision with New Deal policies turned the debate from one of workers
dancing or dancers dancing about workers into one about dancers working; artists were suddenly actively involved as the issue of collective bar-

gaining in the arts took center stage. This issue was complicated by the dancers' relationship to their employer, the federal government.

The splintering of the leftist movement toward the end of the decade, catalyzed by the Russo-German nonaggression pact, and the disillusionment of some activists with the Communist Party—coupled with the impact of Roosevelt's New Deal, which co-opted some facets of the CP agenda—deflected the early militant thrust of the revolutionary dance movement. Issues of American identity now began to define political activity within the dance world as the looming threat of fascism galvanized artists. Martha Graham made several dances in response to the Spanish Civil War and in support of historical American ideals. The vision of the "people"[22] that Martha Graham put forth in *American Document* (1938) joined workers and bourgeois in a panorama of American history; immigrants and minority populations, the downtrodden and the discriminated against, shared space with the Puritan Fathers on Graham's stage.[23] By affirming the country's heritage as many Americans contemplated devastation in Europe, Graham led the way in shaping American modern dance in the 1940s. In many ways it might seem appropriate to conclude this study here. I have deliberately resisted that temptation, however, hoping to show that Graham's work fit instead within the larger dance picture of the 1930s and was influenced by the urgency and vitality of a revolutionary dance movement that ultimately proved more ephemeral. In the aestheticized folk culture of choreographers Sophie Maslow and Jane Dudley, the ideological construct of the "people" continued throughout the 1940s. Leftist dancers as well as other artists, however, seemed to turn their backs on the gritty world of urban life, appropriating instead songs and dances gathered from rural America; the image of the worker was replaced by an idealized agrarian counterpart, the "folk."

Two things are clear. First, while the revolutionary dance movement united many dancers in a shared goal, each dancer also was different—in physical characteristics, in family background, in educational choices, in religious and political commitments, and in choreographic talents and aspirations. Second, because this art movement was really democratic, because so many participants gave themselves, however briefly, to this ideal, because so little concrete evidence remains of how this vision was embodied, it is not possible to document all of the period's activity. Instead, then, I have sought to understand the ideas and forces that helped shape the era, to identify specific approaches and elements that could be characterized as revolutionary, and, most importantly, to provide a voice for dancers who were part of what is now a forgotten movement. What history I do present is indeed "mutilated knowledge,"[24] constructed from the traces that remain: periodicals, some few photographs, the memories of participants. I apologize to all those whose commitment and passion I document but who remain nameless in these pages.

American modern dance is only beginning to acknowledge its roots within this leftist tradition.[25] As the narrative of American dance history was constructed in the 1940s and 1950s, the dancing crusades were overlooked, conveniently disremembered, and the Big Four, Martha Graham, Doris Humphrey, Charles Weidman, and Hanya Holm, came to dominate past and present; Helen Tamiris was acknowledged, but not acclaimed, always somewhat suspect, perhaps because of her social activism in the 1930s. By the 1950s, art—not politics—held center stage. Ironically, however, as the cold war developed, the U.S. government advanced its political interests by exporting American culture, and Martha Graham was named as one of the country's cultural ambassadors. This change came at a time when art—specifically modern art—was linked to an ideal of individual freedom.[26] In the midst of the ideological warfare of the 1950s, Graham acquired a propaganda value to the U.S. government as an avatar of American individualism in the battle against socialist collectivism.

In 1928, when this story begins, American audiences were familiar with the dancing style of Isadora Duncan and the exotic offerings of Ruth St. Denis (Miss Ruth) and Ted Shawn. A few dancegoers may have witnessed early experiments by Graham or the Humphrey-Weidman group. As leisure activity, some Americans would have participated in Delsartian exercises, or performed in one or another of the pageants which proved so popular in the early twentieth century.

Delsartian theory, as promulgated in the United States by Genevieve Stebbins in the late nineteenth century, postulated an intrinsic relationship between movement and meaning.[27] Among early American art dancers, Isadora Duncan in particular shared with the Delsartians the belief that through the physical the spiritual could be reached.[28] To some extent, Duncan's utopian ideas about the power of dancing to create a better, more spiritual world are indebted to such thinking and philosophizing. To some other extent, her extraordinary and luminous performances and her own body's presence on stage, as well as her outspoken and oratorical verbal style—"Madam," she once said, "I believe in the religion of the beauty of the human foot"[29]—contributed to that zeitgeist.

Duncan gave only glancing recognition to the influence of Delsarte on her dance, but Ruth St. Denis openly acknowledged her debt to him, and Delsartian exercises were an important part of the curriculum at Denishawn, the country's first dance academy. Established in 1914, offerings at the school included sequences of movement derived from the work of Delsarte as well as an eclectic array of popular and exotic dance styles ranging from ballet (including pointe work), to ballroom dancing, to yoga and Eastern dance.[30]

~ The early twentieth century promised a kind of liberation of the inner self through bodily efforts, but these genteel opportunities for experiences in movement were generally the province of America's upper and middle classes, white women of Christian background. While the Denishawn troupe occasionally played the vaudeville circuit — a necessity that Miss Ruth much regretted — early examples of art dance in America were mostly patronized by an elite clientele. Ann Daly refers to the early salon performances of Isadora Duncan as a "private performance of class."[31]

The development of "new" dance in America, however, was indebted not only to descendants of the Duncan and Denishawn traditions, but to a generation of immigrant children educated in settlement houses. While "bourgeois" leaders of dance almost always had studied at the Denishawn school, dance radicals were mostly working-class graduates of arts programs in settlement houses and union recreation groups.

As dance historian Nancy Lee Ruyter points out, there is no evidence that the American Delsartian movement affected the working class. But given Delsartism's importance to the development of expressive dance in the United States and the spread of those ideas in interpretive dance classes offered in urban centers, some of his tenets, with the attendant promise of moral and spiritual understanding made possible through movement, undoubtedly reached the daughters of immigrant and working-class families in New York City. Irene and Alice Lewisohn, for example, who came to New York's Henry Street Settlement House in 1905 to lead classes in dance and drama, studied the Delsarte system with Genevieve Stebbins.[32]

Settlement house students also would have been exposed to Duncan dance and to early modern teachers, such as Bird Larsen and Blanche Talmud. Tamiris, once a student at Henry Street, fondly remembered the elegant setting and special atmosphere of Blanche Talmud's dancing classes where the cramped quarters and other grim realities of tenement life might temporarily be forgotten:

> The dancing was called Interpretive dancing. We danced in a large room — with transparent red gold curtains. On the walls were pictures of dancing girls by Botticelli, in long draped costumes — with garlands of flowers in their hair. I loved the soft lights and the little framed pictures in silhouette over the piano [of] little figures leap-

ing over each other . . . . This was a new world far away from the wild life of the streets. We danced in a circle facing each other—Miss Talmud would say—"The Grieg Music"—or "Now we'll have Chopin."[33]

But leaders of the settlement house movement perceived an even more important function for the arts in their work, one that was to provide an avenue of expression for immigrant families traumatized by the upheaval of beliefs and customs in their lives. By performing folk songs and dances from their native countries, it was hoped that children would learn to value and preserve their cultural heritage as an antidote to their sense of alienation.[34] In the settlement houses the children danced their "immigrant gifts," symbolically assimilating their foreignness into the "great melting pot of America" at the same time that they performed their distinct ethnicities; movement thus became a means of resolving conflicts inherent in their identification as new Americans as well as a form of genteel physical exercise.[35]

The single most important distinction between choreographers allied with bourgeois dance and those allied with workers' dance is so self-evident that it is virtually never mentioned in dance history texts. Of the Big Four, Graham, Humphrey, and Weidman were third- and fourth-generation Americans; Holm, although an immigrant, was still a Nordic European, less threatening to Americans in the early twentieth century than the Eastern European Jews who had been immigrating in record numbers. An overwhelming percentage of those involved with the revolutionary dance movement in New York City were children of mostly poor Russian Jewish immigrant families. Beginning in the 1880s, Eastern European Jews had emigrated to some of the larger cities in the United States in record numbers, and after 1896 the influx of these new immigrants far surpassed the numbers of immigrants from Northern Europe. By 1907 the United States was populated by three times as many new immigrants as old, and the American Federation of Labor lobbied for immigration restrictions.

Responses to this phenomenon took two forms. The Americanization movement sought to homogenize the immigrant population through assimilation, even designating the Fourth of July as National Americanization Day in 1915. Countering this seemingly benign agenda was an antiradical and nativist campaign. A resurgent racism, directed against blacks, but also against non-Nordic Europeans such as those from Slavic and Southern European countries created a climate vulnerable to anti-Jewish agitation. Hysteria increased immediately before and after World

War I, producing greater interest in and suspicion toward the activities of radical groups, including anarchists, socialists, radical unionists, and members of the newly formed Communist Party. Since many Russian immigrants in the United States were sympathetic to the new Soviet Union, it is no surprise that Russian Jews became a prime target. They were, in fact, the most prominent symbol of foreign radicalism during the Red Scare. The nativist movement reached its height in 1919 and 1920, and a deportation campaign took place; by 1921 the United States had begun to close the immigration gates, and quotas were instituted favoring Northern European entrants.[36]

Most of the principals in these pages, including Helen Tamiris, Anna Sokolow, Edith Segal, and Sophie Maslow, grew up during these years as children of Russian Jewish immigrant parents. Miriam Blecher's family emigrated from Austria-Hungary. Heir to an idealized vision of the United States as a country that welcomed them and that could assimilate their distinct ethnic identities, they well may have encountered racial slurs and suffered discrimination because of their religious and foreign identities.

In 1928, for example, when the Denishawn School was preparing to open new headquarters in New York City, it developed a set of policies regarding Jewish students. St. Denis declared that Jews should be limited to 10 percent of the student body.[37] The dancer Gertrude Shurr, then a young Jewish student at the school, recalled why she left Denishawn:

> The reason I went with Doris [Humphrey] and Charles [Weidman] when they left Denishawn was because they stuck up for us. Here we were, all of us New York City kids, all of us Jewish kids, in the company, in the school there, and we thought we were going to be taken into the company. And only one tenth of the company could be first generation American. Everybody else had to be from the *Mayflower*. It was just absolutely a crazy thing. And I must say Doris and Charles left because of that issue. And we all left with them. About fifty-eight people left the school just like that.[38]

The Denishawn company may have favored a Nordic "American" look, but the modern dance movement of the late twenties and early thirties could and did unite descendants of Miles Standish and Jewish radicals upon a shared stage, creating a space in which some of the racial and ethnic divisions in American culture might begin to be resolved. Questions about American identity and its relation to ethnicity were central to the work of both bourgeois and revolutionary choreographers during this period. The issue, however, was differently negotiated by proponents of the two movements[39] and changed as the Communist Party redefined its policies and as American Communists and fellow travelers redefined their relationship to the Party.

The Communist Party, seeing Americanization as a means to spread Communist values to the American working class, initially discouraged ethnic identification, but it later came to support a form of American radicalism defined by ethnicity. Marxist ideology constructed a historical place for immigrant workers, which included their own history as well as the history of the United States as a class society.[40] With a bit of creative appropriation, revolutionary dancers were able to stage new and "American" identities for themselves without shunning their pasts.

Martha Graham and Doris Humphrey, the canonical figures in the development of American modern dance, *were* American; they did not have to become American. Graham's choreography proposed a country that encompassed all races and creeds in its past, in its present, and in the future. It was, after all, her America. Humphrey's *New Dance* was inspired by a utopian, class-free vision. Many leftist dancers, however, struggled to join the American dream, to assimilate what were basically urban, foreign, and radical visions into the American historical myths and realities. Because revolutionary dancers needed to make a place for themselves, they could identify with every other person who lacked a place in American mythology: Negroes, workers, immigrants, Okies. This attitude would make it possible to dance about blacks and to move to Negro spirituals without being patronizing. Class ties brought all of these groups together.

While dancers and critics positioned themselves along different lines during the contentious thirties, in retrospect it is clear that they shared common influences and common representational strategies. In particular, the female body was recast as an instrument of force and power — muscles, joints, and sinews at the ready. The decorative, exotic female representations popularized by St. Denis were rejected, as were the maternal representations of "Woman" that Duncan's later choreography constructed.

During the 1930s visual representations of the female body became transformed. The image of the twenties' flapper, slight, frivolous, and fun-loving, was replaced by the capable no-nonsense female figure characteristic of New Deal art. Yet much New Deal art continued to reinforce traditional gender ideology. "Stolid mothers and brawny workers" were but different aspects of a union in which the sturdy female was typically concerned with the domestic, while her equally sturdy husband undertook the "real work." [41]

One of the most radical aspects of the representations staged by New York City dancers is that, for the most part, women stood alone. Whatever the content of the work they produced, the very fact that women were the primary movers was revolutionary. Many fledging groups—revolutionary and bourgeois—were composed only of women, thus explicitly commenting on both the independence of the female body and its power. Experiments with modernism, moreover, allowed the female body to be on stage as an abstraction rather than a representation of the dancer herself. The figure in Martha Graham's *Lamentation* (1930), for example, is not readily identifiable as male or female.

When men shared the stage, as they did in gradually increasing numbers in revolutionary fare, the dance movement was not generally gender-coded. Photographs depict men and women with raised arms and clenched fists doing battle together against the forces of capitalism. The cover of the souvenir program from the first New Dance Group recital shows a group of massed dancers, shoulders hunched, fists tightly clenched, powerful, strong, and united (figure 10). Although the rhetoric of "revolutionary" dance emphasized the fight for social equality, the physical representations argued for equality between the sexes, even if that goal never became part of official oratory. Participants were joined in a kind of union that, unlike the images of men and women popularized in New Deal public art, permitted women the role of warrior in public battle. In an advertisement for antifascist dance, the female body fills the space, threatening to invade its borders (figure 11). It is worth noting that the language of the workers' dance movement was that of virile conquest, although the war was being fought primarily by women.

I want to return to Isadora Duncan, whose presence hovers over so many developments in American dance. For Duncan, the dancing body was a stage on which any number of political and social agendas could be performed, and this inheritance she bequeathed to American modern dance.[42] The forms advocated by dance radicals were bathed in a language that sometimes suggests Duncan's utopian vision of a better world through dance. Mass revolutionary dance was promoted to educate the mover about the workings of the body, to bring the mover into contact with his/her deepest self, to expand the individual consciousness, and to create a communal social experience. Through movement, people would become healthier, proud owners of "bodies functioning naturally,

10. The advanced section of the New Dance Group, an astonishing array of bodies. (Photograph by Goldenberg. Reproduced from the New Dance Group's first annual recital souvenir program, 1933.)

their reactions stimulated, their minds developed."[43] For revolutionary dancers, this nearly religious belief in the power of dance was echoed in commitment to the socialist vision, to an ideal larger than oneself, to a sense of transcendent purpose. Despite the attitude of the Communist Party toward religion as the opiate of the masses, the socialist ideal was a spiritual venture for many followers.

In his account of the Armory Show and the Paterson Strike Pageant of 1913, Martin Green proposes that art and politics are indeed mutual spiritual projects. Radical labor organizer Elizabeth Gurley Flynn explicitly articulated this idea when she spoke of what the Industrial Workers of the World accomplished in organizing textile workers in Paterson: "Stimulation in a strike means to make that strike and through it the class struggle, their religion; to make them forget all about the fact that it is [only] for a few cents or a few hours, but to make them feel it is a religious duty for them to win that strike."[44]

Acknowledging the spiritual base linking "new" dance with radical politics helps to explain the somewhat incestuous relationship between "bourgeois" modern dance and revolutionary dance during this period. In 1934 dancers could march from the Workers Book Shop to the Martha Graham studio in no time, a fact that made it possible to fight the holy war of revolutionary politics and modern dance almost simultaneously. The powerful emotions that ignited dancers' political efforts were in

11. The female body threatens to invade the space. Advertisement for anti-fascist dance, 1934. (Reproduced from *New Theatre,* March 1935.)

some way balanced by the intrinsic passion that infused the style of movement Graham was developing, an internal power allowing dancers to mobilize themselves instantaneously. One member of her company recalled:

> The technique was very passionate. It wasn't cool, it was hot. And it was stripped of any ornamentation; it was like a knife cutting each time. It was stunning. It had an enormous use of space; just the body being flung into space. You had to have a certain amount of dedication because you were doing something nobody else had ever seen before. . . . It takes a person who believes completely, who is totally dedicated, who is fanatical.[45]

Graham's clean, strong, powerful movement could cut through and rearrange the volumes of space in which the body lived, creating a brave new dance world. One telling image of Graham's was that of breaking a rock with the sheer force of personal energy. The revolutionaries were more literal. A William Gropper cartoon from the *New Masses* portrays the power of the worker in an art-revolutionary mode, breaking out of manacles and looming over the capitalists with the kind of force that Graham technique developed (figure 12).[46] The movement, artistic and social, was about power and where power started was in the dancers' own bodies.

12. Worker with broken manacles towering over cowering figures representing clergy, monarchy, and capitalism. Cover of the *New Masses*, May 1933. (Cartoon by William Gropper. Reproduced from the Collections of the Library of Congress, LC USZ62-43324.)

T W O

Proletarian Steps: Workers Dancing

'tis the final conflict
Let each stand in his place
The International Soviet
Shall be the human race [1]

On January 21, 1928, a cast of a thousand workers directed by Edward Massey of the New Playwrights' Theatre performed what was called a Mass Revolutionary Pageant at Madison Square Garden. The Garden was then located on Eighth Avenue, a huge arena that took up the entire block between 49th and 50th Streets and could seat some 20,000 spectators. Host to everything from the circus and rodeo to dog shows and hockey matches, the Garden provided an ideal setting for the political rallies and pageantry sponsored by the Communist Party, USA.

In seven scenes, the 1928 pageant recounted the history of the Russian Revolution: "Russia Under the Czars," "Russia in Revolt," "The Workers Take Power," "Reconstruction Dance," "Lenin Is Dead," "Carry On!," and "1928." The pageant script was written by poet Adolf Wolf, with musical accompaniment by members of the New York Philharmonic Society, and a 200-voice chorus from the Singing Society of *Freiheit*, the Yiddish Communist daily newspaper. [2]

A young Communist, Edith Segal, contributed the dances, which were interlaced with scripted material. [3] In the final scene Segal arranged some fifty dancers in a hammer-and-sickle formation on raised steps at the back of the stage, creating a living incarnation of the young Soviet state's ideals. [4] Because each performer contributed to the creation of the larger symbolic picture, boundaries of individuality were transcended—or so the promoters of proletarian dance must have hoped. Fusing action and belief, this communal ritual nurtured the spiritual aura so essential to the radical cause. The politicized bodies of the participants fostered the new body politic.[5]

Segal's dancers were amateur performers who probably had more enthusiasm than technique. Most were members of the Artef Theatre, a group of Jewish workers who practiced acting in the evenings. As part of their theater training, they took classes with the celebrated ballet teacher Michel Fokine. The other dancers were recruited by Segal on an ad hoc basis. As she put it, "Anybody who would walk decently, I picked."[6] This casual approach to casting assured the appearance of proletarian masses themselves on stage, where in a public ceremony, buoyed by the enthusiasm of comrades who surrounded them, they were converted into the army of a vital new society.

The pageant was trumpeted as a model of proletarian theater, its effectiveness deriving from the twin techniques of mass participation and audience identification. According to Moissaye Olgin, editor of *Freiheit:*

> The performance is significant not only as an experience but also as pointing the way for a real proletarian mass-theatre. Where the actors are workers animated by the class struggle and participating in the battles of the working class, where the plays are giving form to the unclear but powerful strivings of the proletarian masses, where spectators and actors are united by a common bond of class emotions, where the things performed on the stage are of vital importance to all concerned, there the technique will not fail to assume an original form.[7]

Edith Segal was born and raised on New York's Lower East Side, the daughter of Russian Jewish immigrants. Her mother was a hairdresser who specialized in wigs, her father a cigarmaker. They were a "good" Jewish family, decent and hardworking, according to Segal, and while her mother did not approve of dancing, her father enjoyed social dancing, once winning a prize. Perhaps a young Edith was influenced by his enthusiasm. At the Henry Street Settlement House, Segal studied rhythmic movement with Alice and Irene Lewisohn, and she probably performed in festivals staged by them.

Just a few blocks from the Henry Street Settlement stood the Neighborhood Playhouse, which the Lewisohn sisters had established to accommodate their more ambitious artistic efforts. Segal at the age of twelve was selected to study there. The curriculum included ethnic dance styles (she studied with visiting specialists such as the Indian dancer Roshanara), and some form of interpretive dancing. She danced barefoot in

Blanche Talmud's dance classes and was excited by seeing a Duncan performance.

Segal became a dancer on what was called the "public" circuit, performing material such as the "Dance of the Hours" from *La Gioconda* as she traveled around the country. While she was in Chicago in 1924, news arrived of Lenin's death. From there, because she had studied socialism as well as dancing in New York City, she planned to perform in a memorial service scheduled at Chicago's Ashland Auditorium. Although she did not actually join the Party until 1927, she was involved in CP activities at this time.[8]

According to Segal, Party officials were skeptical when she voiced a request to dance at the memorial. But then Charles Ruthenberg, general secretary of the Communist Party in the United States, relented, saying, "Comrade, if you feel you have something to contribute to this meeting, go right ahead."[9]

So Segal danced in what was probably one of the Party's first experiments in the United States involving workers' culture. The dance was in two parts. In the first section she was draped in black and performed to Chopin's Funeral March. In the second section she removed the black material to the strains of the Communist "Internationale," revealing the red tunic she wore underneath; sadness and mourning gave way to a vision of energy and hope.

On her return to New York City, Segal organized a children's dance group—six girls and one boy from the Ukrainian Hall. The children paid 25 cents a month, and she taught them dance at the same time that she taught them the value of work and their history as members of the working class. In 1927 Segal staged a version of the 1924 Lenin memorial dance for this group. Titled *Dance in Four Parts,* the choreography depicted the Russian Revolution, the building of socialism, the death of Lenin, and, in the last section, the future as symbolized by a hammer and sickle constructed out of the dancers' bodies.

The group was called the Pioneers. In 1923 the Communist Party sponsored a youth organization called the Young Pioneers. Formed after the Communist Party had become a legal and above-ground political organization in the United States, the Young Pioneers operated under the Party's aegis and explicitly promoted future membership. Members were children, usually of immigrant parents, between the ages of nine and fourteen; at fourteen, they became eligible to join the Young Communist League. It is not clear whether Segal's group was part of the Young Pioneers, but her work with them and with the children's group of the

International Workers Order, which she later directed, probably would have fit with the Party's program for immigrant children.[10]

Dance in Four Parts was performed by the Pioneers in 1927, and the following year it became the basis for the memorial ballet that Segal's ad hoc company performed at Madison Square Garden. From Moissaye Olgin's review of the 1928 Lenin pageant it is possible to imagine what some sections might have looked like. Setting the stage for the drama of the Revolution were scenes portraying the horrors of prewar Russia. "Under the Csars" featured "the mass of the Russian people, poorly dressed, bent back men and women of the Csar's empire," while "Russia in Revolt" depicted the reigning forces. "Tall posters akin to Russian church banners advance as if moving of their own will. Grotesque figures . . . of the rich man, the priest, the general, the Csar." Then, to do battle with this cast of villains, Segal and her dancers burst on the scene, the revolutionary storm that hailed the future. Segal's movement was designed for clarity, and Olgin reported the electrifying effect on some 20,000 spectators in the Garden:

> There is a stifled cry in the hall. When the young figures draped in red finally appear, driving away the apparitions, one greets them like a true liberating force.
> They are the purifying storm. There is abandon in their sweep. There is release in their abandon. We all know: this is Edith Segal, our own comrade,[11] these are other friends whom we meet every day. But now they are transformed. We are with them in their vigorous gestures, in their flashlike rush, in the turmoil at once harmonious and chaotic like the revolution itself.[12]

At the end of the performance, participants and audience members joined in singing the "Internationale," reinforcing the sense of comradeship within the vast Garden. "Shouts of joy went up," wrote Olgin, "both from the stage and the mass."[13]

In 1930 Segal staged the dance movement for another Lenin memorial pageant at the Garden. Called "The Belt Goes Red," the pageant featured amateur performers from various workers' organizations, including the Workers Dramatic Council, the Workers Laboratory Theatre, the Workers Dance Group, the Freiheit Singing Society, the Workers International Relief Chorus and Brass Band, and members of the Labor Sports Union (figure 13).

Pageant participants massed at the 14th Street side of Union Square at 6 P.M. Carrying banners, they marched to West 50th Street and Madison

Fight Imperialist War Preparations! — Defend the Soviet Union!
JOIN THE COMMUNIST PARTY!

LENIN ◆◆ MEMORIAL MEETING

Wednesday
Jan. 22
at 7 P. M.

At
Madison Sq. Garden
50th St. and 8th Ave.

PROGRAM

1. Singing of the International .... *By the Assembly*
2. Introductory remarks .... *By Chairman I. Amter*
3. Labor Sports Union
4. Lenin Showed the Way for the Negro Masses! ...... *Address—Otto Hall*
5. Greetings
6. Join the Party of Lenin! .... *Address—By Robert Minor*
7. Build Lenin a Revolutionary Monument! .... *Address—By M. J. Olgin*
8. Installation of Communist Recruits
   (a) The Duties of a New Member
   (b) Pledge of Revolutionary Loyalty
   (c) Welcome to the Communist Party
9. The Belt Goes Red
   A Mass Pageant, direction Emjo Basshe; conceived by Edith Segal.
   Dances arranged by Edith Segal. Musical direction, Paul Keller.
   Groups participating: Workers Dramatic Council, Workers Dance Group, Workers Lab-
       oratory Theatre, Freiheit Gesangs Ferein, W. I. R., Brass Band and Chorus, Labor
       Sports Union.

Scene 1—The Belt (dance group).
Scene 2—American Federation of Labor
    Convention.
Scene 3—Revolt (dance group).
Scene 4—Organization!

Scene 5—Strike (dance group).
Scene 6—From the U.S.S.R.
Scene 7—Memorial March (dance group)
Scene 8—Towards Struggle!

13. Program for Lenin memorial meeting, 1930.

Square Garden, where the program officially began with the singing of the "Internationale" and speeches by Communist Party officials; installation of Party recruits and a pledge of revolutionary loyalty followed.

The program's second half was devoted to the pageant itself. Conceived by Segal and directed by Emjo Basshe of the New Playwrights' Theatre, the pageant was structured in eight scenes, with danced episodes interspersed with declamations:

> Scene 1: The Belt (dance group)
> Scene 2: American Federation of Labor Convention
> Scene 3: Revolt (dance group)
> Scene 4: Organization
> Scene 5: Strike (dance group)
> Scene 6: From the USSR
> Scene 7: Memorial March (dance group)
> Scene 8: Toward Struggle! [14]

In "The Belt," dancers portrayed assembly-line workers who take over the machine they have built, a classic version of workers seizing the means of production. A rehearsal photograph shows two lines of dancers facing each other with a single figure in the foreground; upstage left, other figures are massed. Individual dancer/workers moved through the narrow channel defined by the opposing lines, as if passing down an assembly line, before joining the upstage group. Once assembled, the "machine people," as Segal called them, moved in orchestrated patterns; some turned, while others went up and down like cogs in a giant machine. Then: "Through that line came a bolt of red, Turkey red material, which I bought on Canal Street, a whole roll. . . . each [dancer] touched or held the red scarf, the red bolt, and they surrounded the machine which they had built. They took it because they had built it. So that was the belt." [15]

Leftist playwright Paul Sifton's play *The Belt,* a "satire of the American Speed-Up System," had been produced by the New Playwrights' Theatre in 1928,[16] and the assembly line was synonymous with greedy capitalists making money at the expense of American workers. When Segal had the machine circled with the swath of red cloth, it could be taken to signify both the politicalization of the assembly-line workers and the protection offered by the Communist Party. The *Daily Worker* had used the term "red belt" to denote the Party's influence in the suburbs circling Paris in 1929.[17]

Creative efforts by Segal and other pageant participants won Party approval. In a letter to workers' groups that took part in the 1930 memorial a Party official wrote:

> Workers' cultural organizations serving the working-class struggle demonstrate their value on occasions such as our Lenin Memorial Evening. The Communist Party recognizes the merit of working-class organizations of a cultural character and therefore recognizes your place in the class struggle and calls upon you to continue to serve the interest of the working class and thus help to impress upon the minds of those who witnessed your performance the ever-sharpening character of the struggle against imperialism.[18]

The CP's Lenin pageants and other mass entertainments were explicitly propagandistic, but they borrowed techniques from a tradition of amateur performance in the United States in which the political agenda was less clearly defined. Beginning in the late nineteenth century, civic pageantry had been promoted as a means of creating a collective sense of history; pageants involved members of a community in performances of their own past. By the 1910s such pageantry was a nationwide craze, complete with scripts, pageant masters, and organizations to assure the application of proper standards. "Pageantry's most fervent advocates viewed it as no less than an instrument of communal transformation, able to forge a renewed sense of citizenship out of the emotional ties generated by the immediate sensation of expressive, playful, social interaction."[19]

But pageants frequently turned rose-colored glasses on the past, conveniently omitting historical episodes that revealed unpleasant aspects of the collective experience. The St. Louis Pageant and Masque of 1913, one of the largest, simply eliminated the city's historical black population (more than 44,000 at the time)—as well as organized labor—from its treatment of the city's development.[20] Civic pageantry in the United States, then, was essentially conservative, fostering images of an idealized past while sidestepping issues that threatened to expose the country's or the region's or the community's underbelly.

If promoters of civic pageantry were reluctant to draw attention to their propagandistic role, revolutionary pageants, such as the Paterson Strike Pageant which also took place in 1913, openly embraced this mission. The Paterson pageant was sponsored by the radical Industrial Workers of the World (iww) and was organized by such well-known leftists and labor radicals as John Reed, Mabel Dodge, Margaret Sanger, and Big Bill Haywood. Reed four years later would travel to Russia and witness the Bolshevik Revolution; his dramatic record of that tumultuous event, *Ten Days That Shook the World,* was the first major account to be published in the United States. But in 1913 he lived in Greenwich Village and was a contributor to the leftist journal *The Masses*. On the stage of the old Madison Square Garden between Fifth and Madison Avenues and East 26th and 27th Streets, Reed and others staged the pageant to re-enact events of a strike against the Paterson silk mills that was then being fought by the IWW. Praised for its radical politics by unionists and for its avant-garde aesthetics by artists, the pageant depicted the battle between working and capitalist classes. The pageant's text, which called for the silk workers to act out their history, concluded with a meeting in which the strikers determined and voted on their own work rules. By cleverly turning the techniques of civic pageantry to its own more radical ends, the pageant exposed the divisive issue of class in the United States and earned a reputation as a "unique political instrument." "In participating in the pageant they [the strikers] became conscious of their experience as a meaningful force in history, and of themselves as self-determining members of a class that shaped history." [21]

Pageantry was an ideal vehicle for promoting allegiance among its players. Through their actions and words, pageant performers not only projected symbolic qualities, but they assimilated them. By conflating the scripted, symbolic representation with the real-life person who performed the action, both spectators and participants had the opportunity to invent and reinvent their history. The silk workers on stage were playing themselves—striking mill workers—but they could originate an ending more to their liking than actual events allowed. Segal's dancers, as they burst onto the stage draped in red, were comrades playing comrades, acting out an imagined past and promoting a vision of the future.

In constructing memorial pageants, American Communists surely looked to Russian culture as well, to entertainments called mass spectacles that emerged in the Soviet Union after 1917. Such exhibitions involved thousands of participants in episodes celebrating important events in Russian history. Collaboratively written and produced, these spectacles attracted participants from various professional and social orders—primarily soldiers, workers, and artists—who were organized with precision into a glorious whole symbolizing the unifying power of the state. The Soviet spectaculars were distinguished by bold, exaggerated movements, presentational acting styles, clear symbolism, and characters representing good and evil in archetypal terms.[22]

"The Storming of the Winter Palace," for example, staged on November 7, 1920, re-created the actual storming of the palace on the site. On two large platforms joined by a bridge, forces massed. One side housed the red Russians, the other the white. These historical enemies were portrayed in contrasting acting styles, which gave visibility and concrete form to the political agenda. On the red platform, a heroic style of acting prevailed, with grand gestures and elaborate pantomime. Clowning and buffoonery—techniques borrowed from vaudeville and the circus—were featured on the white platform. Action alternated from platform to platform, with the red forces becoming stronger while the white grew weaker. Finally, "as the white stage became wrapped in darkness, the red one was illuminated. Workmen, women and children, soldiers with arms and people of all kinds were seen crowding around a giant red flag."[23] These demonstrations were embraced as a model of Soviet proletarian theater, providing opportunities for expression to thousands of participants and reaching a mass audience.

The idea of a specifically proletarian culture, created not only for workers, but by workers, soon spread to workers' clubs in the United States. Championed by, among others, Mike Gold in the New Masses, artists, writers, and theater people joined forces with workers to create art that reflected working-class life. This effort required new criteria for what constituted a performance. For example, the opening of workers' housing built by the United Workers' Cooperative Association was the occasion for a spectacle featuring mass demonstrations, speeches, a machine dance, and performances by the Freiheit Singing Society and the Freiheit Dramatic Studio.[24] Carnivals, bazaars, floats, and pageantry were the diverse elements combined in these events. Occurring as often as once a month, an upcoming spectacle would be announced in the Daily Worker, accompanied by invitations to participate and schedules for rehearsals. Participants in the May Day celebration in 1931, for example, were scheduled to rehearse every Monday and Thursday evening at 8:30 sharp![25]

Any occasion could be converted into an amateur performance. "Red, Yellow and Black" was produced as part of an anniversary pageant for Freiheit in a carnival pageant at Madison Square Garden in 1928. Written by Adolf Wolf, it had set designs by Boris Aronson and, according to the Daily Worker, featured two thousand actors from the Freiheit Dramatic Studio.[26] Later that year the Worker claimed that 25,000 comrades marched on the Garden for "The Giant Pageant of the Class Struggle," staged to celebrate the eleventh anniversary of the Russian Revolution.[27] For the anniversary in 1930 a pageant called "Turn the Guns" was mounted at the Bronx Coliseum, featuring members of the Workers Laboratory Theatre as well as singers and dancers.[28] And to celebrate a seventy-fifth birthday for Comrade Morris Vinchevsky in November, dancers, singers, and members of the Artef Theatre appeared in a jubilee held at the Garden.[29] Other events reported in the *Daily Worker* included costume balls, bazaars, and features such as the "Miners' Mass Tableaux," with its "Red Sports Number."[30]

Most likely, celebrations such as these employed vaudeville and burlesque acting styles similar to those popularized in the Russian mass spectacles, thus ensuring that audiences could distinguish the good guys from the bad. In "The Giant Pageant of the Class Struggle," clown-like figures represented evil capitalists and drew boos and hisses from crowds of workers as they passed by on their floats.[31] Moissaye Olgin described Tsar Nicholas II and other pre-Revolutionary figures portrayed in the 1928 Lenin memorial as "ludicrous cartoons" who invited ridicule and laughter.[32] This agitprop acting style, developed first in the Soviet Union, then transplanted to Germany, became identified with the workers' theater movement in the United States and soon provided a basis for burgeoning experiments in revolutionary dance.[33]

When revolutionary dance groups claimed that "the dance is a weapon in the class struggle,"[34] they meant two things. First, dance could be used to bring revolutionary content to a working-class audience, educating them about the problems of class warfare in the United States. Second, workers could participate in forms of mass or lay dance, which required little technical training, and through the act of dancing express ideas of social importance and revolutionary significance. Dance was a working person's activity, whether that meant dancing in groups organized by unions and other working-class groups, or becoming part of a new proletarian audience. Examples of revolutionary dance could be seen in union halls, in workers' recreational facilities, and in summer camps organized by workers.

Soon after Segal staged her second Lenin memorial pageant in 1930, she began to present choreographed dances at worker-sponsored events. On February 23, 1930, she danced at an "Art and Dance Evening" arranged by the Workers International Relief Culture and Chess Club.[35] Two weeks later, she appeared with Allison Burroughs in *Dance of Solidarity* and *Revolutionary Dance* at "The International Women's Day Mass Meeting." Sponsored by the Communist Party, the event characteristically opened and closed with the singing of the "Internationale."[36] On March 15 a group called the Red Dancers was first mentioned; the dancers were scheduled to perform a program of American and Russian folk dances for a *Daily Worker* costume ball, held at Rockland Palace in

Harlem.[37] The next day an announcement in the *Worker* placed the Red Dancers at the Bronx Coliseum as part of a mass pageant, "The Soviet Union Forges Ahead," presented by the Workers International Relief.[38]

The Red Dancers was the name for Segal's group, which grew from the nucleus of amateur dancers she had recruited for the Lenin pageants. Although the group was not organized under the aegis of the Communist Party, it was identified with leftist political causes, and the term *red* was chosen to signify its revolutionary status.[39] Segal recalls that the group appeared almost every week during the early 1930s, performing on makeshift stages, once in a space only 8′ × 10′. The dancers saw their role as threefold: "to bring to workers the message of the class struggle thru the medium of the dance, to act as a center for workers interested in the dance as a cultural activity, and to develop leaders for new groups."[40] Emphasizing education and outreach more than artistry, the Red Dancers created performances about working-class issues.

A key issue engaging the Communist press and igniting radical fires during the 1930s was racial discrimination and violence against Negroes. Headlines in the *Daily Worker* reported lynchings and terrorism in the South and pointed to the need for black-and-white solidarity in the class struggle. Negro recruitment was an important theme in the 1930 Lenin memorial at Madison Square Garden. Charging that organizations such as the National Association for the Advancement of Colored People were "in the same boss class with the lynchers themselves," the Party issued a call for Negro workers:

> Our Negro politicians, who fool us into voting for them on the plea of race loyalty are like the white politicians, only tools of the bosses. Neither the republican, democratic, or socialist parties are organized for the interest of the workers, black or white. There is only one Party that can fight for interests of the workers, regardless of race or nationality, and that Party is the Party of the workers, THE COMMUNIST PARTY. [41]

In the *Daily Worker* a poem called "Black Fists, White Fists" by J. C. Eden and a cartoon by Fred Ellis showing a black worker and a white worker standing together express the theme of class unity as a solution to racial divisiveness. In the Ellis drawing, the workers face the world with arms folded across their chests, joined in a show of unity. The caption reads, "And We Will Strike Side By Side on May Day" (figure 14).[42] In like manner, Eden's poem, which announces itself as a commemoration of the first mass meeting of white workers and Negro workers in

14. A black worker and a white worker standing together express the theme of class unity as a solution to racial divisiveness. Line drawing by Fred Ellis. (Reproduced from the *Daily Worker,* April 28, 1930. Courtesy of *Peoples Weekly World.*)

Chester, Pennsylvania, links the equality of the races to their mutual experience as workers.[43]

On March 22, 1930, Segal, a white Jewish woman, and Burroughs, a young Negro woman, appeared in *Black and White Workers Solidarity Dance* as part of an interracial "Harlem Revels" at Rockland Palace[44] (the dance was probably first performed as *Dance of Solidarity* two weeks earlier). After the performance everyone sang the "Internationale"—of course—which was printed on the back of the program, and then, with the Duke Ellington band playing, blacks and whites danced together in the latest ballroom styles.

A week later, Segal and Burroughs performed the dance again, this time at the Manhattan Lyceum for the anniversary of the Gastonia strike.[45] Communists had led a strike at the Loray textile mill in Gastonia, North Carolina, during the spring of 1929, which ended unsuccessfully and violently. Despite the fact that the mill employed only two black workers, the Party made racial equality a central issue and blamed racial divisiveness, in part, for the strike's failure. Setting the tone, a *Daily Worker* headline announced, "Gastonia Points Way to Negro, White Unity."[46] Segal chose the slogan "Black and white, Unite and fight" to accompany her dance.[47]

The dance depicted the history of exploitation that each race suffered and proposed a solution along Party lines. The victims (because each suffered under the capitalist system) found that by supporting each other they could overcome the forces that oppressed them. Composed of literal gestures based on work motifs and tending toward static poses, the dance ended with the black figure and the white figure helping each other rise from the ground, symbolizing the power that each could provide to the other.[48]

Segal's presentation and the accompanying slogan were admittedly simplistic, but the Party *was* in the forefront of the fight against one of the ugliest aspects of American life. By contrasting a white body with a black one, Segal made sure, with scant room for shading or subtlety, that everyone got the message. "To be an effective artist," she stated, "you have to be conscious of the world around you and somehow find a way, if you have opinions about things, to express them so that they're meaningful to a lot of people and not private forms of expression, that are personal, that are purely private."[49]

Over the next few years the dance proved popular and was performed in settings that ranged from workers' camps to legitimate theaters. Negro Communist Angelo Herndon, well-known among leftists after his 1932 arrest in Georgia, praised the dance and Segal's work, emphasizing the theme of class consciousness as a solution to racial discord: "Through the course of our work in the South[,] such dance groups must be developed to weld the unity of black and white workers for struggle."[50] With a speaking tour of working-class camps, Herndon was celebrating his temporary release from jail on what were almost certainly trumped-up charges of insurrection. He was accompanied on the tour by dancers Add Bates,[51] who was black, and Irving Lansky, who was white, performing Segal's *Black and White*. (The two dancers replaced Burroughs and Segal—Segal claiming to have "found" Bates at a gym) (figure 15).[52]

In Segal's construction and in the eyes of Party leaders, workers were a class—black or white did not matter—and their future depended on their ability to confront and challenge their oppressors, the "bosses." Strikes and union politics provided choice subject matter for revolutionary dancers. In a piece called *Sell Out* (1934) Segal portrayed American Federation of Labor President William Green wearing silk overalls, to signify, as she put it, the upper strata of the labor movement separated from the rank and file (figure 16). Until the shift to a United Front policy in 1935, the Party routinely referred to the AFL as a "fascist" organization in cahoots with management.[53] Commenting on a performance of *Sell Out* at a Communist demonstration for textile workers in Paterson, New Jersey, *New Theatre*'s Ann Burlak took the opportunity to point an accusing finger at Francis Gorman, president of the Textile Workers'

15. Cover of *Workers Theatre,* March 1933. Add Bates (on the right) and Irving Lansky in Edith Segal's *Black and White.*

Union, who was being vilified by the Party for his role in the strike. Like Green, he was seen as representing the "bosses" and not the workers:[54] "Coming on the heels of the betrayed national textile strike, the dance, depicting the role of Gorman and the Arbitration Board, demonstrated the great value of groups such as the Red Dancers in the labor movement. It is especially significant that the Red Dancers are up to date in preparing a special dance about Gorman and his sell-out tactics."[55]

    Segal directed a number of working-class dance groups in New York

16. In *Sell Out,* Edith Segal portrayed American Federation of Labor President William Green wearing silk overalls to signify the upper strata of the labor movement separated from the rank and file. (Reproduced from *new dance,* special recital issue, January 1935. Dance Collection, New York Public Library for the Performing Arts, Astor, Lenox and Tilden Foundations.)

City in the early 1930s, among them the Nature Friends Dance Group (an outgrowth of the German recreational and hiking group), the Needle Trades Workers Industrial Union Dance Group (sponsored by the union), and the International Workers Order High School and Children's Dance Groups (also sponsored by the union).[56] The groups consisted of relatively untrained dancers, and initially they were not organized as performing units. Segal seemed to prefer working with nonprofessional dancers—whether as personal preference, necessity, or ideological act is not clear.

In the shules—after-school Jewish religious training programs—Segal taught dance to children, which beginning in 1932 she also did at Camp Kinderland.[57] Camps such as Kinderland, located on Sylvan Lake in New York State, were created as vacation colonies for adults and children, woodsy utopias where the Party's radical program could be experienced in relative isolation from competing ideologies. Herndon had toured three such working-class camps with *Black and White*—Camp Nitgedaigit (literally, "not to worry" in Yiddish) and Camp Unity, both run by the Communist Party, and Kinderland, which had been founded by members of the Workmen's Circle in New York City, a Jewish organization that promoted Yiddish culture and socialist ideology.[58]

Although the camps were important dispensers of the Party's cultural program, unions were still the primary link between workers and workers' dance programs. In a typical workers' dance group, membership came through the union, although outsiders were generally welcome. The unions used this connection to recruit, since discussion groups focusing on radical political ideas served as prelude and postlude to the dancing itself. If necessary, a union representative was available to clarify ideological matters, and the union itself provided classroom and rehearsal space. Leadership from the Workers Dance League also could be requested.[59]

Segal and others deemed it important that the content of the dances be drawn from workers' experiences in the labor struggle such as striking and picketing. The Needle Trades Workers Dance Group developed the following scenario:

1. In a worker's home (morning)
2. In the boss's home (morning)
3. In the shop
4. Speed-up, accidents, discharge
5. Strike
6. On the picket line

7. The AFL misleaders and the boss's henchmen
8. The settlement committee
9. NTWIU, the leader of the needle trades workers[60]

This script pointed to inequities between workers and "fat cat capitalists," showed the exploitation and reckless endangerment of workers' health and the attempts by workers to organize, their subsequent betrayal at the hands of the "fascist" AFL, and their salvation under the Communist-led NTWIU.

Clearly, one purpose of such groups was to get workers moving politically and to prime them for actual strike actions and picketing. Workers' classes made up scenarios that they danced in a kind of rehearsal for the real thing. They also met and discussed the implications of their work.

Writing in *New Theatre,* dancer Jane Dudley outlined a procedure for putting dance practice to revolutionary use.

> Large groups of lay dancers, even at times the most superficially trained people[,] can by careful direction, set simple but clear patterns of group movement into a form that presents our revolutionary ideas movingly and meaningfully. The dancer learns to move communally, to express with others a simple class conscious idea. In this way large numbers of people can be mobilized not only to dance but to observe and through the discussion of the theme and the problems of movement brought forward by the leader and dancers, clarity of ideology can be given. Certainly the clarification that will come with the discussion of the theme at the end of the class, plus the experience of dancing in groups of twenty and thirty people such a theme as strike or anti-war, cannot fail to educate (propagandize) the members of such a mass class.[61]

Bracketed by discussion groups in which the theme was analyzed and reviewed, the procedure Dudley suggested was encumbered by committees for organizing the class and for delegating responsibilities such as selecting the theme and a leader. Bureaucratic red tape abounded.[62]

From the beginning of her formidable career as a dancer, Dudley was both activist and artist. She was an anomaly in the workers' dance movement. While many of the most active revolutionary dancers were from working-class backgrounds and had experienced firsthand the devastating effects of the depression, Dudley came from an upper-middle-class family, mildly privileged, with a smattering of bohemian tradition; her father was in public relations, her mother once had danced. Educated at the Walden School in Manhattan, a private institution that was a hotbed of radical ideas, and later in Chapel Hill at the University of North Carolina, she went to the Wigman School, not to a settlement house, to study dance.[63]

The revolutionary dance class she proposed began with simple movements aimed at evoking a sense of community in the group. With the warmup complete, sequences of movement could be introduced based on activities such as walking, creeping, marching, hesitating. Whenever possible, these movement structures were used to relate to some predetermined theme, such as striking or picketing. Gradually, a dance was built. As an example of mass dance, Dudley provided a scenario in which workers, pickets, and militia played assigned roles. She suggested different movement themes for each group: a rhythmic swing to the workers; walking motions for the pickets; abstractions of shooting motions for the militia. The stereotyped movement vocabulary clarified dramatic intentions and identified participants in each group. According to her outline, the dance would begin with pickets passing back and forth between rows of workers who would be busily engaged in a repetitive task. While the pickets moved randomly at first, gradually their patterns coalesced and they became a unified group. The first section culminated in three sharp accents. First, the picketers gestured forcefully to the workers. Next, the workers abandoned their labor. Finally, the militia raised their weapons, taking aim at the idle workers.[64] The dance was to reach a climax with the workers surging toward the picketers, and then workers and picketers together pressing the militia back.

Radicals hoped that mock demonstrations such as this one would prepare workers for actual confrontations as well as engage their sympathies and raise political consciousness. One dance that Segal made for the Needle Trades Workers Dance Group was called *Practice for the Picket Line*. Based on a folk dance called the "Oxen Dance," which she had learned in her settlement house days, it consisted of two lines of dancers moving in opposing directions and using motifs that suggested fighting.[65]

Although there was clearly some kind of hierarchical structure underlying the composition process in the revolutionary dance groups, the leader's role was more that of group facilitator than of dictator, and rehearsals often progressed through mutual decision-making. Writing in *New Theatre*, Segal proposed a revolutionary dance community developed through group discussion and shared ideas of movement. In 1933 she had made a dance, *Southern Holiday*, for the Red Dancers, and she described her approach, which included discussions about the various roles (the lynchers and the victim, the Negro) and experiments with plot and movement.

We decide the dance will start with a hunt by the lynchers for the Negro. We try various ways of running, leaping. Some do it with the torso erect, some with the back straight but in a horizontal position, some crouched, some with head going from side to side. We try it in groups and singly. After the director has seen them all, it is decided to choose the leap with the torso low and energized, because it best emphasizes the animal-like nature of the lynchers.[66]

Segal's writing clearly proposed collective solutions—"we try," "we decide," "the dancers contribute." She downplayed the director's authority, and an effort was made to involve participants in the work's composition. In groups such as these, an egalitarian spirit prevailed. Workers participated in creating dances, chipping away at traditional and hierarchical relationships between director and dancer, between professional and lay dancers, and between performer and audience. Because masses of workers often performed, the distinction between those who danced and those who watched was minimized. One article in *New Theatre* went so far as to propose eliminating the role of the audience. "As long as the dance remains a visual experience, it is separate from the people, whereas it should be part of everyday life. Large groups of people can be taught to dance to take part in vast mass dance spectacles. Then there would be no audience in the sense of onlookers at a performance because this enthusiastic group of people would also be participating."[67] In a sense, no audience really was present, if by audience one assumes a distinct and critical body. There was little difference ideologically or professionally between those on stage and those out front.

On June 4, 1933, many workers' dance groups took part in the First Workers Dance Spartakiade held at the New School for Social Research on West 12th Street. The Spartakiades were patterned after German competitions, and this particular event was sponsored by the newly formed Workers Dance League. Participants included the dance group of the Needle Trades Workers Industrial Union, the Artef, the Rebel Arts Dance Group, the Nature Friends Dance Group, the New Dance Group, and the International Workers Order Dance Group as well as the Red Dancers. On the program the NTWIU Dance Group performed *Practice for the Picket Line,* while the Red Dancers did *Southern Holiday* and *Scrubwoman's Dance* about the lives of the mostly Polish and Ukrainian women who made their livelihoods cleaning offices at night. Segal performed *Third Degree,* portraying a comrade who refused to speak. Subtly or not so subtly altering the lyrics of the Negro spiritual, Segal's dance prefigured events of the McCarthy era.

What are your comrades' names
And he didn't say a mumblin' word
Where do your comrades live
And he didn't say a mumblin' word[68]

Segal covered her mouth with one hand and did a long, slow back fall to the ground, which she sustained through the duration of the dance, a technique she had learned from her studies with Martha Graham.[69]

For the Spartakiade in June 1934, held at New York's Town Hall, the Red Dancers performed *Comintern* and *Scottsboro*. The Scottsboro case outraged Northern liberals. Nine young black men, age thirteen to twenty-one, had been accused in March 1931 of raping two white women in Alabama, and they were hastily convicted by an all-white male jury. A long legal struggle followed, led by the Communist Party. "Free the Scottsboro Boys" became a rallying cry for leftist organizations, which were bolstered by one of the young women repudiating her rape charge a month before a new trial. Still, the defendants again were found guilty. Segal wanted to protest this great injustice.

The Nature Friends Dance Group performed Segal's *Kinder, Kuche, and Kirche*.[70] An explicit critique of Hitler's program for women (children, kitchen, and church), the group chose that theme because it reflected the members' own experiences—most of them were German-born. A twelve-year-old child, the granddaughter of one of the group's women, appeared at dance's end as the spirit of the future.

Although audiences continued to be large and enthusiastic, in many ways concerts such as these signaled the end of this first period of revolutionary dance. Emphasis increasingly shifted toward the visual experience of dance, away from the kinesthetic and experiential—the participatory. When workers took their dances onto the proscenium stage, out of union halls and workers' clubs, the elements that had made their work vital to other workers—clarity and ideological stance—were suddenly criticized as crude and obvious.[71] Reviewing a performance of *Black and White* at Town Hall in December 1934, Edna Ocko wrote:

> Put any negro and white performer on the stage, show them struggling under similar conditions, show their initial enmity and their final heroic handclasp and fist salute, and you have ideal conditions for applause. *Black and White* by the Red Dancers recreates a slogan in pantomimic movement, but surely no one can claim for it an imaginative or original approach to the negro question, despite the fact that it evokes lusty applause.[72]

17. The Nature Friends Dancers in Edith Segal's *Kinder, Kuche, and Kirche.* Note the formal spatial patterns and abstract use of gesture. (Reproduced from *new dance,* special recital issue, January 1935. Dance Collection, New York Public Library for the Performing Arts, Astor, Lenox and Tilden Foundations.)

Although Ocko was a fierce defender of revolutionary dance, she was also a supporter of the "new" dance and an advocate of modernism. She had her own agenda, and she found Segal's too predictable, too simplistic. Yet despite the clear symbolism and exaggerated stereotypes characterizing much of Segal's work, her formal use of space and design in a photograph of *Kinder, Kuche, and Kirche* suggest the extent to which she did transform elements borrowed from pageantry and agitprop theater into a unique style that used elements of modernism (figure 17). The figures in the photograph are placed in formal spatial patterns, not realistic designs, and the positions, while reminiscent of actual gesture, are in fact highly stylized and abstracted.[73]

Workers' dance, despite its status as "revolutionary," functioned most successfully within a self-selected community, uniting audience and performers in a shared ideological vision. Performers did not have the burden of attempting to shift audience allegiance; instead, dances reinforced existing belief systems. When the radical dance movement expanded onto the proscenium stage, however, attracting a wider audience that was not specifically, or only, working-class, it was perceived as agitprop theater meant to provoke and incite, and it was criticized for the same elements that had been praised.[74]

Segal, intending "to dance the kind of dances that workers understand,"[75] now earned stinging criticism. In a way, Ocko and other critics were changing the rules of the game; the purpose of workers' theater and dance, after all, never had been the creation of professional artists, accomplished performers in a repertory of socialist drama or dance. Participation of the masses in artistic and cultural endeavors had been the goal.[76]

In 1935 the Workers Dance League changed its name to the New Dance League[77] in an attempt to broaden its influence and downplay class associations. Amateur performances by workers' cultural organizations in proscenium theaters virtually ceased. Segal left for Detroit in 1936 to establish a Midwestern New Dance League, and there she was employed by the Federal Theatre Project, staging movement for productions such as *One Third of a Nation* at the same time that she made various attempts to organize FTP workers and take her place in sit-down strikes and picket lines. Returning to New York in 1939, she resumed her association with Camp Kinderland, where she continued to teach until 1972, the camp's final summer at the Sylvan Lake location.

To some extent, the workers' cultural program continued at places like Kinderland, where the outdoors became Segal's stage. In a pageant called "Immigrants All, Americans All," she used the lake to stage the arrival of immigrants from Europe, creating a model of the Statue of Liberty on a raft.[78] Actors from the Artef and singers from the Freiheit Singing Society were on the camp's staff, and Segal was quick to make use of their talents, but as always she coaxed amateurs into performing, finding ways to pull casual onlookers into the thick of things, where they were taught bits and pieces of the folk dances she had learned at the Neighborhood Playhouse. One former camper remembered: "'39 was the first time I got in touch with Edith because she was the one who got me involved with dancing. She got all the guys down to the campfire and she said, 'I need guys,' and we made up a dance around Indian Village."[79]

Large pageants, most with explicit political agendas, also continued the tradition of amateur performance, relying primarily on choreographers associated with workers' dance to stage the movement. In 1936 Bill Matons, who appeared on concerts sponsored by the New Dance League and with the Humphrey-Weidman company, choreographed a May Day pageant at the Bronx Coliseum in which he appeared with his own Experimental Dance Group. Directed by Charles Friedman of the Theatre Union, this pageant depicted "memorable scenes in Labor's history," and amateur singers and dancers were recruited to perform.[80] The *Daily Worker* assured readers that the dances were one of the program's highlights, praising in particular the scenes portraying the trial of Sacco and Vanzetti, whose execution in 1927 had inspired liberal and leftist outrage.[81] Another May Day pageant that year, staged at the Polo Grounds, featured amateur dancers from the International Ladies Garment Workers Union in "Brotherhood," a work choreographed by a Virginia Mishnun.[82]

Pauline Koner and Fanya Chochem staged dances for the Lenin-Liebnecht-Luxemburg memorial event sponsored by the Young Communist League on January 15, 1937, at St. Nicholas Arena. Chochem, an early member of the Workers Dance League, was associated with the Rebel Dancers of Newark. Koner's long career as an artist is well-known, her early association with the left less so. Five days after the YCL-sponsored event, on January 20, a Lenin memorial was organized to take place in support of the Loyalist cause in the Spanish Civil War; dances once again were to be by Maton and direction by Friedman. A Living Newspaper, an agitprop technique that issued from the workers' theater movement, was scheduled to depict the siege of Madrid. Accounts in the *Daily Worker* to the contrary, it appears that this event never actually occurred because New York City fire marshals closed the doors of Madison Square Garden before the performance could start.[83] For a jubilee at the Hippodrome in March 1937, dances were staged by Lillian Shapero, a dancer with the Martha Graham company until 1934 and the director of the Artef Dance Group. Later that year, Shapero contributed the choreography for *One Sixth of the Earth* (the population of the Soviet Union).[84] It included a ballet, set to composer Marc Blitzstein's "Moscow Metro," about the Soviets' ten-year plan for electrification.[85] Anna Sokolow, active in the revolutionary dance movement from its inception, staged "Dance of All Nations" at Madison Square Garden in 1938, using members of her group, the Dance Unit, to commemorate the fourteenth anniversary of Lenin's death.[86]

Accounts of Edith Segal's work in the 1940s and 1950s indicate that she continued her association with amateur dancers. In 1943 she began work on a piece called *The Magic Fountain*. The idea for the dance was sparked by a picture of a fountain in Stalingrad circled by the idyllic dancing figures of six children holding hands. In the dance's scenario the fountain came to life once a year, on May Day, and children came from all over to witness the magical event. Divided into three parts, the dance began with a celebration of the monument. In part two the fountain was destroyed by the invading German army, and in part three the statue was rebuilt by the Red Army after its victory over the enemy.

Initially, Segal used participants from Camp Kinderland, adding more dancers from her classes at the shules—one hundred in all—for a Carnegie Hall performance in December for Russian War Relief. The dance ended with dancers moving in concentric circles, one group circling clockwise, the next moving counterclockwise, suggesting the powerful forces that could join participants into a single dynamic community.[87]

Clearly, the utopian ideal of making a better world through dance was still informing Segal's work. Interviews reveal her perception of herself as teacher and educator with a missionary impulse to introduce children and young people to a world where the value of labor is understood and where peoples of diverse colors and religions live together harmoniously. In a book of poetry first published in 1952, *Be My Friend and other poems for boys and girls,* Segal envisioned a world joined in a utopia of movement:

A Different Language

I met a little girl
    Who came from another land.
I couldn't speak her language,
    but I took her by the hand.
We danced together,

> Had such fun,
> Dancing is a language
> You can speak with anyone.[88]

In a note to dance teachers at the end of the volume Segal explained that she had developed this particular poem into a festival of dances from all nations ending with a dance of peace and brotherhood.

The complicity of the body in the openly propagandistic exercises of dancers like Segal was always enveloped in a system of beliefs: through dance would come the fulfillment of the Soviet vision. Like Isadora Duncan's, Segal's vision may have seemed grandiose, yet an underlying commitment to the rights of those most often ignored—children, blacks, immigrant workers—remained at its core.

T H R E E

Dancing Red

Those dancers who were party members were the ones who got the idea and the ones who generated and caused it to go. Later it spread out to people who were more politically naive, but more artistically mature.[1]

Idealistic visions of a new socialist world buoyed by the collective mus-culature of hundreds of dancing bodies collided head-on with questions of form and aesthetics as they were developing in the "new" dance. Under the eagle eye of Louis Horst, mentor to Martha Graham and musi-cal director for Graham, Doris Humphrey, and Helen Tamiris, American modern dance struggled to define principles of composition, to estab-lish standards of professionalism, and to earn respect within the artis-tic community. The goals of "new" dance were often in conflict with the impassioned, aesthetically naive danced treatises that flourished in workers' groups, at union gatherings, and at Communist Party rallies. The principles of modernism—abstraction and distortion—complicated the social message.[2]

The Workers Dance League claimed that all art was really propaganda: "No artist, if he is honest, can fail to recognize that no matter what he is saying, he is saying something . . . which he expects to evoke some response from his audience."[3] Yet the League did allow that not all pro-paganda was art.

Although the League claimed to be a nonpolitical, nonsectarian orga-nization, with Communist dancers accounting for only twenty of its 800 members in 1932,[4] its official line on art and propaganda echoed Party rhetoric. Many dance groups were modeled on the CP's political cell,[5] and the League's program emphasized class struggle as the central issue in all artistic endeavors.

We definitely have something to say. We are aware of sharp social conflicts. We are on the side of the oppressed people, the workers[,] and we rally with them in their revolutionary struggle for the overthrow of the oppressors, the capitalists. We see the forces of progress, of peace, of universal freedom choked by the black forces of fascism, the naked brutal dictatorship of the capitalists. And this conviction . . . is the inspiration of our work.[6]

Although the Lenin memorials and celebrations of Russian and Soviet history continued throughout the decade, workers' dances were increasingly concerned with issues directly affecting Americans—not Lenin's death, but the struggles of working-class poor in the streets of New York City. League members' dances focused on a "disintegrating social system,"[7] the psychological alienation of the underclass, and the unequal distribution of power within the American capitalistic system. Dances such as *Strike* (1933) by the New Dance Group depicted the revolt of the worker, while Nadia Chilkovsky's *Parasite* (1934) denounced a greedy, fat-cat capitalist. The emotional and physical wreckage left in the system's wake was the subject of Jane Dudley's *Time Is Money* (1934), Chilkovsky's *Homeless Girl* (1934), and at least two works by Anna Sokolow, *Strange American Funeral* (1935) and *Case History #* (1937). The growing threat of fascism in Europe was another subject of concern. *Van der Lubbe's Head* (1934) by the New Dance Group was made in response to the rise of National Socialism in Germany, and Sokolow's *Anti-War Cycle* (1934) "took the entire canvas of imperialist war and diplomacy and translated it into a three-partitioned dance."[8]

While harsh political and economic realities were standard subject matter in most League concerts, occasionally a writer lobbied for a touch of levity to lighten the mood—for instance, a dance about nature or love sandwiched between the class struggle. A member of the New Dance Group who signed himself Ezra Freeman A.B. (able-bodied seaman) gently chastised the earnest revolutionaries: "Nor need we fear that the proper amount of gaiety and humor will detract from our revolutionary strength of purpose. Beware! ye gods and masters of rebels who laugh and sing."[9] *New Theatre* failed to appreciate his sense of humor and shot back: "When the greatest battle of all has been fought and won: when oppression and exploitation shall have become history, then we shall dance of the sea and the stars."[10] In other words, until the class struggle was resolved, no frivolity was to be allowed.

By the mid-1930s the agitprop style and the participatory form of the tributes to Lenin sponsored by the Communist Party, USA, and en-

acted by workers' dance groups had been altered by aesthetic consider-
ations borrowed from bourgeois art. Among League members, the New
Dance Group and the Theatre Union Dance Group, affiliated with the
working-class Theatre Union and under the direction of Anna Sokolow,
proved most successful in realizing the marriage of social conscience
with emerging professional and artistic standards in "new" dance. These
groups earned critical acclaim from John Martin and from Louis Horst's
newly established periodical, *Dance Observer,* as well as from the leftist
New Theatre.

In February 1934 *Dance Observer* published its first edition, stating its
mission as an advocate for serious dance in the United States and arguing that no other publication existed to fill this need. *New Theatre* was
providing fairly complete coverage of the revolutionary dance scene at
the time, so *Dance Observer* almost certainly was intended to provide
an alternative critical voice, one more tuned to aesthetics than politics.
Although the first issue of *New Theatre* was published only five months
earlier, in September 1933, it replaced an earlier periodical called *Workers
Theatre,* which had been in existence since 1931, publishing articles on a
variety of dance activities.

Sokolow's *Anti-War Cycle* was praised by *Dance Observer* for its "com-
mendable choreography and [its] fine sense of interpretive balance, despite its avowed purpose of propaganda." [11] In the *New York Times,* Martin
proclaimed it "a fine piece of work when judged by almost any standard."
"Any standard" meaning aesthetic as well as political. Overall, Martin was
impressed by the distinction between the "first-rate" work produced by
the New Dance Group and Sokolow's Theatre Union Group and what he
judged to be the amateur contributions of other workers' groups, such
as Segal's Red Dancers.[12] In *New Theatre,* Edna Ocko agreed, pronounc-
ing the New Dance Group and the Theatre Union Dance Group the only
ensembles that belonged on a concert stage.[13]

The dance content presented by these groups was not so different
from that developed within union settings, except that real workers were
absent. Borrowing techniques gleaned from the world of theater and
collaborating with leftist artists from other fields, these groups molded
didactic themes into modernist works of art.

The New Dance Group was formed in February 1932 by dancers from
the Mary Wigman School,[14] including Fanya Geltman, Miriam Blecher,
Nadia Chilkovsky (figure 18) (who sometimes wrote under the pseudonym Nell Anyon), Becky Lee, Grace Wylie, and Edna Ocko.[15] Ocko wore
many caps in the revolutionary dance movement. She played piano ac-

18. Nadia Chilkovsky of the New Dance Group. She sometimes wrote under the pseudonym of Nell Anyon. (Photograph by William Stone. Courtesy of the Dance Collection, New York Public Library for the Performing Arts, Astor, Lenox and Tilden Foundations.)

companiment for classes, danced, and wrote, using a variety of pseudonyms; besides her own byline, her criticism appeared under the names Eve Stebbins, Elizabeth Script, Marion Sellars, Francis Steuben, and Edna Poe.[16]

An article in *New Theatre* listed the aims of the New Dance Group:

1. performing before workers, students, and the regular dance concert audience;
2. performing for the purpose of educating and stimulating the audience to significant aspects of the class struggle;

3. training performing troupes to undertake this task;
4. training the individuals who are to make up these performing troupes;
5. themselves becoming a part of the class struggle through practical and theoretical education.[17]

Dancer Fanya Geltman recalled the group's first days: "We handed out these leaflets. . . . We went to all the factories, the garment industry . . . the ILGWU. The first night I shall never forget. They came in hordes, 10 cents we charged, 10 cents a dance. And they came and they came and they left their machines at night, you know, and they came to dance." [18]

By 1933, membership counted three hundred, and organizational strategies proliferated. The group was administered by an executive committee consisting of representatives from the dance sections and committee heads, including dance, which handled teaching and repertoire; business, in charge of publicity and finance; and education, responsible for the library. A secretary and an individual known simply as the organizer (initially this task fell to Grace Wylie) completed the committee (figure 19).[19]

From the beginning, the New Dance Group foresaw the need for a working-class dance academy, a center devoted to training dancers. The New Dance Group school was probably unique at this time, established outside the structures of unions and workers' recreational clubs but untainted by the elitism and social isolation that the radical press attributed to "established" modern dance schools such as Graham's.

These early classes were inexpensive, 10 cents for a three-hour class. Each group numbered about thirty students and was led by an executive committee member. Classes included technique and improvisation —modeled after the teachings of the Wigman School—and concluded with a political discussion.[20] Members were encouraged to read revolutionary literature and to participate in demonstrations: "It is our task as a workers' organization to knit our membership together in the revolutionary movement through the dissemination of working class literature, the institution of study circles, and participating in workers' demonstrations." [21] Dancing and politics—they were really the same thing.

The group prided itself on its heterogeneous membership. One report on occupations lists six sales clerks, a shoe worker, a needle trade worker, a food worker, a social worker, a dress designer, a professional housekeeper, a dress cleaner, six office workers, a milliner, four students, a laboratory technician, an artist, a hairdresser, two beauticians, a physical therapy technician, fifteen teachers, two lawyers, a model, a chem-

19. By 1933 the New Dance Group's membership counted three hundred, and organizational strategies proliferated. (Photograph by Kessner. Reproduced from the New Dance Group's first annual recital souvenir program, 1933.)

ist, and a sailor (probably the outspoken Ezra Freeman).[22] These classes must have included an astonishing array of bodies and shapes.

Often, the individuals who were most politically involved in the group's activities were the least accomplished dancers. "They got too involved in the organizational work," said Jane Dudley, who joined the group early on. "You can't do both. You have to do your pliés and your leg beats. You have to put in so many hours a day."[23]

Classes were open to everyone, and membership was actively solicited. Struggling with ways to involve amateurs while producing dances of "artistic integrity,"[24] the New Dance Group formulated a policy in which professional members performed together but made it their mission to develop a new cadre of trained dancers. Anyone in the group therefore could aspire toward a position in the performing troupe, but standards of professionalism remained in force.[25]

The group promised to perform "anywhere, at anytime, with dances suitable to the occasion";[26] its aim was to become a full-time paid professional group. No precedent in American dance existed, however, for a fully independent, self-supporting group; in fact, "American" dance really did not exist yet.[27] Ocko argued for a shock troupe, professionals who would live and work collectively, supported by the other members. Free to devote themselves entirely to creative activities, members of the troupe would compose new dances in support of the revolutionary cause and present them to workers everywhere.[28] Ocko probably took the idea of a shock troupe from the Workers Laboratory Theatre, which had successfully established a full-time performing group in 1933, supported by members of its evening section.[29] While it must have seemed a compelling goal, the New Dance Group was never able to make a dance shock troupe a reality.

The first New Dance Group concert took place at the Heckscher Theatre on March 26, 1933 (figure 20). Concerns with contemporary social issues are evident in the dance titles. Sections of *Strike* were called "Uprisings," "Hunger," and "War Trilogy: Breadlines, War, On the Barricades," while the suite *Satires* contained dances called "Parasite," "Charity," "Jingoisms: Traffic, Politicians, Peace Conferences" (figure 21).[30]

In theory, anyone who had an idea could direct or choreograph a dance for performance by the group. And anyone within the group could contribute to the making of the dance. While this arrangement fit nicely within the vision of egalitarianism promoted by the Party, in practice a single individual usually directed the choreographic process. Generally, this was not publicly acknowledged as most of the group's early programs did not single out individuals for choreographic credit.[31]

Attempts were made to solicit ideas for dances from artists in other fields as well. A set of the Little Lenin Library was offered as a prize in a New Dance Group contest open to workers as well as artists. "The contest calls for a prize winning dance scenario or libretto for a ballet or mass dance. . . . One need not know how to dance or direct dances in order to participate in this contest; leave that problem to the League. This is for writers, poets, thinkers, scenarists, who have ideas they would like to see danced."[32]

Initially, the *Daily Worker* had praised the New Dance Group as an antidote to the "theories and outworn ideological energies of the principal schools of the modern dance,"[33] discreetly sidestepping the issue of what was being taught at the school under the generic title of "dance." In fact, the school's approach was "bourgeois," its philosophy consistently emphasizing the usefulness of the newly established dance techniques. At first, those techniques were influenced by Wigman/Holm principles, but later into the 1930s, classes in Graham technique were taught by Sophie Maslow. Maslow, a dancer of great social conscience performed with the Martha Graham company beginning in 1931 and came to the New Dance Group in 1935 to teach technique to the group's professionals.[34] Thus, an eclectic array of strong "bourgeois" classes for its

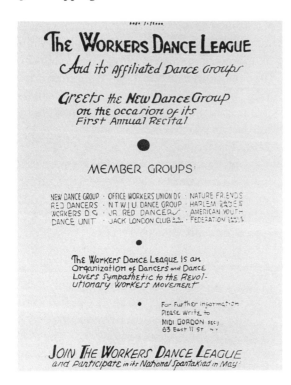

The Workers Dance League

And its Affiliated Dance Groups

Greets the New Dance Group
on the occasion of its
First Annual Recital

●

MEMBER GROUPS

NEW DANCE GROUP · OFFICE WORKERS UNION DG · NATURE FRIENDS
RED DANCERS · N T W I U DANCE GROUP · HARLEM DANCER
WORKERS D G · JR RED DANCERS · AMERICAN YOUTH
DANCE UNIT · JACK LONDON CLUB ·· FEDERATION

●

The Workers Dance League is an
Organization of Dancers and Dance
Lovers Sympathetic to the Revol-
utionary Workers Movement

● For Further information
please write to
MIDI GORDON secy
63 East 11 st n y

JOIN THE WORKERS DANCE LEAGUE
and Participate in its National Spartakiad in May

20. The Workers Dance League greets the New Dance Group. (Reproduced from the New Dance Group's first annual recital souvenir program, 1933.)

working-class students was the school's hallmark, while some technical prowess was a must for the performing group.

Although the group was sometimes criticized for its association with "bourgeois" technique, members familiar with self-criticism as part of the Party regimen faulted themselves for not mastering those same skills sufficiently. In an article in *New Theatre,* Grace Wylie charged that uneven technical abilities and lack of adequate rehearsal caused the group's performances to be ragged, while lack of political sophistication made the content of the dances murky.[35] Reacting to a rash of generic revolutionary dances presented by the Workers Dance League, she wrote: "We hope that by next year all our groups will have gotten a *Revolt* [sometimes called *Uprising, Upsurge,* or *Red Tide*] off their chests and find means of bringing forward themes which are of direct import to our audience."[36]

This critique of proletarian efforts appeared about the same time that the Communist Party was promoting its new policy of socialist realism, urging revolutionary artists to make use of the professional know-how of bourgeois theater to make the Party's message more understandable and enjoyable to a wider audience. While this was surely an attempt to lure dancegoers with the flash of technical skills and smooth professionalism, the irony was that "bourgeois" schools of dance were experimenting with material that was hardly understandable or enjoyable to a naive audience. Popular audiences were indeed mystified — if not dumfounded — by "new" dance at this time. The musical comedy star Fanny Brice created a spoof called "Rewolt" for the 1935 *Ziegfeld Follies* in which Graham's work was the object of humorous ridicule. Nevertheless, the new policy meant that dancers could aspire with a clear conscience to greater technique within working-class groups.

Early efforts by the New Dance Group were similar to dances being composed by the Red Dancers, the Nature Friends Group, and the Needle Trades Workers. The production of *Charity,* for example, was lambasted by Louis Horst in *Dance Observer:* "as crude and illiterate an example of bad taste as could possibly degrade a great and powerful art." [37] Based on the Wobbly song "There'll Be Pie in the Sky By and By," the dance proposed to expose the false promise of religion by satirizing the Salvation

21. Concerns with contemporary social issues were evidenced in dances such as "On the Barricades," part of a suite entitled *Strike.* (Reproduced from the New Dance Group's first annual recital souvenir program, 1933. Courtesy of the Dance Collection, New York Public Library for the Performing Arts, Astor, Lenox and Tilden Foundations.)

Army; in one section a man dressed in a cleric's black suit stood on a platform making "fake generous god bless you motions."[38] The dance met with an enthusiastic response from Communists and fellow travelers in the audience. Horst, accompanied by Martha Graham, walked out of the performance.[39]

While no specific demographics were produced for the composition of workers' dance audiences, the extent of Communist influence was often alluded to by reviewers in *Dance Observer,* generally to discount favorable responses to material that the reviewer may have found questionable. Acknowledging the "large and enthusiastic audience of Communists in varying states of leaning," for example, Paul Love chided the dancers, likening them to "obstreperous children. . . . The Workers' Dance League at present," he wrote "sways nobody but its own coterie— and that through Communist patriotism, not through dancing."[40] But no one could deny that Workers Dance League performances were popular. An article by Ocko in *New Masses,* for example, reported that from October 1933 until April 1934, 240 requests for paid performances by the League were received, of which some 140 were accepted.[41]

The Workers Dance League mandated political content, but that content was not easily framed within the emerging modernist aesthetic. How to dance the oppression of the working class, the exploitation by a capitalist society, the threat of fascism, and the horrors of racism, yet not depend upon mimetic action? On one hand was the Marxist concept of art as a literal reflection of reality, on the other, the modernist project that demanded the viewer's participation in the creation of meaning.[42]

When *Van der Lubbe's Head* (1934) won first prize in the Second Annual Spartakiade of the Workers' Dance Festival, it established the New Dance Group's role as standard bearer of artistic and social practice among workers' dance groups. According to the collective ideology of the day, the choreography was credited to the New Dance Group, although, in fact, Miriam Blecher directed the dance.[43] Blecher, like other principals in the revolutionary dance scene, had been raised on the Lower East Side by immigrant parents;[44] her father was a tailor and a religious Jew. Introduced to dance through settlement house programs she studied and performed at the Neighborhood Playhouse before immersing herself in classes at the Wigman School (figure 22).

Blecher described her approach to the social issues of the time as intuitive rather than analytic,[45] and she composed dances that celebrated the energy and life of New York's teeming streets. Surely, her experience growing up on the Lower East Side was important in her politicization,[46]

22. Miriam Blecher. (Photographer unknown. Courtesy of the Dance Collection, New York Public Library for the Performing Arts, Astor, Lenox and Tilden Foundations.)

and later she would be influenced by her husband, the radical playwright George Sklar.

Van der Lubbe's Head told the story of Marinus Van der Lubbe, who was made the scapegoat for the Reichstag fire in February 1933. He was beheaded by order of the new German chancellor, Adolf Hitler, in an effort to consolidate the Nazi Party's hold on governmental power. A 1934

23. An uneasy stillness before some inescapable act of violence. The New Dance Group production of *Van der Lubbe's Head,* 1934. (Photograph by Alfredo Valente. Courtesy of Judy Sklar Rasminsky, Daniel Sklar, and Zachery Sklar.)

photograph shows five dancers dressed in long black skirts (figure 23). The faces of four of the women are hidden behind masks, while the exposed and vulnerable features of a fifth dancer set her apart. The masks disguised the perpetrators of the Reichstag arson at the same time that the absence of a disguise identified and isolated the falsely accused, thus communicating the story's most obvious elements. Spatial formation and exaggerated gesture played parts in the creation of an ominous picture; three of the masked figures point accusing fingers, while a fourth figure looms over the unmasked dancer, who appears unaware of the menace. The photograph suggests an uneasy stillness before some inescapable act of violence.

The masks worn by the dancers were suggested by Blecher[47] and were reminiscent of the New Dance Group's German Expressionist roots. Wigman used masks in *Ceremonial Figure* (1925), *Witch Dance* (1926), and *Totenmal* (1930), among others. Not surprisingly, considering the Wigman/Holm principles taught at the school, the movement style borrowed elements of German dance.[48]

Ocko, a dancer in the original production, but now wearing her critic's cap, was anxious to establish the group's modernist credentials. Comparing this depiction of German fascism with the agitprop style of Segal's Nature Friends Dance Group in *Kinder, Kuche, and Kirche,* she wrote, "*Van der Lubbe's Head* . . . projects the horror and viciousness of the Hitler regime, not through literal movement, but through distortion."[49]

The New Dance Group may have embraced the project of modernism in *Van der Lubbe's Head,* but the broad mimetic style of agitprop dance would have been redundant in any case. The dance was accompanied by Alfred Hayes's poem of the same name, which provided the political text.[50]

In the *New York Times,* John Martin reluctantly praised *Van der Lubbe's Head,* pointing to Blecher's gifts as a choreographer and composer. But the reviewer could not resist a jibe at the audience:

> From the standpoint of perfection this success is debatable, but in the particular dimensions in which the Workers Dance League builds its entire repertoire, it is significant. The major complaint commonly raised against "propaganda" dancing is its literalness and lack of essentially choreographic form. With a definite literary message to deliver, it customarily sacrifices without hesitation such vital considerations as good composition and kinetic design and defends itself by classifying them as aesthetic abstractions and flights from reality, and drowns all criticism with three rousing cheers from the proletariat.[51]

From Martin's standpoint, *Van der Lubbe's Head* succeeded because it assigned the burden of propaganda to the poem's ringing words. He offered the following suggestion to radical dancemakers: "If, therefore, one were bold enough to offer a formula to these groups it would be that they compose all their dances to spoken words and then omit the words in performance. Thus everybody would be satisfied with the possible exception of the poet."[52] So much for the social message.

Clearly, the combination of text and movement solved a lot of problems for radical dancemakers. A dance could unfold according to the rules of composition developed by Horst, and leave the task of political education to the words. Dancer Jane Dudley recollected "the most important thing about that whole period was that some very good dances were done, mainly using words because it was through the words that the content got made specific."[53] Many of her dances at the time relied on some form of text. *The Dream Ends* (1934) was set to a song by the German composer and revolutionary Hans Eisler,[54] while the words of left-wing poet Sol Funaroff accompanied Dudley's 1934 *Time Is Money.*

Dudley had studied with Ruth Doing and at the Mary Wigman School, and she had danced in Hanya Holm's demonstration group. Through their studies at the Wigman School, she knew Miriam Blecher, and it was Blecher who introduced her to the New Dance Group.[55] Appearing with the group for the first time in June 1934, Dudley contributed three compositions to the Workers Dance League solo concert in November 1934; these included *The Dream Ends* and *Time Is Money,* which juxtaposed images of exploited workers, their exhaustion, and the monotony of their jobs with the ticking of a clock, while Funaroff's words were recited offstage. In *New Theatre,* Steve Foster singled out this dance as one of the best in the repertory of solo dances by Sokolow, Maslow, Blecher, Segal, and Chilkovsky, praising Dudley's "insight into the social scene" and noting that she made no attempt to act out the poem.[56] *Dance Observer,* however, found Dudley's interpretation literal and accused her of having nothing to say.[57]

The two periodicals' reactions were perhaps predictable. Still, the New Dance Group was gradually succeeding in creating a unique space for itself in a kind of middle ground, a place where its dances might presumably satisfy two disparate sets of audiences and critics: the "bourgeois" concertgoers who were following the development of the "new" dance and applauding modernist experimentation, and the enthusiastic working groups whose halls and unions still provided stages for numerous performances.

This attempt at artistic and political balance occasionally created misunderstandings between dancers on stage and workers in the audience. While some League performances occurred at the Brooklyn Academy of Music, or St. Nicholas Arena, or the City College auditorium, many still took place on makeshift stages on the workers' own turf, where, after long subway rides, the dancers would traipse in, costumes stuffed into brown paper bags, to face the task of turning a union hall into a temporary stage.[58] And here a performance of *Van der Lubbe's Head* for an audience of striking shoe workers had some unexpected results. According to Ocko: "The dance begins with a bare leg coming out of the curtain. . . . and the shoe workers said . . . don't you have any money for shoes, ladies? We'll give you some shoes. That's why we have to be on strike. They don't wear any shoes."[59] Duncan's spiritual legacy—the religion of the naked human foot—proved puzzling to the audience of shoemakers. Yet surely some members of this unorthodox audience continued to follow the development of modern dance in more conventional settings where they may have sat side by side with the dance avant-garde.

The contributions of dancers such as Miriam Blecher, Jane Dudley, and later Sophie Maslow in the New Dance Group point to the transitional character of the movement at that time. The group had begun as "a laboratory for the study and development of proletarian culture in the form of the dance,"[60] but by the mid-1930s increasing emphasis was being placed on artistic matters. Workers' issues were subject matter, something to dance "about," rather than to be embodied in an actual presence. The school continued as a resource for working-class and amateur students, offering an eclectic array of classes, including ethnic dance styles, but the group's composition gradually changed. Fanya Geltman and Nadia Chilkovsky left to become part of the Federal Dance Project. Edna Ocko stopped dancing and concentrated on writing. In 1937 Blecher (the only one of the original six still active in the group) and Dudley appeared in a program at the Grand Street Playhouse. Blecher did *Two Jewish Songs* and *The Village Without Men,* a dance about a German village where all the men had been killed or sent to concentration camps,[61] while Dudley danced *Four Middle Class Portraits,* a psychological study based on poems by Kenneth Fearing. Appearing as "Swivel Chair Hero," "Dream World Dora," "The Aesthete," and "The Liberal," Dudley was beginning her work with character study in movement.[62] A program sponsored by the American Dance Association in 1938[63] featured Blecher dancing *East Side Sketches, Mask Dances,* and *Three Jewish Songs* in concert with Dorothy Bird of the Martha Graham company and Si-lan Chen.[64] Photographs of Blecher in *East Side Sketches* hint at the lyricism, the emotional warmth, and the enthusiasm and professionalism that inspired her audience (figures 24, 25, and 26). In April at the Brooklyn Museum the New Dance Group appeared along with an independent group headed by Maslow,[65] and a 1940 performance at the Grand Street Playhouse featured works by Dudley and Maslow as well as Marie Marchowsky and Frieda Flier—all four at that time dancing with Martha Graham.[66]

In 1940 Blecher left New York, moving to California with her husband, and none of the original group members remained.[67]

It is not clear how Anna Sokolow came to be associated with the Theatre Union. Larry Warren, her biographer, suggests that the Theatre Union approached Sokolow in the summer of 1933, after a Union representative saw some of her creations at a Workers Dance League concert.[68] A dance group from the Theatre Union made an appearance soon thereafter at an Anti-War Congress at St. Nicholas Arena. Another account posits that Sokolow and Jane Dudley approached the Theatre Union's executive board and proposed a dance unit after the Theatre Union had presented a solo recital by dancer Sophia Delza.[69] (Delza was the sister

24, 25, 26. Miriam Blecher in *East Side Sketches*. (Photographer unknown. Courtesy of Judy Sklar Rasminsky, Daniel Sklar, and Zachery Sklar.)

of leftist filmmaker Leo Hurwitz, who would later marry Jane Dudley; radical artists formed a close community.)

Sokolow was an important member of Martha Graham's early company and a significant force in both the revolutionary and modern dance movements, so there may well have been mutual explorations. In any event, a dance group was organized within the Theatre Union with Sokolow as its director. The original group included Ethel But-

ler, Marie Marchowsky, Anita Alvarez, Ronya Chernin, Celia Dembroe, Ruth Freedman, Eleanor Lapidus, Florence Schneider, and Ethel Solitar. Marchowsky as well as Aza Cefkin, who joined the group a year later, had both danced at Camp Kinderland.[70]

The Theatre Union, which shared the social conscience of other working-class groups, had two basic goals: (1) to produce plays with working-class content and (2) to provide theater experiences of a high caliber to working-class audiences at working-class prices.[71] The Union was distinguished by its artistic ambition and embrace of professionalism. From its inception, its productions involved professional actors who were both socially conscious and artistically ambitious. Describing her experience in a production called *Peace on Earth,* one actress said: "I've always felt that the theatre should be a means of political and social expression. This is the first play in which I had a chance to express that feeling myself. No other play ever did it. A few plays attempted it with a slightly satirical approach; but no other play involved both the actors and the audience like *Peace on Earth.*"[72]

Sokolow's group, which also would distinguish itself through its emphasis on professionalism, was initially called the Theatre Union Dance Group. Performing under the Theatre Union aegis in a number of concerts sponsored by the Workers Dance League in 1934 and 1935, as well as on union stages, the group took second prize in the League's 1934 Spartakiade with *Anti-War Cycle.* In the *New York Times,* Martin questioned the very idea of a workers' dance competition; he then allowed, however, that the judges had probably picked the wrong winner. He preferred Sokolow's *Anti-War Cycle* to *Van der Lubbe's Head,* which won first prize. He did not even mention Segal's *Kinder, Kuche, and Kirche,* which earned third prize.[73] Although the dance group was soon disbanded, Sokolow continued her work with another group—the Dance Unit—and with most of the same dancers.

With *Strange American Funeral* (1935), Sokolow contributed to the growing debate surrounding the marriage of poetry and dance.[74] The dance was set to a poem called "Strange Funeral in Braddock" by Michael Gold and to a musical score written by leftist composer Elie Siegmeister. Gold's poem was an example of what he called proletarian poetry. In his column for the *Daily Worker,* he urged writers to use simple vocabulary and concrete ideas or, as he put it, the kind of words that "work every day, and not words that live only in the library." His poetry was geared to "arouse that emotion of solidarity, class loyalty and courage, which is the red beating heart of a mass movement," and he berated writers who wrote "not for the masses, but for the narrow circles of the overeducated."[75] His chief target was T. S. Eliot, a naturalized British citizen, born in St. Louis, with aloof, patrician airs, who became a dedicated anticommunist.

In "Strange Funeral in Braddock" a steelworker is immolated and his body turned into steel. The poem splices images of the Pennsylvania spring and the suffering of the worker's widow with scenes of the steel mill; softness and pathos are layered between hard, unfeeling metal. Accounts of Sokolow's dance suggest that she also depicted the harsh, external reality of the steel mill alongside the widow's emotional experience.

Using the metaphor of steel forming, melting, and reshaping itself, a reviewer described the dance:

> The solid steel block of dancers, locked at the elbows, coming heavily downstage, fixed the meaning of the dance. Breaking and shifting to dance the steel-puddler, Jan Clepak, who is buried in his trough, and resolving again to steel, breaking to dance spring in Pennsylvania and the resolution made at Clepak's grave, and becoming steel again, they contributed an effective and popular success.[76]

The choreography seems to have been basically formal: group arrangements, phalanxes of dancers moving with implacable force, the "solid steel block of dancers" breaking and re-forming. I can imagine linear formations; cold, clean angles, architectural designs, all dividing into narrative vignettes.

The Gold-Siegmeister collaboration had been performed in 1934, a year earlier, for the Workers Music League, which also took as its primary task the development of art as a weapon in the class struggle. As an avant-garde composer, Siegmeister must have found himself in an awkward position. But the Party line verged on schizophrenia, allowing the CP to decry what Gold called the elitism of the "narrow circles of the overeducated"[77] —that is, composers like Siegmeister—yet advocate classical (and/or avant-garde) techniques whenever such techniques could prove useful to proletarian purposes or as the policy of socialist realism dictated. So the collaboration was praised for "using a twentieth century musical idiom of the bourgeois concert stage as the vehicle for a proletarian text."[78] The *Daily Worker* reported that the mass of workers were "thoroughly 20th century in musical taste in spite of the lack of their musical training under capitalism" and that "the 'untutored' workers almost unanimously acclaim[ed] the tractor of 20th century modern music,"[79] a clumsy, social realist metaphor suggesting a marriage of working-class life and high art. The *Worker* thus effectively executed a rapprochment between proletarian culture and avant-garde aesthetics after the Party's earlier attempts to designate modernism as elitist and decadent. Interestingly, the reviewer was the modern composer Charles Seeger, writing under the pseudonym Carl Sands.

Gold's poem, said the *Worker,* was even more powerful because of the addition of Siegmeister's music. In a 1936 recording the mournful strains of a funeral march are mixed with jazzy undertones as a sonorous voice inflects "the story of a strange funeral, a strange *American* funeral." Placing heavy emphasis on the word "American" underscored the situation's irony. A worker's life in the United States, it implied, was far removed from the ideals of equality and opportunity that composed the American dream.[80] Gold's poem, with its concrete social message and strong emotional appeal, carried the burden of Siegmeister's modern music and Sokolow's modernist choreography.

Collaborations such as *Strange American Funeral* exemplified how artists in different fields undertook projects based, at least in part, on their shared political beliefs. Such collaborations also proved problematic for some advocates of the new modern dance. In some of the earliest modern dance experiments such as those of Humphrey and Tamiris, even music seemed to threaten the development and primacy of movement. John Martin, who genuinely admired Sokolow as an artist, felt overwhelmed by all the elements of *Strange American Funeral.* The work simply did not fit within his construction of "new" dance:

> Though it is a composition of great interest and strengthens beyond any question the belief that Miss Sokolow is one of the most gifted young choreographers in the field, it cannot truthfully be called a complete success. The problem of building dance forms on verbal forms is still far from solution and the Siegmeister music further complicated matters by making the poem unintelligible. Nevertheless there are powerful phrases in the dance, and much of it is original and compelling.[81]

The marriage of text and movement was one answer to the dilemma posed by revolutionary content in dance form. Another approach came about because of the close connections between leftist theater and dance groups. Theatrical techniques, such as those advanced by the "bourgeois" Konstantin Stanislavsky, director of the Moscow Art Theatre, proved useful for modern dancers like Anna Sokolow seeking to communicate emotionally powerful material. With carefully etched, dramatic characterizations, perhaps influenced by the work of the Russian master, Sokolow was able to bring contemporary newspaper headlines to her audience without using any words at all, and with an intensity that was alarming.

In *Case History #*, Sokolow's 1937 solo dance about a young boy from the Lower East Side, she confronted her audience with a haunting character study of alienation and isolation. Louise Mitchell described the dance in the *Daily Worker:* "Anna Sokolow depicts the lifetime of thousands of youths who roam this country as vagrants and petty criminals, who live in the slums of New York[,] Chicago or Detroit. She dances with boyish bravado, their willfulness, frustration, desperation, the hunted suspect, the third degree, the cringing crying boy-killers, the last mile."[82]

The street kid whom Sokolow portrayed might have been a familiar sight to her from her youth. Although she had been born in Hartford, Connecticut, her family settled in New York's Lower East Side when she was a small child, later moving uptown to the East 80s. Like many others in the workers' dance movement, she was the daughter of immigrant Russian Jews. Her mother worked in the garment industry, was active in the ILGWU, and was a member of the Socialist Party; when the factory workers went on strike, Sokolow marched on the street with them.[83]

I think Sokolow must have felt enormous empathy for the disaffected youth she danced. She played hookey from school,[84] eventually was a dropout, and might easily have found herself labeled a case history of the burgeoning experiments in social science that were popular in the 1930s.[85] *Case History #* could have been her own story.

But Sokolow had danced instead. Receiving her first training at a settlement house called the Emanuel Sisterhood, she later attended the Henry Street Settlement House, and the Neighborhood Playhouse School, where she studied with Martha Graham.[86] She used the developing Graham technique in the dances she composed and performed as part of the Workers Dance League. Pictures of Sokolow's early group show well-trained bodies in disciplined arrangements. The ideological content of her dances, not any commitment to mass or amateur participation, made her a part of the workers' dance movement.[87]

A review in *New Theatre* by Leonard Dal Negro attributed the success of Sokolow's group to the efforts of the dancers—pointing out that they approached the work of dancing as artists and professionals: "What differentiates it most is that its small membership is made up of young women whose exclusive occupation, often at great sacrifice, is the dance. The majority of the other groups are workers in industry and in offices, who dance as an avocation, though one that plays an important part in their lives."[88]

Most members of Anna Sokolow's Dance Unit were students at the

Martha Graham school,[89] and more than a few were subject to Louis Horst's exacting eye for form and structure in the composition classes he taught at the Neighborhood Playhouse where Sokolow was his first assistant. Horst would have made sure that they knew the difference between art and politics, while urging them to attend concerts and museums and other cultural activities.[90]

Critic Margaret Lloyd called Sokolow's approach sociological,[91] but it was never didactic. Her dances about society's problems were primarily an emotional and, I think, personal response to the domestic and foreign situation. I imagine that she *was* alienated from the American dream; with the exception of New York City, she has said, she felt estranged from the United States.[92] But despite her affection for the Soviet Union, which she visited in 1934 with leftist composer Alex North, she was not a joiner. Edith Segal tried to get Sokolow to become a member of the Communist Party, but Sokolow declined,[93] preferring the idiosyncrasies of her own responses to the coherent political philosophy advocated by the Party.[94]

Sokolow's responses seemed emotional, but her dances emerged within the disciplined frame of the new art form, made for an audience to view and not for audience participation. Her dances were often about political situations—the horrors of war, the rise of fascism, the horrendous domestic situation—but they did not propose solutions or answers in the way that Segal had attempted in *Black and White*.[95] Instead, they exposed the human cost involved in the dance of politics; the alienation and desperation of the underclass, the debris left behind in the pursuit of the American dream.

For *Case History #* to move an audience, its members had to believe and empathize with what they saw on stage. Sokolow's performance was the medium through which the social message had to pass if her viewers were to feel the desperation of a street child in the New York slums. Essentially, hers was and is an actor's problem, and the solution to be found during this period was in Stanislavsky's teachings.

As outlined in a two-part article in *New Theatre*, "Stanislavsky's Method of Acting" (December 1934, January 1935), his system of training aimed at making actors' emotions "real" by analyzing character motivation and breaking roles down into actions and beats.[96] The goal was to bring a character's inner life into external focus for the audience. The Method, as it came to be called in the United States, was advocated at this time in the Soviet Union as part of the policy of socialist realism that allowed techniques from "bourgeois" theaters to be used in proletarian dramas.[97]

In the United States the workers' theater movement embraced "bourgeois" theater methods in the same way that dancers adopted "bourgeois" movement techniques:

> The workers theatre now understands that it must study the technique of the theatres of the past, adapting the best of the old to the service of the masses—experimenting—studying—criticizing itself . . . [bourgeois artists] must be attracted to the revolutionary theatre, where they can give technical training to the workers, farmers and students, and where they can practice their art in a more socially useful way than they ever could before.[98]

Realism in acting and the seductive power of empathy replaced the broad caricatures and mass chants in some workers' theater groups. Originally, Stanislavsky's methods had found an American home in the Group Theatre, and since Group members also were involved with workers' theater groups such as the Theatre Union, the Method permeated the movement.[99] The Theatre Union embraced acting techniques, "without which no theatre can hope to achieve telling propaganda."[100] To borrow John Martin's figure, it was hare for the hare pie.

During the first year after the Theatre Union Studio was established in January 1934, actors met three times a week for two-hour afternoon periods on the stage of the Civic Repertory Theatre.[101] Their technical studies centered on what they called the improvisation method as introduced from the Soviet Union by the Group Theatre—in other words, Stanislavsky's techniques. Playwright Clifford Odets of the Group Theatre was the first director.[102] His classes in scene study included exercises in affective memory and sense memory; development of character and ensemble playing were emphasized.[103]

Sokolow's distinctive style of movement characterization began to develop during her association with the Theatre Union, and Stanislavsky's ideas almost certainly influenced her work. Odets's play *Waiting for Lefty*, which was highly praised for its performance realism, was produced by the Theatre Union in 1935 on a program that also featured Sokolow's *Anti-War Cycle*. In addition, Sokolow probably saw performances of the Moscow Art Theatre during her visit to the Soviet Union in 1934.[104] In any event, if the credo of the Method is transmitting interior psychology through external behavior, that is exactly what Sokolow's danced studies did.

The imperatives of the "new" dance were consistent with the kinds of principles advocated by Stanislavsky. Martha Graham, defining her art in 1927, wrote that "out of emotion comes form."[105] In modern dance the interior experience came first. Dance writer Valentina Litvinoff described Graham as a living embodiment of Stanislavsky:

> Her every movement on the stage . . . is an illustration of the use of the Method . . . big gestures and small are all motivated, emotionally honest, colored by a sense of history and period, driven by an organic logic. . . . Furthermore Graham's movements are an identity of the act and its qualities—as distinct from an action which is merely done with this or that expression.[106]

Litvinoff singled out Graham, but in fact the writer could have been describing Sokolow or any of a number of early modern dancers. On a physical level, the emphasis on kinesthetic awareness and the workings of the body's interior in, for example, Humphrey's fall and recovery required dancers to re-create a feeling within exacting boundaries and disciplines. Paying attention to the sensations of a movement rather than its visual shape, and reproducing the interior experience to create an observable exterior structure, both have much in common with the methods advocated by Stanislavsky. The idea of motivation in movement, another pillar of expressive dance, also dovetails with Stanislavsky's credos. For the early modern dancers, movement could not be separated from an internal dynamic. Motivation could be physical or psychological, but the imperative that every movement have a reason for existence was always present. A kind of substratum, an underlying experience out of which both words and motion flow, shapes expressive modern dance as well as Method acting.

Stanislavsky's techniques offered a way to produce emotion on stage in a manner that avoided self-indulgence, and these approaches also would have interested modern dancers. In the Method, feelings and impulses have no value in and of themselves; instead, they provide the actor with the basic materials for creating a character on stage. Exercises in sense memory are practice sessions aimed at strengthening the actor's ability to recall at will. The parallel in dance is not interpretive dance, based on feelings, but expressive dance, composed of dynamically motivated and carefully chosen segments of movement.

Probably the fact that Stanislavsky was Russian also was attractive to many revolutionary dancers. Members of the New Dance Group, for example, experimented with the possibilities of Stanislavsky's technique, and Jane Dudley made deliberate use of the Method in creating her character of the Ancestress in Graham's 1940 *Letter to the World,* analyzing the spine of the performance and finding the long line that connected the various beats and actions—all terms borrowed from the Method.[107]

How Method techniques crossed from theater into dance is another example of the ways in which shared political ideals facilitated the exchange of artistic visions. Among many leftist artists this shared perspective was as important as their distinctive art forms, making collaborations of all sorts both possible and exciting in the service of a larger, transcendent purpose. Such visions were surely responsible for the many alliances between dancers and poets, dancers and musicians, and dancers and actors during the 1930s. *New Theatre,* after all, was a magazine devoted not to dance or to theater exclusively, but to leftist theater, leftist dance, and, later, leftist film.

For Sokolow and members of the Theatre Union Dance Group and dancers of the New Dance Group, despite their deep commitment to political issues, the embryonic modern dance was first an art form and only secondarily an instrument of social change. These dancers took the charged political atmosphere of the 1930s as fodder for artistic ambition. In many cases their impression of political issues was emotional and intuitive, but the dances always reflected their need to understand and communicate. What established their credentials as revolutionary artists was the content of the dances, the political and social commentary that emanated from the percussive thrust of a heel or a head's abrupt turn. Radical dancers may have openly embraced bourgeois technique, but they did not dance about "the life of a bee."[108] They danced about the lives and concerns of working people.

The "worker," however, was increasingly absent from the stage. In the most artistically successful efforts by revolutionary dancers, the worker was the imagined inhabitant of a trained body rather than a participant in the experience. This construction allowed the scales that weighed the merits of propaganda against those of aesthetics to be balanced, and for a brief period some radical dancers could satisfy the demands of both art and politics. What established their art as revolutionary was content; in essence, their dances were narratives about the social crisis affecting the worker.

F O U R

How Long, Brethren?: Dancers Working

Webster's New World Dictionary defines "worker" as a "person who is employed to do physical or mental work for wages, esp., in order to earn a living." And work—or the lack of it—was undoubtedly the most pressing issue affecting millions of unemployed workers. In 1935 Roosevelt's Works Progress Administration (WPA) was mandated to provide government employment to masses of out-of-work Americans. Envisioned as an alternative to relief payments, the WPA aimed to put needy people into jobs that would be genuinely useful to the community and in ways that upheld workers' morale. In general, the administration made an effort, particularly with the middle-class unemployed, to ensure that the jobs provided were within workers' fields of expertise. In the arts, four programs were originally set up: the Federal Arts Project, the Federal Theatre Project, the Federal Music Project, and the Federal Writers Project. A fifth program, the Federal Dance Project, came into being directly as a result of efforts by New York City dancers, and it enjoyed a short though impassioned history.

The federal projects in the arts carried a distinctive mission. Not only were they to provide relief to unemployed artists, but they democratized American culture, creating "art for the millions."[1] While controversial subjects were often presented, the projects were not designed to promote a proletarian culture or to focus on the class struggle; they were meant to be popular. Still, the WPA mission to democratize art carried an implicit attack on elitist art forms, and through it some goals of the workers' dance movement were advanced.

Initially, the Federal Theatre Project (FTP) was the most radical of the arts projects. Forms developed within the project such as the Living Newspaper exposed social inequities to mass audiences. *One Third of a Nation,* which premiered in New York City in January 1938, was a sweeping indictment of slum landlords and the problems of tenement housing; exposés such as this one made the project especially vulnerable to assaults of the Dies Committee—better-known as the House Committee on Un-American Activities. Accusing the Federal Theatre of being dominated by Communists, the committee was influential in causing Congress to withdraw funds for the project in 1939.[2]

Dancers were originally employed under the Federal Theatre Project. Three units operated in New York City: one headed by Don Oscar Becque, another by Gluck Sandor, and a third unit designed to supply dancing bodies for theatrical productions as needed.[3] When the campaign to establish a separate dance unit within the Federal Theatre Project began, followed by an effort to employ *all* unemployed New York City dancers, it was shaped by the sense of mission characteristic of the federal projects in the arts and by the special commitment to left-wing politics that governed the New York theater project.

Among the modern dancers, Helen Tamiris's interest in group action and administrative solutions best prepared her to plead the unemployed dancers' cause in Washington and to lobby for establishing a Federal Dance Project (FDP). Like Segal and Sokolow, she was the child of Russian Jewish immigrants. Her family was poor, her father a sweatshop tailor, and she grew up on the Lower East Side. Tamiris did not romanticize poverty. She knew it firsthand. Her father worked sixteen-hour days, and her own summers were spent working in a factory. "For the one who survives, thousands die— For the one who battles through, too many fall by the wayside," she later wrote.[4]

Organizing and uniting forces was one way to equalize the odds in the battle between haves and have-nots. Tamiris engineered the ill-fated Dance Repertory Theatre of 1930 and 1931 in an attempt to reduce the financial burdens of performing in a Broadway house. The leading moderns (Graham, Humphrey, Weidman, and Tamiris) shared a first season and the costs of production at the Maxine Elliott Theatre on West 39th Street. Joined by Agnes de Mille in 1931, the DRT played for two weeks at the Craig Theatre on West 54th Street.[5] Fierce loyalties (among dancers and audiences), however, contributed to the DRT's demise after its second season.

Tamiris was also on the board of directors of the 1930 Concert Dancers' League (de Mille was president), an organization formed to repeal Sunday blue laws forbidding certain forms of commerce, theatrical dancing among them, on the Sabbath. Since Sundays were dark nights on Broadway, those nights offered the only times when theaters were available for dance; individual dancers or groups had neither the funds nor the audience to afford a full week's rent. On January 19, 1930, the city's Sabbath Day Committee served summonses on three Sunday dance events, precipitating a crisis within the dance world and a flurry of political activism.[6] The Concert Dancers' League argued that dancers should not be considered entertainers, but rather as concert artists, like musicians and singers, who were permitted to perform on Sundays.[7] By successfully negotiating the repeal of the blue laws, the ad hoc league demonstrated dancers' ability to organize effectively and take collective action.

Although the league dissolved once its express purpose had been achieved, other organizations in which Tamiris was involved continued to promote concert dancers' economic interests. Government employment for New York City dancers would clearly advance their prospects and in 1936 a group called the Dancers Association, with Tamiris at its head, was instrumental in winning a place for dancers as an independent unit in the Federal Theatre Project.[8]

Efforts began with the Provisional Committee for Unemployment Relief for Dancers. On November 23, 1934, Tamiris, along with some thirty other dancers, gathered in response to a call to initiate a dance project. Although professional artists in other fields were included in various government relief projects by this time, dancers had been systematically excluded from such undertakings. The dancers voted to establish a dancers' union, electing Francis Bordine as their secretary and putting forth the following demands:

> 1. Jobs for dancers, dance teachers, etc. in CWA [Civil Works Administration] projects.[9]
> 2. Jobs for performing units of dancers in CWA projects.
> 3. A central theatre of dance where performing units are salaried to put on dance programs regularly.
> 4. Establishment of more schools resembling the unit of Drama, Music and Dance at 117 West 46th St.[10]
> 5. Immediate cash relief for needy cases.[11]

A second meeting was held a month later[12] at Tamiris's studio on West 8th Street to elect a grievance committee and to designate a spokesperson for the group. In a letter to *New Theatre*, Bordine urged all dancers to support the newly formed group:

> Such activity on the part of the dancers sounds a progressive note in this profession. A militant organization of dancers can procure immediate relief and aid for the unemployed. It can also establish a

much needed unity among dancers in all fields, which can work for the raising of standards all along the line. All dancers, unemployed or otherwise, are urged to support the Dancers Union.[13]

The Dancers Union (sometimes referred to as the Dancers Emergency Association or the Dancers Association) was championed by the workers' dance organizations as a means for dancers to experience firsthand the struggle to achieve economic demands.[14] Section 2 of its constitution listed the following objectives:

(a) The expansion of governmental appropriations for the teaching and presentation of the dance as a cultural activity which may benefit the community at large.
(b) The right to suitable employment at the prevailing rate of wages for the work performed.
(c) The right of teachers, students and professionals to join organizations of their own choosing and the right to bargain collectively if such organization is an economic one.[15]

Membership in the association was open to "anyone connected with any branch of dance activity," [16] and meetings at the Union Methodist Episcopal Church on West 48th Street, headquarters for the association, were jammed; clearly the issues were important and timely.

Efforts to assert control over their economic lives—to organize and to acquire economic power through collective action—were part of the larger labor movement energizing the 1930s, but for dancers such actions must have been particularly heady. Employment on the WPA could give New York concert dancers a chance to practice their art and get paid for doing it, an opportunity so far denied them. Technically, they were not even unemployed because most of them had never been employed as dancers who were paid for their skills.

The Federal Theatre Project began to function in New York City late in 1935. Soon after its inception, Elmer Rice, who was in charge of New York's Regional Drama Project, announced that dance would be included in FTP plans; dancers Doris Humphrey and Charles Weidman were considered likely to head the program. New Theatre credited the insistent Dancers Union with getting the government to take their situation seriously and with winning dancers a place in WPA relief efforts:

We are convinced that were it not for the activities of these militant young dancers who fought the category of boon-dogglers, who repeatedly urged . . . the necessity of a dance project, who even now are fighting to have the State School of the Dance continue as a free project, the dance would still be considered—by the authorities at least—on a par with whittling and jig-saw puzzles.[17]

The dancers, however, were not so satisfied. For them, it was not enough to be part of the Federal Theatre Project; they wanted their own unit. They politely wired Hallie Flanagan, national director of the FTP: "The needs of the dancers of New York are not adequately covered by the present setup under the municipal drama project. We therefore request the formation of an independent dance project with its own administrative staff and permanent theatre."[18] By January 29, 1936, Flanagan was in the city consulting with Don Oscar Becque, her choice as supervisor of an autonomous dance project.[19]

Becque's appointment was plagued by controversy; many dancers disliked him, and his qualifications in modern dance were suspect. Born in Oklahoma, he studied ballet with Enrico Cecchetti in London and with Michael Mordkin in New York. He was an important concert dancer in the late 1920s, creating works based on geometric shapes, and he was working at the Federal Theatre Project at the time of his appointment. But he never would have been considered "one of the founders of the modern movement,"[20] as the WPA claimed. One of his first acts was to propose a "common denominator" modern technique, a kind of generic modern dance.[21] Given the fierce allegiances that characterized students of Graham, Humphrey, Tamiris, and Holm at the time, his notion of a single modern technique undoubtedly contributed to the scorn that WPA dancers later heaped on him.

The initial budget for the Federal Dance Project was set at $155,000, an amount that was to cover operating costs until June 1, 1936; included were appropriations for costumes and scenery for eight productions, a theater for performances, a support staff of administrative and office workers as well as theater workers, and 185 dancers, all of whom were to be on home relief. A Home Relief Act had been passed by Congress on March 31, 1933, and initially, to qualify for employment on WPA projects, participants were required to be on relief rolls. Fortunately, a loophole existed. Creative projects were given a 25 percent allowance for nonrelief personnel, which made it possible to hire working artists in leadership positions.

In addition to Becque, other choreographers were appointed to the project, including Doris Humphrey and Charles Weidman, Felicia Sorel, Gluck Sandor, and Tamiris. They represented a broad range of approaches to dance. Humphrey and Weidman were leaders in the new modern dance, as was Tamiris, while Gluck Sandor was best-known as a theatrical and ballet choreographer. He had trained with Blanche Talmud at the Neighborhood Playhouse and had danced with the Metropolitan Opera Ballet. Gluck Sandor and Sorel (who were married) had formed a group earlier in the decade called the Dance Centre, which fused ballet and modern training. Sorel also had come from an eclectic background that included ballet with Michel Fokine, modern dance with Mary Wigman, and Spanish dance with Vicente Escudero.

Other personnel included as chief musical director, Donald Pond, a young English composer who had been musical director for the Dartington Hall School. His associates on the dance project would be Genevieve Pitot and Wallingford Riegger. Grace Duncan Hopper, previously affiliated with the Neighborhood Playhouse, served as director of personnel.

Plans for the first year were ambitious, probably overly ambitious. Among the productions anticipated were Tamiris's *Walt Whitman Suite*, which she had premiered in the summer of 1935, and a new version of Weidman's 1933 *Candide*. Gluck Sandor planned to produce *The Prodigal Son* and a composition called *Tempo*, while Sorel would choreograph a ballet to Strauss's *Till Eulenspiegel*. Don Becque would be working on a piece called *The Young Tramps*. Project leaders expected to assemble the first production within six weeks. It was a tall order.[22]

The creation of an independent Federal Dance Project introduced the dancers to a union shop. The actors had their own professional union, Actors Equity Association, and Chorus Equity spoke for dancers in musicals, but concert dancers had no union representing them.

When they were hired onto the project, concert dancers were represented by the City Projects Council (CPC), which had been formed to represent all project workers who did not belong to a professional union.[23] The CPC was a subsidiary of the Workers Alliance, a highly militant organization later accused by the Dies Committee of being a Communist front. WPA dancers were immediately introduced to confrontational bargaining techniques; they proved to be enthusiastic students. Wages themselves were not central, but the right to work, the elimination of unemployment for all dancers, and the means to redress arbitrary administrative decisions were the issues that project dancers fought hardest for.

For dancers, the first step was to get on the project, and the way to do that was to get on relief:

There was a certain procedure. You left home if you wanted a job and you went on relief. And you joined the Unemployed Council,[24] which was an organization that was made up of the unemployed. They organized all the picket lines and the whole strategy. . . . to open up the Project for more jobs for dancers.[25]

I had to go on relief and it was organized by [the] Workers Alliance. . . . The conditions to get on relief were such that no human being who was alive could ever fit them. It was impossible to fit them. We were made caricatures and you couldn't be born. You couldn't have parents. You couldn't have a place where you lived. You had to be in some kind of limbo.[26]

My family was on relief to begin with.[27]

[Fanya][28] said "Listen, this is what you have to do to get on the Project." . . . Get on relief first . . . I needed that job, you know. I had no job. It was very legitimate really. So I got on relief and she said "Now you apply for the Project," and that's how I got on the Project.[29]

So I told them to apply for Home Relief . . . not the relief we speak of today, welfare, but Home Relief. Well, we had a dance project full of orphans . . . I told them what to say. And we got the Project, that was the main thing.[30]

Getting on relief was a means to an end, and the end was dancing and getting paid for it. Working.

On March 5, 1936, registrations for work on the dance project halted; the federal government was no longer hiring. Only eighty-five dancers had been hired at this time, although the quota had been set at a hundred more.[31] A few months earlier, dancers had courteously requested a place of their own on the project, but now they were not so polite. The Dancers Association petitioned Becque for immediate fulfillment of the government quota of 185 dancers and for expansion of the project to include all unemployed dancers.[32] In April a couple dozen dancers trouped to the offices of Philip Barber, director of the FTP's New York office. When they found his response to be less than satisfactory, they picketed his office, returning again the following day when ten of them were arrested. In a letter to *Dance Observer,* Fanya Geltman, one of those arrested, described the events:

The picketers marched in the rain, first the unemployed who were later joined by the employed. Mr. Barber heard their voices and passersby read their placards. The next day police tried to disband the line. The next afternoon the police, together with the Veterans League Guards, arrested two of the dancers. (They thought the rest would be nice little girls and run along home.) For a fraction of a second the marchers were puzzled and angered, then up went the placards again and the line reorganized, more determined to win than ever. Before they had gone a few steps the police were at them again and this time arrested eight more dancers. A patrol wagon arrived to take the desperate criminals away, charged with "walking a coicle and shouting somethin' about unemployed dancers wantin' jobs."

The trial came up on the 22nd of April. The dancers on the Project were excused to attend. Mr. Barber wrote to the judge that the picket line was no "distoibance of the peace," the courtroom was packed. So many dancers were there, much to the undisguised chagrin of the Judge, that he ordered the courtroom cleared. The policeman on the witness stand wasn't very sure exactly what happened; he just thought his duty was to arrest people on a picket line. The lawyer for the girls suggested the case be dismissed; the Judge cautiously agreed. The picket line was [formed again] the next day.[33]

Geltman was one of the more outspoken project dancers, and perhaps her account is biased. But it reveals the pugnacious quality of working life for the project dancers. Pauline Tish (Bubrick) recalled that the dancers often gave false names to arresting officers, identifying themselves as such members of the pantheon of modern greats as Isadora Duncan or Mary Wigman.[34]

Grant Code, who chronicled the project's history for *Dance Observer* in 1939, called the April trial "the first recorded public performance of the dance project."[35] (There had yet to be a single performance on stage.) Code was the head of the Brooklyn Museum of Art during the 1930s, and he strongly supported the art of dance and the rights of professional dancers to make a living. In a 1936 letter to Harry Hopkins, head of the Works Progress Administration, Code endorsed the expansion of the Dance Unit of the Federal Theatre Project, and he was instrumental in getting the Young Choreographers Laboratory of the Federal Dance Project to make its home at the Brooklyn museum.[36] Code was a shrewd observer of project life, and his article points out how the dance offstage, orchestrated by the techniques of organized labor—pickets, sit-ins, delaying tactics—became as fundamental to the project's identity as anything that took place on stage.

New Theatre carried accounts of benefits to be won by organized efforts. Dancers engaged for a modern dance number in *Sweet Surrender,* a film shooting in Astoria, Long Island, had signed contracts that failed to specify either hours or rates of pay, depending instead on a verbal agreement that management soon renounced. A walkout just before actual shooting of the film had assured the dancers of overtime pay and seemed to promise the success of a strong dancers' union. Another article reported a successful strike by chorus girls at a Spanish-language theater in what was then the heart of the Latin American section of New York City, West 116th Street and Fifth Avenue. The strike, masterminded by the Unemployed Council of Lower Harlem, led to a 50 percent pay raise for the dancers.[37]

In a 1978 interview Geltman summed up the project worker's position: "Today we can't work because we have to go on the picket line."[38] Other wpa dancers remembered:

> It seemed to me that we were daily picketing.[39]

> Picketing and marching and going to and writing letters and 100 percent with the political movement, which was very, very radical and extremely well organized, extremely well organized.[40]

> I just remember one occasion when we all went in there [Philip Barber's office] and sat in. And I remember getting up and making a speech . . . and saying, "We'll stand here without leaving until we get"—I don't know what. I don't remember what.[41]

> The marches that people went on, the picket lines, were extremely peaceful. People were singing and holding up slogans and that was where you met your friends. "I'll meet you on the picket line. When are you going to meet?" "See you tomorrow on the picket line." "We'll have lunch together." And you know, you took turns. So many would go off for an hour or so and have lunch and then the next group would go off.[42]

> They [the Unemployed Council] organized all the picket lines and the whole strategy. . . . to open up the Project for more jobs for dancers.[43]

For the most part, the rhetoric employed by the dancers was strident and combative. When John Connolly, acting as representative for the unemployed dancers of the Dancers Association, presented a plan to Hallie Flanagan for the expansion and revision of the project, he concluded with large, handwritten capital letters, "WE DEMAND THAT ALL

UNEMPLOYED DANCERS BE PUT ON THE DANCE PROJECT BY JULY 1ST."[44] According to Connolly, the delegation represented five hundred unemployed and organized dancers. There had never been appropriations for more than 185 dancers, and eighty-five of those slots were now filled. Connolly was either exaggerating the situation or demands were escalating.

On April 22, 1936 (the day of the trial), Becque sought an appointment with Flanagan to discuss the dancers' demands. "The delegations," he wrote, "are becoming so large and unwieldy that our headquarters here will not accommodate them, and they are taking my time from my productions." But, he added "I am, of course, in sympathy with them in a great many of their demands."[45]

By August, Becque was no longer so sympathetic. He sent a memo to Philip Barber about his increasing impotence in the face of the militant dancers and their mounting attacks; the dancers' delegation was creating so much chaos that guards had to be sent from the main office. In a petulant passage Becque complained that "the racket the unemployed group is allowed to make is inexcusable. . . . I think we should have some system put into effect whereby people cannot walk right into our offices and park themselves, crippling office routine completely."[46] But, judging by the memo's conclusion, the dancers' activities produced the desired results. "I will call you in the morning," Becque wrote, "to see when we can talk over the situation of putting the one hundred people on, for it is truly becoming acute."[47]

The following day Hallie Flanagan approved a press release, written by Becque, which called for employing one hundred additional dancers to fill the Federal Dance Project's original quota; the release also suggested an auditions board to screen applicants:

> Dancers will be employed on a basis of need and professional ability. Applicants need not necessarily be on relief, but must be certified as needy by the Emergency Relief Bureau. Two Audition Boards, consisting of prominent people in the dance world, who are not associated with the project, will determine the fitness of the applicants. More than three hundred applications have already been received at the Dance Theatre headquarters, 254 West 54th Street. Dancers applying for jobs are receiving thorough physical examinations at a WPA clinic. Auditions are expected to begin this Thursday.[48]

The Unemployed Council of the Dancers Association celebrated victory, giving credit for the increase to their "unceasing militant front"— the picket lines, sit-ins, and disruptions. The council further boasted that it was responsible for increasing the Dance Unit's personnel while other projects were being cut.[49] Nobody seemed to anticipate the new disruptions that would follow an auditions board's creation.

The auditions board set standards for dancers who hoped to become part of the project. The guidelines called for a minimum of five years' dance experience, which could be a combination of technical training at accredited schools and professional appearances. On the list of schools recognized by the Federal Dance Theatre (FDT) were studios run by Tamiris, Humphrey-Weidman, and Becque, as might be expected; but it also acknowledged the studios of Duncan dance, Wigman, Sokolow, Edwin Strawbridge, and Fokine, and the schools of the Metropolitan Opera Ballet, to name only a few. Would-be dancers were given the choice of auditioning before either a ballet or nonballet board.[50]

Some dancers already on the project were asked to audition a second time in an attempt to ensure professionalism. Needless to say, the affected dancers considered this request an affront, a tactic engineered by Becque—who was now heartily disliked—to keep them in line. A lengthy hearing was held on September 17, 1936, in which Oscar Fuss of the Communist-dominated City Projects Council challenged Becque's auditions and the practice of transferring those who had not requested transfers. For example, Fanya Geltman, who had worked for Becque on his production of *The Young Tramps,* was transferred out of the Federal Dance Theatre altogether, to the Federal Children's Theatre, and she was convinced that Becque was punishing her for criticizing his policies.[51]

The principal subject of the hearing was the proposed dismissal of dancer Ruth Allerhand. Allerhand, who had been active in Workers Dance League productions, had a history of trouble with Becque in the Federal Dance Project. Initially employed by the FTP, Allerhand had expected to be transferred into the Federal Dance Project when it was formed. Apparently Becque often shifted her around from one directing job to another, and she felt that she had no chance to complete any of the work she had started. Most recently, Becque had asked her to take over a group headed by John Bovington,[52] and she was in the middle of that effort when Becque demanded that a number of her dancers audition again. Allerhand rebelled, defending the dancers' qualifications in a letter to the auditions board and noting that she was satisfied with their work. For this act, she was charged with insubordination and given notice of dismissal. At the hearing, the Communist challenger Fuss accused Becque of a history of discriminating against Allerhand; Becque accused Allerhand of agitation; Fanya Geltman threatened a walkout by the dancers; and Fuss's proposal to stop the auditions was left unsettled.[53]

In truth, Becque had accomplished little in nearly eight months of project life. Three productions (Weidman's *Candide*, Tamiris's *Salut au Monde*, and Becque's *The Young Tramps*) had been staged, only one of which might be considered original. *Candide* was a restaging of Weidman's 1933 production, with a young José Limón starring as Candide, opposite Lily Verne as Cunegonde and Lily Mann as Paquette (figures 27 and 28), while *Salut au Monde* was based on one of Tamiris's earlier productions, *Walt Whitman Suite*. Only *The Young Tramps*, about America's disinherited youth,[54] was created specifically for the WPA. And no production had achieved more than a limited run.

According to *Dance Observer*, the policy of second auditions was "a bit of rotten politics; an attempt to shift the burden of the so far comparative failure of the Dance Theatre onto the heads of dancers who realize more than anyone else the value of the Federal project and grant, and work accordingly." The *Observer* lashed out at the WPA administrators and at Don Oscar Becque:

> We had expected more from the WPA Federal Dance Theatre. Now eight months old, a well developed repertory should have been established, a routine of performances, and not, as is the case, the necessity for an almost complete revamping of the organization. Something is wrong somewhere. We should like to know why it is necessary after all these months of what might have been preparation for a permanent theatre for the WPA to announce "approximately 100 dancers have been auditioned these last few weeks, and are at present being hired to fill the dance project's original quota of 185 people. New companies will be formed from those new dancers hired. . . ." Certainly there has been time enough since the Works Progress Administration set aside (in January [1936]) $155,000 to carry on the work of the Dance Theatre until the first of June, time enough to have filled this quota of 185, and filled it again. . . . We should like to know in the face of the splendid activity on the part of the related theatre arts under the supervision of the government, what has held up the number of dance productions that were scheduled for early appearance; what has limited this number to three compositions and to no more than ten performances.[55]

Shortly after, at a public hearing at the Union Methodist Episcopal Church, dancers joined in the attack on Becque. Ironically, the dancers' offstage disruptions must have been partially responsible for the project's

27. José Limón and Lily Verne in *Candide*. (Photographer unknown. Reproduced from the Collections of the Library of Congress.)

28. Lily Mann as Paquette in *Candide*. (Photographer unknown.
Reproduced from the Collections of the Library of Congress.)

A PETITION

For the Removal of Don Oscar Becque

To HARRY L. HOPKINS, *Federal Administrator, Works Progress Administration*

To MRs. HALLIE FLANAGAN, *National Director of Federal Theatre*

To PHILIP W. BARBER, *Regional Director of Federal Theatre*

We, the undersigned, in sympathy with the workers on the Dance Project support them in their demand for the removal of Don Oscar Becque as Supervisor of the Dance Unit of the Federal Theatre Project of N. Y. C. because of his

1. Failure to fulfill the Dance Quota.
2. Retarding productions.
3. Dictatorial methods in dealing with the staff.
4. Discrimination against organized dancers.
5. Attempted coercion of the Dance Audition Board.

As dancers and dance audience we maintain that Mr. Becque has proven himself incapable of administering a Federal Dance Theatre.

We authorize the designated Committee to submit suggestions for a Supervisor capable of furthering the development of the Dance.

COMMITTEE

DAISY BLAU   DORIS HUMPHREY
ANN DODGE   LUCILLE MARSH
ELISA FINDLAY   KLARNA PINSKA
LOUIS HORST   GLUCK SANDOR
                   TAMIRIS

29. The upshot of the controversy within the FTP's Dance Unit was the circulation of a petition to Harry Hopkins, Hallie Flanagan, and Philip Barber for the removal of Don Oscar Becque as supervisor.

failure; a lot of work time was undoubtedly lost to pickets, sit-down strikes, arrests, and night court appearances. And with hindsight, Code later reflected, Becque had faced an impossible task to begin with.

> To anyone at all familiar with the work involved in dance production, the original project of creating a completely new dance theatre, bringing together dancers who had never worked together before, creating well-organized companies of groups and soloists, and designing, rehearsing and producing eight productions in six months was an impossible project under any circumstances.[56]

At this point, project choreographers Tamiris, Gluck Sandor, and Humphrey added their voices to the debate. Tamiris accused Becque of being uncooperative and dictatorial. Gluck Sandor charged that Becque knew nothing about choreography or theater, and Doris Humphrey declared her sympathy for the dancers. The upshot was the circulation of a petition to Harry Hopkins, Hallie Flanagan, and Philip Barber "For the Removal of Don Oscar Becque" as supervisor of the New York City Dance Project (figure 29). Grievances included:

1. Failure to fulfill the dance quota.
2. Retarding productions.
3. Dictatorial methods in dealing with the staff.
4. Discriminations against organized dancers.
5. Attempted coercion of the Dance Audition Board.[57]

Becque responded by accusing Tamiris of manipulating the entire hearing, and then, true to form, he called for her immediate dismissal.[58] Oscar Fuss of the CPC countered with a request that Becque be dropped from the project, declaring the proposed dismissal of Tamiris a "stupid reprisal." [59]

Ultimately, Becque's attempts to shore up his waning authority by manipulating the auditions board proved unsuccessful. The dancers won. On December 24, 1936, the New York Times reported that Becque had been replaced by Lincoln Kirstein. Alas, Kirstein's regime was short-lived. Perhaps he too lacked the temperament for sparring with the peppery dancers. As one of his first projects, he envisioned a danced panorama of the history of American dance. He probably thought he was complimenting Tamiris when he suggested that she could dance the great Isadora Duncan, but it was a little like Becque's suggesting that Tamiris (or Humphrey, or Weidman) pursue a common denominator technique after each had struggled for years to define an individual dance style. Both men were out of touch with the imperatives of modern dance. Tamiris reputedly eyed Kirstein coldly when he proposed the idea to her and asked, "And who will dance Tamiris?" [60]

Shortly thereafter, Kirstein resigned, and Stephen Karnot, who had been active in the Workers Laboratory Theatre took over, continuing in this role for the remainder of the life of the dance project. Interestingly, Karnot's wife Greta had taught dance to the Lab Theatre's Shock Troupe. Perhaps Karnot had a better understanding of what made the dancers tick.

The creation of an auditions board brought to the fore important issues about the purpose of the Federal Dance Project and the implications of creating "art for the millions." The central mission of the arts projects— the extension of culture to a mass audience—had as its corollary the employment of artists on a mass basis. This meant that project workers would be chosen from among artists of eclectic backgrounds, training, and accomplishment.

Aesthetic ideals were not the sole criterion governing the Federal Dance Project in its employment practices or in its artistic productions, but to the extent that other goals were considered, those ideals were never clearly articulated. Was the project basically a form of relief for the needy, in which case it mattered little whether the dancers were trained professionals or whether they could articulate a distinctive line in space or understand the nuances of a tricky rhythm? Or was the project's mission to create a national dance theater, in which case the artistry of the performers should have been the most significant feature, and the degree of their economic need or deservedness less important. Were they dancers or unemployed people? Artists or simply hungry people?

Ambiguity of purpose haunted the Federal Theatre Project as well. In her autobiographical book, *Arena*, Hallie Flanagan wondered where the emphasis should be placed—on theater or on relief?

> Historically and functionally we were a work project in which the primary concern was for human values. We believed that these human values could best be attained by focusing efforts on theatre. Many people within wpa offices, however, still thought and spoke of the program as relief. It was perhaps the greatest handicap of the arts projects that the wpa in spite of many utterances by its leaders never succeeded in explaining to the public that when people came onto the projects they were no longer relief clients, but people doing work useful enough to be paid for out of government funds.[61]

The question of who would be included or excluded was always politically charged. Recognition of a dance unit by the federal government confirmed the status of dance as a serious art form; employment bestowed prestige as well as a wage. The Dancers Association and the City Projects Council were blatant in their attempts to influence the composition of the project, but so were other groups. Lucile Marsh of the National Dance League argued that the project employed "amateurs" and that it was controlled by the "Modern group."[62] At one point, Tamiris and Becque got into a scuffle because Tamiris claimed that the Humphrey-Weidman group was being given preference in auditions. Becque vehemently denied the charge.[63]

It was painful for board members to insist that standards be enforced if enforcing them meant denying a hungry person a job. For Nadia Chilkovsky, one of the founders of the Workers Dance League and the New Dance Group, functioning on the auditions board was particularly onerous. She remembered:

People were hungry; the nicest people were hungry. The very gifted
and intelligent people were hungry. And if there is one thing that
united this country it was hunger. . . . When I was asked to be on
the Auditions Board . . . I felt it as a responsibility and I accepted. . . .
And I thought then, well I'm here and if my vote is going to get
them something to eat, I'll vote for them. And that's what I did and
other people did the same thing. But others, and I can't remember
who it was, put forward the idea that this is supposed to insure the
future of choreography in this country. That was, I thought, a pecu-
liar notion and the wrong timing for this kind of thing. . . . A little
group of people who are given permission, who are delegated to say,
"You should eat and you should not, and you are a dancer and you
are not."[64]

Eventually, she resigned.[65]

Because the project's goals were unclear; because it *was* a humanitarian
effort; because no clear standard of professionalism existed among the
dancers as it did, for example, among the actors (who at least could point
to union membership as a means of determining professional status);
and because the dancers' militant tactics often were successful in pro-
tecting jobs—the technical expertise of the dancers who were employed
was uneven. John Martin remarked on the absence from the project of
some of the best young dancers and the presence of many who would be
better off (he thought) in another profession. Photographs of some Federal Dance Project productions show stocky figures, undancerly legs, a
general lack of tension in the bodies, and a lack of attention to detail,
that is, the height of the leg, the angle of the head, the ways in which
the hands and fingers are held. But when Martin alluded to the "delicate
problem of what kind of critical standards should be used to measure
such presentations as these," and he asked, "Are they to be considered as
self-contained works of art, or are they rather to be treated as work-relief
projects, pure and simple[,] and given the benefit of the doubt when
their accomplishments fall short,"[66] he once again was trying to define
the boundaries of American dance. The Federal Dance Project created a
critical dilemma for him, just as the workers' dance movement had. In
Martin's construction, the dances could be either art or relief, not both.

Helen Tamiris's production of *How Long Brethren?* was both. It was relief and it was theater, and it fulfilled Flanagan's imperative. It brought
culture to the masses at the same time that it provided employment on
a generous pay scale to dancers and singers. It was one of the most successful and long-running productions of the Federal Dance Theatre.

Based on the *Negro Songs of Protest* collected by Lawrence Gellert, the production opened on May 6, 1937, along with Weidman's *Candide,* as the FDT's fifth presentation. Creating work for a cast of twenty dancers (including Tamiris) as well as for a choral group of twenty (members of the Federal Theatre Negro Choir), it played to packed houses from May through early July—an unheard-of run for a dance production—and reached an audience of 24,235.[67] In December 1937 *How Long Brethren?* was revived, and it ran for another three weeks[68] in a program that included a selection of solos by Tamiris, based on parts of a suite of Negro spirituals on which she had been working since 1928.[69] The Federal Theatre Negro Choir performed on this bill as well.

Divided into seven episodes, "Pickin' Off De Cotton," "Upon de Mountain," "Railroad," "Scottsboro," "Sistern' and Brethren," "Let's Go to the Buryin'," and "How Long Brethren?"[70] the dance provided an opportunity for performers and audiences to empathize with the struggles and the spirit of Negroes[71] in more subtle ways than Segal's agitprop approach in *Black and White* had allowed. Genevieve Pitot's score incorporated elements of jazz, and Tamiris's choreography included vernacular dance steps. Pauline Bubrick, one of the original dancers in *Brethren,* remembered a loose, angular style and a "swashbuckling" pattern of arms and legs in "Let's Go to the Buryin'."[72] Members of the audience could enjoy some relief from the stark angularity of 1930s modern dance as well as a rousing good vocal chorus. According to contemporaneous accounts, spectators responded with outbursts of applause and excited shouts.[73]

In a photograph from one of the episodes, Tamiris lunges toward the dancing ensemble, one arm high, but curved, so that the line of her arm and hand direct attention back toward the group. The fingers become a conduit for transmitting her energy to the group's assembled bodies, while her focus—direct and intense—repeats the motif of powerful forces converging on the ensemble. With one foot placed in front of the other, the bodies of the dancers form a long line, each dancer fitting snugly and compactly against the next one. They are poised to move forward, yet their heads turn back toward Tamiris, awaiting her direction. In all, the tableau replicates the relation between Tamiris as leader, as organizer, and as choreographer, and the dancers who look to her. Production notes called for the ensemble to march off into a "red dawn,"[74] with Tamiris leading the way (figure 30).

Yet a conspicuous absence is apparent in the array of faces that stare from the photographs of *How Long Brethren?* Although songs lament "Laborin' fo' white folk" and pointedly observe that "White folk he aint Jesus, he jes' a man grabbin' biscuit out of poor darkie's hand,"[75] the

30. The WPA presentation of *How Long Brethren?*. Production notes called for the dancers to march off into a "red dawn," with Tamiris leading the way. (Photographer unknown. Reproduced from the Collections of the Library of Congress.)

irony that white dancers were grabbin' the spotlight from poor darkies' faces apparently never was noticed.[76] The Negro choir received no credit in the original program,[77] although reviews consistently pointed out that the singers' glorious voices made the exclusively white dancers almost superfluous.[78]

The Federal Theatre Project voiced an ideal of racial equality, but in fact it was modeled along separate-but-equal lines.[79] Most New York Negro dancers, as well as Negro actors, were employed at the Negro Theatre, which was operating in Harlem's Lafayette Theatre. Although efforts may have been made to recruit Negro dancers for the dance unit,[80] the unit's basic self-definition restricted their presence from the start. Dancers trained in traditional ballet schools or at any of the newly emerging modern dance schools could qualify to work on the project. But many dance studios were segregated. Negroes faced discrimination in training and within concert dance companies.[81] While Flanagan was committed to representing both modern dance and ballet on the project, vaudeville and musical comedy dancing—where Negro dancers most often found employment—were specifically discounted: "The Dance Project aims to put to work unemployed dancers of the several schools of the dance, such as ballet, modern, interpretive, etc., which are usually classified as an *art* group, in contrast to dancing as entertainment; such as musical comedy, vaudeville or variety."[82]

Federal criteria also excluded dancers who were getting their training on the spot in places like the Savoy Ballroom in Harlem. Some white modern dancers, such as Edna Ocko, trouped uptown on a regular basis in the early thirties to see the hottest dancers and to learn the latest steps.[83] Mura Dehn, a project dancer, was a regular at the Savoy from 1930 on.[84] But such dancing, no matter how spectacular and inventive (an implicit rule among the Savoy's elite dancers was that no one was to copy anyone else's routines),[85] did not qualify under the guidelines established by the Federal Dance Project.

The Workers Dance League had made efforts to include Negro dancers, sponsoring a forum called "What Direction Shall the Negro Dance Take?" at which Hemsley Winfield and the Negro Ballet performed, but Negro dancers were virtually absent from New York's Federal Dance Project[86] and from Tamiris's work at this time. Dehn remembered working with dancers at the Savoy and learning about African dance, partly through contact with Negro drummer and dancer Asadata Dafora Horton.[87] Dafora had created the highly acclaimed *Kykunkor* (1934), a production deemed "exciting" by John Martin and "more rewarding than any other recital" by Lincoln Kirstein.[88] Dehn also recalled that her identification with Harlem styles and jazz dancing made her feel like an outsider in the WPA. [89]

In *Arena,* Flanagan points to numerous efforts of the project that demonstrated commitment to Negroes and to an ideal of racial equality. Orson Welles's highly successful production of *Macbeth* with the Negro Theatre at Harlem's Lafayette Theatre in 1936 is a prime example.[90] The project certainly never intended its policies to be discriminatory or racist, but it was creating standards for "art" dance and incomes for concert dancers; Negro dancers were by and large excluded.

Perhaps they did not dance side by side, but many white dancers identified deeply with the Negro struggle, seeing in it a parallel to the entire country's economic struggle. They too were struggling to stand on their feet. Like the chillun' in "Up de Mountain," they were tired of starvin', and if their own shoes were not yet worn out, there was ample evidence on the streets of New York of people who had given up the fight. Revolutionary dancers identified with Negroes because they believed they were members of the same class and because Negro protest songs echoed their determination to take control of their economic lives.

Many white activists in dance were drawn to Negro songs. Miriam Blecher composed dances to Negro spirituals as early as 1934, and Jane

Dudley was working to some of the Gellert collection in 1937. But of all the white dancers, Tamiris was most closely and enduringly associated with Negro themes. Early on, she considered Negro songs and music as a vital medium for her talent. In January 1928 she had performed the first two of her Negro spirituals (eventually she composed nine of them), "Nobody Knows de Trouble I See" and "Joshua Fit de Battle ob Jericho," earning praise for her efforts. In her journal she wrote, "I understand the Negro people so well."[91]

It is tempting to criticize Tamiris's efforts from today's vantage point. She was a white woman who could never really know what it was like to be a Negro in the United States. Moreover, her dances continued a tradition in which white professionals borrowed elements of Negro culture to create their own stage character.[92] Strutting down the diagonal in "Swing Low, Sweet Chariot," chest lifted high, arms making darting motions while her feet dig into the stage, Tamiris does borrow elements of the cakewalk popularized in minstrelsy. At the same time, however, the integrity of Tamiris's purpose still shines through.[93] Tamiris with her working-class Eastern European Jewish background and her progressive politics would have empathized strongly with Negro interests. In a Nordic and Protestant country, she too was "other," and perhaps she felt the language of movement was more significant than any difference in skin color.

Tamiris expressly stated her desire to capture the Negro "spirit" in her dances, the Negro's oppression and subsequent struggle to overcome.[94] She had never enjoyed the rarefied atmosphere of high art—every account suggests that she was different in some ways from her modern dance contemporaries—and performing to Negro spirituals would have provided just the right opportunity to display her more flamboyant style.[95] She had been a showgirl, played in nightclubs and revues, and she was a very beautiful woman.

Descriptions of her dancing focus on sensual elements. Martin called her a "magnificent creature,"[96] a "vivid passionate young animal,"[97] and referred to her "lust of motion."[98] Margaret Lloyd wrote about her "animal vitality" and her "extravagant sheaf of shining curls,"[99] while *Time* magazine described a "symbol-minded, mop-headed Tamiris [who] shook substantial thighs beneath a raspberry sundae skirt."[100] More than that, she sometimes smiled when she danced. She enjoyed moving, she relished it, and she communicated her pleasure in her way of moving. As a performer, Tamiris combined art with entertainment, and in this regard she was a natural for the Federal Dance Project with its avowed intention of creating a mass audience.

At the same time, Tamiris did share many characteristics with the other early moderns. Interested in defining her own style of dance, she wrote in a 1928 "Manifesto" that "the dance of today is plagued with gestures, mannerisms, and ideas borrowed from literature, philosophy, sculpture and painting."[101] If she enjoyed and took advantage of a certain show business aura, she still aimed to discard the decorative and move toward modernism.

With the Negro material, Tamiris could display her ebullience and sexiness and showiness, yet stay within the intellectual modern dance fold. In "Go Down, Moses," one of the earliest Negro spirituals, she combined weight and effort with a generous second position plié as imaginary forces of oppression hammered her into the ground. Then, as she began to rise, rocking from side to side, the active use of weight became passive and sensuous. Her hips swung from one side to the other, and the unity of the torso was broken. When Tamiris moved her hips, the asceticism of early modern dance became laden with ripe promise. While Martha Graham's vocabulary was built around pelvic initiation as well, her technique at this time did not segment the torso and rarely gave in to weight.

Christena Schlundt captured the popular interpretation given to Tamiris's affinity for the Negro material when she wrote, "the uninhibited nature, the extemporaneous air, the free flowing life of the Negro as expressed in their songs appealed to her love of the impromptu, and the unpremeditated."[102] Tamiris might have been a modern-day primitive, her dances stirring the cauldron of sexual innuendo. In *Time and the Dancing Image,* Deborah Jowitt argued that both ballet and modern dance history were replete with dancing images that promised the audience a glimpse of mysterious and foreign lands but whose real function was to provide an outlet for homegrown libidinous desires.[103] From the violent sexuality of Fokine's harem world in *Schéhérazade,* to Maud Allan's bloodthirsty *Salome,* to Ruth St. Denis's spiritual *Incense,* the public enjoyed strange worlds made safe because they were enclosed within the boundaries of the theater. The New York press dubbed Tamiris the "Harlem savage,"[104] a term that enfolded her sensuality within the boundaries of an exotic "other."

Undoubtedly, this kind of reception made it more difficult for Tamiris to be taken seriously as a modern dance choreographer and as an activist for dancers' rights. The press reported strikes and picketing by the dancers, providing ample coverage that often included a generous expanse of dancerly bodies. "It's Scientific, It's Rhythmic, and It's Worth $23.86 Per" reads the headline of a newspaper account of dancers auditioning for WPA jobs, while the photograph features the bare legs and bare midriffs of youthful applicants.[105] Efforts at organizing and picketing were met with amusement. "They danced right out of their jobs" is the caption of a newspaper photograph that showed a group of project workers engaged in social dances during a sit-down strike.[106] Another picture captured dancers on a hunger strike in front of the Federal Theatre lounging in the sun, bare-legged.[107] Clearly, the press seemed to be saying, no one should take these sunbathers seriously, either as artists or as activists.

The presence of the dancers as part of the government labor force continued to make its own revolutionary statement, however. Becque's real failure as head of the Dance Unit was that he never understood the political or moral fiber of the WPA dancers. Most of them brought to the stage the expectations of workers in a rapidly changing labor movement. As working dancers they were tied to the working class not only through their ideology but through their labor, and they insisted on their right to some control over the institutions that employed them. Unfortunately, Becque did not respect these ambitions.

The WPA dancer was a new breed, down-to-earth and assertive where most dancers were trained to respond obediently to a choreographer's demands. As workers, dancers like Fanya Geltman lobbied for fair wages, good working conditions, and job security, and she and others let everyone know right off that they would not be nourished by dance alone.

On May 19, 1937, project dancers staged what the New York Post referred to as "The Theatre's First Sit-In Strike."[108] The dancers had fought from the beginning to be a part of the project, to expand the quota of dancers, and to protest dismissals. Their reputation as one of the most militant groups in the WPA was well-earned. With characteristic verve and more than a touch of bravado, they now fought to keep the Federal Dance Project alive. As the curtain descended on Candide at the Nora Bayes Theatre, Charles Weidman stepped forward and addressed the audience. "The show is in danger," he said, "in danger of all of us losing our jobs and having the Federal Theatre done away with."[109] The expiration date for the act of Congress that had authorized the project was approaching, and rumors circulated that the federal government would cut appropriations.[110] Dancers, along with other workers in the federal arts programs, were apprehensive, and they were not about to take anything lying down. They were ready to go another round with the government to protect their weekly paychecks of $23.86.

The Daily Worker championed the activism of both dancers and audi-

31. Demonstrators outside the WPA Dance Theatre where *How Long Brethren?* and *Candide* were playing, May 1937. Note the price of tickets, 25 and 55 cents. (Courtesy of *Peoples Weekly World.*)

ence, claiming that the show only began when Weidman "stepped out of the role of Candide and addressed the audience as a WPA choreographer and dancer."[111] In urging the audience to join with the striking dancers, "the line of the footlights was crashed and audience and performers were joined in a common protest."[112]

The impulse to stage the strike originated with the project dancers, who asked Weidman to join them and to encourage the audience to stay. They reasoned that this display would prove public support for WPA cultural activities, such as these dance dramas, and for WPA prices of 25 to 55 cents.[113] About half the audience remained; significantly, many were friends and relatives of the dancers on stage and had been organized into an informal strike contingent. Fanya Geltman was one of the ringleaders.

> We were at the Nora Bayes Theatre with *How Long Brethren?* and *Candide.* And I must say Charles Weidman was the greatest. We wrote the thing for him and we told him we were going to sit in that night, and we were not going to leave. And at the end of *Candide,* he was to get up and read this thing, a sort of proclamation. Of course, we had all of us told friends and relatives and husbands,

32. WPA dancers on a hunger strike, June 1937.
(Courtesy of *Peoples Weekly World*.)

et cetera, you know, to come that night, to come to the theater that
night, and that they were going to stay. And that was one of the first
sit-ins, I think, ever.[114]

Outside the theater, pickets gathered, singing, "Hail, Hail, the Gang's
All Here," and the area was roped off by police.[115] Sympathizers hoisted
sandwiches and hot coffee all night to the strikers inside, and folksinger
Earl Robinson entertained them.[116]

In June, more demonstrations occurred. To protest a 25 percent layoff
of musicians employed in the Federal Music Project, audience and performers staged another sit-down strike. A photograph shows picketers
outside the WPA Dance Theatre, while inside, tired of sitting, audience
members and performers sang and danced in the lobby. From June 21 to
25 the dancers went on a hunger strike to express their solidarity with
the musicians. Incidents such as these capture the important themes
that shaped the Federal Dance Project's history: the sense of public mission that animated those involved with the project, the dancers' focus on
economic issues and their willingness to employ techniques of collective
bargaining, and the eagerness of the press to exploit the dancers' image
(figures 31, 32, and 33).

33. "The audience at the WPA Dance Theatre at 54th Street, New York City, joined with the cast of performers in protesting a 25 percent layoff of musicians employed on a Federal Music Project and staged a sit-in-strike, June 16. Tired of sitting down the sit-inners enjoy a bit of singing and dancing in the theatre lobby to pass the time away." (UPI/Corbis-Bettmann)

The Federal Dance Project was absorbed back into the FTP in October 1937 as a result of congressional cutbacks.[117] Many New York dancers, however, continued to be employed by the government. Tamiris choreographed two more projects, *Trojan Incident* (1938) and *Adelante* (1939), and Doris Humphrey used project dancers to mount *With My Red Fires, Race of Life,* and *To the Dance.* At the Brooklyn Museum of Art as part of the Young Choreographers Unit that Code had established, Lily Mehlman composed *Folk Dances of All Nations,* Nadia Chilkovsky made *Mother Goose on Parade,* and Berta Ochsner and David Campbell did *Fantasy 1939.* Anna Sokolow was working on *Sing for Your Supper* when the project's final act began in 1939.

In Washington, D.C., Tamiris delivered petitions protesting project cuts (figure 34), and Hallie Flanagan battled for the life of the Federal Theatre.[118] Pink slips of dismissal started to roll in, and in New York City dancer Paula Bass helped organize the Pink Slip Soup Kitchen at 321 West 41st Street to make sure that those artists who had been dismissed would not have to live by art alone. "Those who were working would

34. Delivering petitions to the White House to protest cuts in the Federal Arts Projects, 1939. Left to right are Phoebe Brand; Helen Tamiris; Marvin McIntyre, a White House secretary; Frances Farmer; and Artie Shaw. (UPI/Corbis-Bettmann)

35. At the Pink Slip Soup Kitchen in 1939. From left to right are Helen Tamiris, Leif Erickson, Zorino, and Paula Bass. (Courtesy of *Peoples Weekly World*.)

contribute $1.00, so that they could eat and it would give ten meals to people who were out of work." [119] With help from the Workers Alliance, a sympathetic taxi driver, and a cook from the Cafeteria Workers Union, food was provided (figure 35). [120]

F I V E

Dances for Spain, Dances for America

For a dancer educated in more or less wealthy and secluded surroundings, filled with the philosophical and esthetic culture of a liberal individualistic environment, suddenly to go in for proletarian dances, just because intellectually he or she has been convinced of the validity of Marxian philosophy—such a procedure seems fated to remain barren of vital results.[1]

Martha Graham was not a proletarian. She could trace her roots to the *Mayflower,* and her family had money; her father had been born with a trust fund. "Through all my childhood, all my education, I had no privation," she once recalled.[2] Graham, as a doctor's daughter, was a member of the country's educated and professional elite. However much she may have sympathized with some of the positions and ideals articulated by the socialists, she did not ally herself with working-class culture. Workers' issues were not her issues.

In his analysis of "Art and Propaganda," composer Dane Rudhyar revealed the dilemma facing artists such as Graham who lacked the "vital experience" to produce "art with vital content."[3] What could Martha Graham know about limited economic vistas and poverty of choice? As an artist, she may have been poor, and she probably did not always have enough to eat; Gertrude Shurr, a devoted and loyal member of the early Graham company, recalled bringing packages of food to Graham after Shurr returned from visiting her own family.[4] Still, for someone like Graham, a safety net existed back home.

Rudhyar's article, featured on the front page of the December 1936 issue of *Dance Observer,* tries to explain why dancers like Graham remained comparatively aloof from the class struggle of the revolutionary dance movement.[5] In Rudhyar's judgment, artists of her economic background could respond only with empty polemics and propaganda to the economic and social crisis of the time, and Graham's position on political oratory was well-known. In a 1934 interview she bluntly declared: "Propaganda is one subject I will not allow to be discussed in my studio."[6]

Rudhyar's article appeared just as a new vanguard of artists were emerging in the United States, artists galvanized by events in Europe and outraged over the fate of their colleagues in other countries. Working-class issues that had defined leftist political action in urban centers like New York gave way to concerns over the threat of war in Europe and the spread of fascism. Americans of all kinds were drawn into the political fray, including Martha Graham.

Graham gave her first independent concert in 1926 at the 48th Street Theatre before a sizable audience that included artists and students.[7] The program's dances had such titles as *Maid with the Flaxen Hair, Clair de Lune,* and *Désir.* In the next years, while Segal and the Red Dancers were playing to audiences gathered for Workers International Relief, celebrating International Women's Day, commemorating the Gastonia strike, and trouping off to Coney Island for May Day dances, Graham performed at a number of Broadway houses: the Guild Theatre on West 52nd Street, the Little Theatre on West 44th Street, Maxine Elliott's Theatre on West 39th Street, the Booth and the Klaw Theatres on West 45th Street, and the Craig on West 54th Street. She may have scoured 14th Street and the Lower East Side for fabrics to design her costumes,[8] but she made her performing home in the legitimate theater district—uptown, on Broadway.

Of nearly a hundred dances that Graham composed before the explicitly antiwar *Chronicle* (1936), only a few hinted at social turmoil. *Immigrant* (1928), for example, had sections entitled "Steerage" and "Strike." *Poems of 1917: Song Behind the Lines* and *Dance of Death* (both 1928), *Vision of the Apocalypse, Sketches from the People,* and *Heretic* (all in 1929), might also be considered dances of social significance, along with *American Provincials, Act of Piety,* and *Act of Judgment* (1934), and *Panorama* (1935). But Graham's approach could never be called revolutionary, as defined by the radical dancers. In most cases she stood for the individual and not the group. "One must always remember that Martha's protest was for the individual against an unthinking society, and never against a class or social order," explained fellow artist Agnes de Mille.[9]

A film record of *Heretic* provides insight into Graham's treatment of social conflict.[10] In the opening tableau a mass of eleven women stand with arms clasped firmly across their breasts. They form a semicircle that encompasses and imprisons a lone individual—Graham—who has separated herself from their community. Time after time Graham appeals to

them, seeking release. The women group and regroup—solid, impene-
trable masses—forming barriers beyond which Graham cannot go. They
act to restrict and contain her. By the end of the dance, the force of the
group has proved overwhelming. Graham slides to the ground, makes
one final appeal, and the struggle is over.

The roles of the participants were carefully coded. Graham wore white,
her dark hair hanging loosely down her back; the group was clothed
in dark jerseys, their hair constrained at the nape of the neck in dark
snoods. While the press routinely referred to the group as twelve less
expert Martha Grahams[11] (implying they were somehow intended to
function as look-alikes), they actually appear as studies in contrast and
opposition to Graham. The dance is about Graham's valiant effort, the
glory of the individual spirit *against* the group. Graham's movements
are infused with breath, providing sharp contrast to the deadly force of
the group as they erect one architectural barrier after another with their
bodies. Although the group triumphed, Graham was the heroine. Simi-
larly, in *American Provincials,* Graham played a solitary Hester Prynne
figure condemned by an unfeeling group. In Graham choreography, audiences identified with the individual, not the mass, which amounted to a
kind of heresy within the workers' dance movement.

Offstage as well, Graham placed her interests apart from group endeavors. Early efforts to organize dancers such as the Concert Dancers
League took place without Graham's support, although she faced the
same problems with regard to the illegality of performing on the Sabbath. Agnes de Mille, president of the league, recalled Graham's refusal
to join forces, her insistence on maintaining a sense of separateness and
doing things her own way.[12] In those days, according to de Mille, "anybody who was anybody was a Communist, of course,"[13] but Graham
refused to be defined by the group. She was always for the individual.
So, in a way, *Heretic* was her own story, the struggle of the solitary artist
when confronting any monolithic organization.

While Graham showed little interest in group efforts and revolutionary dance movements in the early 1930s, the dancers who were making
such a commotion appearing barefoot before striking shoeworkers or
raising money for the *Daily Worker* had considerable interest in her. Rec-
ollect that many of them were members of her company. By 1930 Anna
Sokolow was appearing with Graham. Lily Mehlman and Sophie Maslow
joined in 1931, Marie Marchowsky, another Workers Dance League member, became associated in 1934, Jane Dudley in 1935. And most of the
dancers in Sokolow's Dance Unit came from Graham's studio. Miriam
Blecher, Nadia Chilkovsky, and Edith Langbert of the New Dance Group

were all part of Graham's *Panorama* workshop at Bennington, Vermont, in the summer of 1935. Despite Graham's political aloofness, these young radical women idolized her and dedicated themselves to her work.

Yet sometimes it must have been hard for them to reconcile the two worlds. *New Theatre* carried an interesting account by Blanche Evan of her experience during an intensive summer course at Graham's studio in 1935:

> Long before class begins each day, there is a hush in the studio comparable only to the tense moment before a curtain rise in the theatre. The girls quietly seat themselves on the floor and begin to stretch. I don't dare fling a "hello" to a class-mate across the room. It would seem out of keeping in this solemn atmosphere. Martha enters dressed in a beautifully designed costume of white silk wearing white fur slippers to match. It's only eleven A.M. but she has already completed her private rehearsal and practice period. She quietly reclines on the divan, wraps a thin blanket around her, one of the three studio dachshunds snuggles in beside her, and the class commences.[14]

Evan, a dancer who appeared in at least one of the League concerts as part of the revolutionary dance movement's amateur army, was probably more of an educator than a performer. Most of her article is devoted to analyzing Graham's technique, her technical progressions and pedagogical approach—this about the same time that Evan was offering her own courses in "Dance Analysis."[15] Evan found Graham's approach overly formal, even didactic, and she yearned for some explanation of the principles involved rather than an insistence on what she perceived as rote learning. In addition, the article explored Graham's mysticism and the way that students worshiped and followed her without question. Graham, in her white silks and furs, must have been part goddess and part Hollywood glamour girl—a figure evoking the image of her own idol, Miss Ruth. Did Evan mean to satirize Graham's explicitly bourgeois appearance in her matching white rehearsal costume, or did it simply escape her editorial blue pencil?

Graham was criticized within the revolutionary press. Her dances were too personal and too individual; moreover, she had a predeliction for "past periods, lost civilizations, and ancient or medieval art forms." "She will be on one night," wrote Edna Ocko, "medieval, pre-Aeschylean, pre-white man Indian, and more recently, pre-classic."[16] Ocko, who persistently scolded Graham for a lack of social conscience, tried to educate revolutionary readers and dancegoers about how to interpret Graham's work. Dances like the 1928 *Strike,* Ocko said, were misconceived because they gave the impression that immigrants caused strikes. *Heretic,* Ocko concluded, portrayed the masses as unsympathetic, brutal, and above all ignorant of the Byronic "artist." [17]

At the same time, Graham's artistry and status were attractive, and critics like Ocko tried to woo her. Despite her fierce criticism, Ocko considered Graham a singular influence on the entire modern dance scene, and she genuinely loved Graham's work. She searched for excuses to claim Graham as a revolutionary artist because, as she recalled, "I always knew she was good." [18] Surveying some timely Graham repertory—*Prelude* (1932), *Satyric Festival Song* (1932), *Ekstasis* (1933), *Frenetic Rhythms* (1933)—Ocko seized on the third section of *Frenetic Rhythms* as an example of Graham's emerging social conscience. *Frenetic Rhythms* was about the "possession of the mind and soul by the rhythms of contemporary decadent living with its vice, its abandon, its gripping and sinister cruelty, its jazz and mechanical intimations." [19] The audience had reserved its most enthusiastic applause for this dance, she said, because it expressed something about their lives and the madness of contemporary life.

"More and more of Miss Graham's ever provocative recitals," Ocko wrote, "deal however impersonally and abstractly, with social conditions and social change." [20] Reviewing Graham's November 11, 1934, performance at the Theatre Guild, Ocko called *Celebration* a revolutionary dance and praised Graham's group choreography. *Celebration* was the first dance Graham made in which she did not appear. Consequently, no central figure appears; every dancer assumes equal importance. Critics such as Ocko could interpret this dance as a celebration of the power of the group and as an ideological advance for Graham, who previously had pitted herself against the masses in her choreography. It must have been a welcome sign to the socialists.

A barrage of jumping patterns begin the dance, strong vertical thrusts that emphasize the body's linear characteristics. From a cluster in the middle of the stage, dancers break away and return; swirling spatial patterns pull dancers back in toward a central force, then spray them out into the larger space. Graham apparently was thinking about contemporary urban life when she made this dance. She talked about architecture, the upward thrust of buildings, the percussiveness of modern life, the energy of modern industrialism. [21] Jowitt points out that modern architectural ideas were particularly interesting to dancers like Graham at this time.[22] The dance must have seemed bold and new, the essence of pulsing urban life, but all of its effects were achieved through formal patterns and virtuosic energy.

The dance was devoid of content—any content, let alone social content—but the energy, the ferocious passion that defined Graham's style made it seem revolutionary. It might have been called *Demonstration,* wrote Ocko, evoking images of May Day parades and union organizing.[23] Moreover, Ocko continued, Graham had admitted in conversation that her dances could be interpreted as a form of social commentary. She had even considered "May Day" as a subtitle for *Celebration.* Ocko speculated that when leftist dancers Lily Mehlman and Anna Sokolow appeared as the figures in red in Graham's *Course* (1935), they were meant to symbolize communism.[24]

Did Graham actually have these conversations with Ocko? The evidence is less than decisive, but Ocko's intention is clear. To the revolutionary dance movement, Graham was a prize worth winning. Ocko issued a challenge to Graham:

> Martha Graham must decide for whom, for what society she speaks. Is it for a nation? Is it for a class of people? If so, when will she reach out to that class of people and dance for them? Whatever confusions exist in the work of Martha Graham, this much is true: her technic has elements which make it ideal for depiction of militant evaluations of society, her dances more and more approach realistic social documentation and her verbal sympathies are avowedly one with the revolutionary dance. Will she openly assume leadership in the vanguard of revolutionary art, or will she be the last stronghold of a departing social order, and let her disciples champion new causes? This she must decide for herself.[25]

New Theatre and *Dance Observer* were essentially antagonists in the mid-1930s. With each periodical trying to define and capitalize on the development of the new American dance, they vied for readership and audiences. While Ocko was wooing Graham in *New Theatre, Dance Observer* was setting out to cast her work as revolutionary despite its formalism. In retaliation, *New Theatre* accused its rival of trying to discredit the revolutionary dance movement. Mignon Verne, the dance editor, slyly proclaimed that "dancers and dance critics who do not participate in the revolutionary dance cannot remain 'observers' without being partisans."[26] *Dance Observer,* Verne maintained, was trying to ride the coattails (or the audience) of the revolutionary movement by couching their descriptions of Graham's work in vague and nonspecific revolutionary language. If they succeeded in casting her as a revolutionary artist, Verne implied, working-class audiences would be more likely to attend her concerts.

Henry Gilfond's criticism in *Dance Observer* is what alarmed Verne. In a series of articles Gilfond tried to build support among readers for Graham as a social critic and to deflect criticism of her as a formalist. Writing about *Course,* Gilfond emphasized "the touch of the masses . . . in its sweep." He found *Imperial Gesture* (1935) to be an example of Graham's social conscience; no matter that some might interpret it in purely formal terms, it could not, he wrote "have been created by an artist who is not thoroughly aware of her social and economic environment." [27]

Gilfond (husband of Edythe Gilfond who designed costumes for Graham later in the decade) had made his debut in *Dance Observer* with a letter to the editor critiquing the state of dance criticism. Apparently *Dance Observer* invited him to contribute articles, because in December 1934 a scathing criticism of the Solo Workers Dance League concert at the Civic Repertory Theatre appeared under his name. He grudgingly acknowledged the fervent audience response, but he noted that "applause is not always a measure for merit." [28] Gilfond argued that Martha Graham and Mary Wigman were the only real artists around, even if they were not the most popular.[29]

In January an editorial in *Dance Observer* drew its readers' attention to another problem, namely, the "swift movement amounting almost to flight on the part of the young dancers into the ranks of the various workers' dance movements with varying shades of red and pink at their mastheads." [30] Gilfond was now on the board of *Dance Observer.*

It would be incorrect, however, to assume that the editorial and critical policies of *Dance Observer* represented a strictly conservative perspective. In fact, all of its principals were liberals. When Ocko accused Gilfond and Ralph Taylor, also of *Dance Observer,* of trying to discredit the revolutionary dance movement, Gilfond wrote a spirited reply, "Redder Than the Rose," in which he said he espoused the movement's aims. He simply wanted proletarian dance to fulfill the goals it had set for itself.[31] Taylor was a member of the Socialist Party in New York City, and Louis Horst, the founder of *Dance Observer,* was a liberal, although according to Taylor he hated the Communists.[32] Some of the aesthetic controversies therefore that played themselves out in the two periodicals were related to arguments between Communists and socialists that characterized the decade's early years.

The truth is that Gilfond and Ocko were both interested in finding a way to unite Graham with the vital workers' dance audience, although perhaps for different reasons. Ocko proposed to change Graham. She prodded Graham to join the movement. Gilfond wanted to change the way the audience perceived her. He wanted the movement to join Graham. In fact, both things happened. Graham's choreography became more explicitly political, and the workers' dance movement made efforts to broaden its membership and to be more inclusive.

By April 1935 the Workers Dance League had changed its name to the New Dance League (NDL), trying to consolidate an increasingly shaky position and to disassociate itself from the amateurism that the term "worker" was beginning to denote. The group's members wanted to correct what they considered to be the false separation between agitprop and concert dance. To this end, since every dance performed was to be considered a concert dance, establishing a review board with criteria for judgment was proposed. In this way the standards imposed, both artistic and ideological, would be the group's own and not John Martin's or Henry Gilfond's or Louis Horst's.[33] The New Dance League welcomed "all those who are striving, in their way, for freedom of expression and the perpetuity of dance culture,"[34] and in this guise it attracted some dancers not previously aligned with the workers' cause, including Ernestine Henoch (Stodelle), Lil Liandre, and Eleanor King.

In 1937 the American Dance Association (ADA) was formed, an amalgamation of the New Dance League, the Dancers Association (the organization that had proved so influential in getting the Federal Dance Project under way), and the Dance Guild, a broadly defined alliance dedicated, simply, to furthering the dance.[35] The ADA's platform was devoted to securing dancers' rights, promoting world peace, and fighting fascism — purposes so general that it is hard to imagine any dancer rejecting membership on the basis of political ideology.

Dance Observer also transformed itself during the later part of the decade, instituting changes that broadened its influence. The magazine initially saw its mission as championing modern dance — indeed, contemporary American dance was modern dance within the journal's pages. But in May 1936 Edna Ocko, writing as Eve Stebbins, sounded a populist note. Surveying the U.S. dance scene, she found it vital, exuberant, and varied, featuring jazz, tap, and square dancing as well as ballet and modern dance. Unfortunately, Ocko wrote, advocates of one form were often blind to the merits of other kinds of dancing. "The interested devotee of modern dancing deplores the persistence of the balletomane, and the culture-hungry worker is constantly pitted against the sated esthete."[36]

In October 1937 *Dance Observer* announced a change in editorial policy designed to bridge the divisions among advocates of different dance forms. Significantly, *New Theatre* was out of business, publishing its last issue in April 1937. In the future, *Dance Observer* would include not just contemporary modern dance, but ballet and folk.

A further change at *Dance Observer* saw Lincoln Kirstein welcomed as a member of its editorial board. For some time, Kirstein had tried to make ballet more palatable to American workers. In a lengthy 1934 article in *New Theatre* he claimed ballet could be revolutionary and popular; all that was necessary was working-class content.[37] In 1936 he formed Ballet Caravan to produce American ballets, and with dances such as Lew Christensen's *Filling Station* (1937) he demonstrated that ballets could be made about working-class people.

To write on folk dance, *Dance Observer* employed May Gadd, director of the English Folk Dance Society of America. Although the English folk dance and ballet were essentially foreign in their origins, they had taken root in native soil, and as *Dance Observer* redefined the limits of "American" dance, these forms came to be included.[38]

Dance Observer's changed editorial policies and the efforts of the revolutionary dance movement to include "all progressive, forward-looking dancers" were ways of being inclusive rather than exclusive, of laying aside divisive policies. Dancers—indeed, most Americans—seemed to want to huddle together in the face of what was going on in Europe. War was coming. In a rush of American themes and evocations of what America was, or could be, or might have been, distinctions between revolutionary and bourgeois artists virtually disappeared.

Within this context, Martha Graham emerged as a political choreographer, first of *Chronicle* (1936), then of *Immediate Tragedy* (1937) and *Deep Song* (1937). While *Immediate Tragedy* and *Deep Song* were created in response to the Spanish Civil War, Graham made it clear that she danced as an "American," thus paving the way for the nationalism that made its appearance in her 1938 production of *American Document*.

In December 1935 Graham had danced on a benefit program for the International Labor Defense at Carnegie Hall, appearing with groups headed by Humphrey, Weidman, Tamiris, and Sokolow. *New York World-Telegram* columnist Heywood Broun, now a socialist, spoke, while Angelo Herndon, seated in the audience, received an ovation.[39] It was just the kind of soapbox electioneering that had occasioned John Martin's scorn at the New Dance League concert a few months earlier when he had compared the event to a medicine show.[40] Graham did *Celebration, Imperial Gesture,* and *Course*; Humphrey presented parts of *New Dance* (1935); Weidman did *Stock Exchange* (1935); Tamiris performed

Harvest (1935) and *Work and Play* (1935); and Sokolow did *Strange American Funeral*. Note that with the exception of Sokolow, none of these choreographers had been explicitly connected to the revolutionary dance movement, although Tamiris had been instrumental in other aspects of organizing, and Weidman had appeared on one or two concerts of the Workers Dance League. The dances (with the exception of *Strange American Funeral* and perhaps *Stock Exchange,* Weidman's comical depiction of the 1929 Wall Street crash) were not the usual revolutionary fare. But in this atmosphere, even the abstract *New Dance* was perceived as a dance of social significance, its ideal community a model of a better world. Among the Graham contributions were compositions that Ocko had singled out as socially conscious; despite their formal values, they had earned the tentative approval of left-wing ideologues. A new army of dancers was marching onto the political scene as a result of the looming fascist threat.[41]

The courting of Graham and other politically moderate dancers was related to changes within the Communist Party and its shifting relationship to the American scene. The Party's policy of socialist realism had set the stage for an appreciation of Graham's technique and artistry, and the Popular Front—the alliance of all those groups opposed to fascism— provided a home for artists who might never have become Party members. In 1935 the Party had begun to show signs of support for Roosevelt's New Deal, and some socialist-supported programs, such as the Social Security Act, were passed by Congress. The Party's interaction with New Deal philosophies made it increasingly acceptable to large segments of the American public. During this period the Party actually extended its influence, with membership rising from approximately 10,000 at the beginning of the 1930s to 65,000 by 1940, with a marked increase among native-born Americans.[42]

In 1936, certainly influenced by the Popular Front, an American Artists Congress was formed to combat the reactionary forces that were perceived to be threatening the destruction of contemporary culture. No prominent Communists were in the organization, which instead was composed of some four hundred artists and intellectuals, including Stuart Davis, Meyer Schapiro, and Martha Graham,[43] while the prominent dance photographer Barbara Morgan was recording secretary.[44] Significantly, in making her politics public, Graham chose to unite with artists, not workers.[45]

An awareness about events in Europe and the fate of dancers and artists in Germany contributed to a growing political consciousness at home. In August 1935 *New Theatre* ran a piece reporting that the German dancer Mary Wigman was a fascist.[46] Apparently this caused no great apprehension in the offices of *Dance Observer* because in October the magazine carried a long letter from Virginia Stewart reporting on the German dance. Stewart was "America's Business Representative" of the Central Wigman School, and she organized tours of American dancers to study at the Wigman school in Dresden.[47] She was the coauthor of an early book on modern dance in which she described and analyzed German and American modern dance.[48] In her letter, Stewart provided information about the activities of important German dancers, including Wigman and Rudolf von Laban, her mentor. Over the summer of 1934 Laban had staged a work called *Camp March* for the new Tanz Buhne (dance stage), a department of the chamber of culture under Joseph Goebbels. Stewart lauded it as a symbol of "the new work of the dance in Germany today."[49] Was Stewart naive? Did business interests influence her? She concluded her letter with an announcement of plans for the next summer's international dance festival. Wigman and her group were to perform in an *Olympic Youth* pageant to be staged as part of the opening festivities of the 1936 Olympic Games in Berlin.[50]

The next month *Dance Observer* featured Wigman in a lengthy article by Hanya Holm that failed to question any of Wigman's recent activities. Did Holm know? Did the board of *Dance Observer* know?

Ocko knew. She wrote a furious response, pointing out the failure of *Dance Observer*'s editorial policies: "Even now, in all parts of the world, trade unions, [which] surely are not peopled by athletes, are agitating for a boycott of these Olympics, yet this parallel situation in the dance does not elicit an editorial comment from a dance magazine."[51]

In *New Theatre,* Ocko declared that Wigman was lost and urged that "all ties be severed between those dancers teaching the German method and Mary Wigman."[52] Ocko suggested that in exchange for a tour through Germany and Poland, Wigman had complied with the new Nazi regime rather than flee the country as so many of her fellow artists had done. American dancers must boycott the German-held festival, said Ocko. "What dancer in America today wishes to be the guest of a government that does not hesitate to torture and murder artists because of their religion, their anti-fascist sentiments, their progressive approaches to art."[53]

Faced with increasing evidence, the New Dance League mounted a campaign, and a committee was formed to encourage dancers to boycott the Summer Olympic Games;[54] Lily Mehlman and Jane Dudley of the

Graham company were on the committee.[55] Perhaps Graham learned of the boycott through their activities, or perhaps she followed these events herself. At any rate, Graham's refusal to take part in the 1936 Olympic Games has become canonized in dance history. She did not hesitate to take a strong stand for her group, but though it was for the group, it was the act of an individual.

> I would find it impossible to dance in Germany at the present time. So many artists whom I respect and admire have been persecuted, have been deprived of the right to work for ridiculous and unsatisfactory reasons, that I should consider it impossible to identify myself, by accepting the invitation, with the regime that has made such things possible. In addition some of my concert group would not be welcomed in Germany.[56]

The American dance community responded in force. Besides Graham, Doris Humphrey, Charles Weidman, Helen Tamiris, Anna Sokolow, Sol Hurok, and Lincoln Kirstein supported the boycott. In November 1936 the Wigman school changed its name to the Hanya Holm School.[57]

Martha Graham had not joined in earlier efforts by dancers to improve working conditions or to create jobs, but as the political landscape changed, her attitude toward group efforts mellowed. From May 18 to 25, 1936, the first Dance Congress in the United States took place in New York City with conferences, discussions, demonstrations, and performances. Participants included dancers such as Humphrey and Tamiris, and critics like John Martin and Henry Gilfond.[58] Graham spoke and led her group in a dance demonstration on one of the evening programs.[59]

Descriptions of the congress hint at organizational problems and antagonism between groups, although resolutions passed at the session's conclusion stress solidarity and support among the dancers. In particular, Martin was disturbed by the way meetings progressed, complaining that "young Left-wingers kept the Congress in their own hands."[60] Edna Ocko retaliated, pointing out that any attempts at collective bargaining and joint action by dancers were being viewed suspiciously and labeled "Red."[61]

Probably the Dance Congress was the site of some heated discussions, based in part on the fact that the dancers represented a broad cross section of activity in the United States; the evening performances included ballet, folk, and theater dance as well as modern. Also, representatives were present from outside the working-class dance movement, which had dominated earlier attempts at organizing. The fact that Graham was willing to let her name and her dancers be associated with this effort, even though she did not play a significant role in the congress, suggests that she viewed its goals as compatible with her own artistic and political interests.

Amid all the resolutions for fair wages, more dance critics, support for the Federal Dance Project, and just about everything else was Resolution IV:

> Because the forces of Fascism lead inevitably by the nature of Fascist policy to a stagnation of all art forms and creative endeavor and to wars of aggression, because the forces of war are patently destructive both to human life and the development of art and culture, the Dance Congress resolves that its members, in the interest of a free and uncensored growth of the dance, go on record as being opposed to war, fascism and censorship and to all efforts that foster such retrogressive policies.[62]

Graham's dances began to reflect her fears for the world. *Chronicle* premiered on December 20, 1936 (figures 36, 37, and 38).[63] The dance was lengthy—forty minutes—and divided into three sections: "Dances Before Catastrophe: Spectre—1914 and Masque"; "Dances After Catastrophe: Steps in the Street and Tragic Holiday"; and "Prelude to Action." As her program notes reveal, Graham clearly intended the work to be a form of social commentary: "'Chronicle' does not attempt to show the actualities of war; rather does it, by evoking war's images, set forth the fateful prelude to war, portray the devastation of spirit which it leaves in its wake, suggest an answer."[64]

Full of symbolism, and relying on lighting, props, background, and costume to produce its effect, *Chronicle* was a theater piece. "Dances Before Catastrophe" was performed in front of a red, white, and black background—no accident, said Henry Gilfond, "but rather conscious selection and condemnation,"[65] apparently referring to Graham's explicit display of the Nazi colors (a black swastika in a white circle on a red field). In the solo "Spectre" Graham appeared dressed in black and red, suggesting rivers of blood to one reviewer;[66] in "Tragic Holiday" she waved a black flag, mocking ceremonies destined to honor war dead. Gilfond praised Graham for showing new interest in concrete subject matter and moving away from abstraction.[67]

Still, some critics found her content obscure and her style elitist, despite the explicit program notes and dramatic costume and background effects. A disappointed Ocko critiqued Graham's technical approach and

36, 37, 38. Martha Graham's dances began to reflect her fears for the world. "Spectre 1914" from *Chronicle*. © Barbara Morgan.

her "icebound formalism." Graham's interest in counterpoint in "Steps in the Street" had rendered the dance an "unrecognizable abstraction,"[68] Ocko lamented.

"Steps in the Street" is a dance for a group of women and a soloist (originally May O'Donnell). As the dance section begins, the women back onto the stage, their torsos hollowed out in a high Graham contraction — not a mimetic depiction of hunger but an expression of its essence. With long, lean steps, the women cross the stage. Diagonals form and re-form, evoking images of breadlines, of aimless wandering, of endless despair.[69] These images are coded in the systematic language of Graham's developing technique and unfold through formal manipulations of space, without the aid of literal gesture, but with enormous emotional intensity.[70]

Ocko felt that Graham's infatuation with elements of form robbed the dance of its potential power. Predictably, Ocko and Gilfond took antagonistic positions. Ocko wished Graham were more accessible, while Gilfond hoped that explaining Graham's work to the audience would clarify its underlying intent. Graham continued to evade easy categorization.

The real problem was that despite its powerful emotional appeal, "Steps in the Street" failed to establish an entirely sympathetic view of the masses. As in *Heretic,* a solo figure challenged the power of the group, "continu[ing] to resist the mass movement even as the curtain falls."[71]

The Spanish Civil War triggered an avalanche of artistic opposition to fascism, from Picasso's *Guernica* to Hemingway's script to the film *The Spanish Earth* (1937), to Martha Graham's *Immediate Tragedy* and *Deep Song* (both 1937). Lily Mehlman did a suite called *Spanish Woman* (1937), which included "Lullaby for a Dead Child," and Sophia Delza made *We Weep for Spain* (1937) and *We March for Spain* (1937). Jane Dudley and Sophie Maslow collaborated on *Women of Spain* (1938), a dance in two parts, "Caprichos" and "Evacuación." "Caprichos" examined the relationship between peasant women and the Spanish aristocracy, while "Evacuación" dealt with women forced to leave the land. Dudley made *Cante Flamenco* (1940) and Graham made *War Theme* (1941), improvising to a poem by William Carlos Williams. Images by Barbara Morgan vividly document Graham's dancing defense of human rights, while working relationships such as the Morgan-Graham-Williams collaboration attest to the creative energy released in such shared political visions (figures 39, 40, 41, and 42).

On May 23, 1937, the American Dance Association sponsored the first "Dances for Spain" concert at the Adelphi Theatre for the benefit of the Medical Committee to Aid Spanish Democracy. The evening featured an array of dance styles: ballet, Spanish, modern. Ruthanna Boris, from the American Ballet, and Polanca, a Spanish dancer, performed alongside Tamiris, Sophia Delza, Lazar Galpern, Mehlman, Miriam Blecher, and Anna Sokolow.[72] Graham did not perform on this first evening, but in January 1938 she took part in a second "Dances for Spain" concert at the Hippodrome Theatre, where she shared the stage with Lincoln Kirstein's Ballet Caravan, Sokolow's Dance Unit, Helen Tamiris, and Hanya Holm. In February another benefit evening was arranged by the American Dance Association at the Mecca Temple. Humphrey, Weidman, Tamiris, Sokolow, and Graham took part. At the conference that preceded the performance, Graham as well as Kirstein and Louis Horst were listed as speakers.

Graham's involvement in the political arena came at a time when the leftist agenda no longer was defined primarily by working-class issues and rights; she was responding to a situation that she believed threatened all peoples. As one reviewer pointed out, the dance *Chronicle* was about "the looming horror of a universal catastrophe and its moral breakup."[73]

Immediate Tragedy and *Deep Song* were composed in response to the Spanish Civil War, but Gilfond argued persuasively that the two solos depicted more than events in Spain and that Graham danced more than only Spanish women's despair. Over and over in his review, Gilfond returned to this theme: Graham rose above the strictly representational; her dances were not merely descriptive; the Spanish tragedy was not unique. "It is not Spain that we see in her clean impassioned movement; it is the realization that Spain's tragedy is ours, is the whole world's tragedy. The dedication is not a Spaniard's; it is an American's."[74] Graham universalized the tragedy, he claimed.

Graham's prestige had spread beyond New York cultural circles. In the spring of 1936 she had taken a solo repertory on tour across the country. Merle Armitage's book on Graham was published in 1937 and included articles by leading artists and critics: John Martin, Lincoln Kirstein, Wallingford Riegger, Stark Young, Edith Isaacs. The same year Graham was invited to appear before President Franklin D. Roosevelt, becoming the first American dancer to perform for a U.S. president in the White House.[75] When a representative of American dance was sought to perform at the 1938 preview pageant of the New York World's Fair, Graham must have seemed a logical choice. *Dance Observer* applauded the selection. It was appropriate, they implied, she "being a direct descendant, on her mother's side, of Miles Standish."[76] So much for the American melting pot.

39, 40, 41, 42. The Spanish Civil War triggered an avalanche of artistic opposition to the Fascists, who were supported by Fascist Italy and Nazi Germany. (39) Martha Graham in *Immediate Tragedy.* © Barbara Morgan. (40) Jane Dudley in *Cante Flamenco.* © Barbara Morgan. (41) Martha Graham in *War Theme.* © Barbara Morgan. (42) Poster for the second annual dance for Spain benefit at the Mecca Temple.

Graham had been defining her dance as "American" and indigenous for some time. Discreetly downplaying the contributions of the German school, she placed the origins of modern dance in the United States; its style of movement was characterized by American rhythms, which were "sharp and angular, stripped of unessentials."[77] Graham was also, of course, describing the characteristics of her own dance and distinguishing it from all things European. In such dances as *American Provincials* (1934) and *Frontier* (1935), Graham's ode to the experiences and feelings of the American pioneer woman, she danced moving testimony to a "spirit which was willing to face a pioneer country."[78] And, as Gilfond pointed out, it was as an American responding to international events that she created *Immediate Tragedy* and *Deep Song*. Now she produced *American Document*.

American Document premiered at Bennington College in the summer of 1938. Since 1934 Bennington had been the site of summer programs, gathering eminent dancers such as Graham, Humphrey, Weidman, and Holm. (Tamiris was noticeably absent.) Also teaching at Bennington during these summer months were John Martin (dance criticism), Louis Horst (dance composition), Arch Lauterer (stage design), and John Cage and Norman Lloyd (music). In addition to their teaching responsibilities, choreographers were given space and opportunity to create new works, and it was in this setting that Graham devised her new creation.

The dance was Graham's tribute to her American heritage. Texts that accompanied *American Document* were drawn from actual historical records such as the Declaration of Independence, the Gettysburg Address, and the Emancipation Proclamation as well as lesser-known examples such as Jonathan Edwards's fire-and-brimstone sermons and the lament of Red Jacket of the Senecas. Program notes indicate that Graham believed such documents contained the essence of the nation: "Our documents . . . our legends—our poignantly near history, our folk tales."[79]

Edythe Gilfond, making her debut as a designer for Graham, devised costumes that featured the colors of the American flag, while the dramatic structure that Graham chose—unique to American dance up to that time—was borrowed from the American minstrel show.[80] The musical score by Ray Green was based on American and African folk songs. The central question posed by the dance, which introduced four out of its five sections, was "What Is an American?"

An Interlocutor, played by Housely Stevens, inaugurated the dance.[81] "The place is here in the United States. . . . the time is now." Each of the dancing principals was then presented:

The characters are:
The dance group, led by Sophie,
You, the audience,
The Interlocutor—I am the Interlocutor,
And Erick and Martha.[82]

The company, which had been onstage throughout this introduction, now exited, and the Interlocutor spoke again, setting up the dance's central theme—the construction of an American national identity:

These are Americans.
Yesterday—and for days before yesterday—
One was Spanish,
One was Russian,
One was German,
One was English.
Today these are Americans.

The first episode, "Declaration," presented members of the cast in succession, presumably suggesting the waves of immigrants who had forged new identities as Americans. This was followed by "Occupation," an ode to the virgin country that was once America and to its original inhabitants. "We do not remember the Indian Prairie before these states were," said the Interlocutor. "But my blood remembers, my heart remembers." Graham did a solo, looking like a "tribal maiden," according to Agnes de Mille, with her hair braided down her back,[83] and the group danced "Lament for the Land." May O'Donnell recollected that in this section they were asked to move like animals in a forest.[84] "Puritan Episode" followed, a duet for Graham and Erick Hawkins (who was appearing with the previously all-female company for the first time), and then "Emancipation Episode," in which the liberation of the slaves was presented.

In the fifth and final episode, originally titled "AfterPiece," the uncertainties and tragedies of contemporary life were depicted. A photograph by Barbara Morgan captures dancers Jane Dudley, Sophie Maslow, and Frieda Flier with outstretched arms, beseeching the audience, an obvious reference to the destitute and hungry still wandering the country's streets (figure 43).[85] Stevens recited, "We are three women . . . we are three million women. . . . We are the mothers of the hungry dead. . . . We are the mothers of the hungry living." The women's dance was followed by a Hawkins solo portraying the struggles of the work force, probably the most explicit representation of working-class America in Graham's

43. The AfterPiece. "We are three women. . . . We are three million women."
Frieda Flier, Jane Dudley, and Sophie Maslow in Martha Graham's *American
Document*. © Barbara Morgan.

dances, but here the representation was enlarged to the universal. "I am
one man . . . I am one million men," the Interlocutor repeated.

Graham did not end her dance on this note. The critique of contemporary society gave way to an affirmation of American ideals, a call to
rally round.

> America! Name me the word that is courage.
> America! Name me the word that is justice.
> America! Name me the word that is power!
> America! Name me the word that is freedom!
> America! Name me the word that is faith.
> Here is that word—
> Democracy!

Lincoln's Gettysburg Address was the final document: "that government
of the people, by the people, for the people, shall not perish from the
earth."

Most scholars are convinced that the final episode was significantly
altered between 1938 and 1942 when Graham's libretto was published

in *Theatre Arts.* A review by George Beiswanger noted references in the original text to the "things we are ashamed of . . . Sacco-Vanzetti, share-croppers, the Scottsboro boys."[86] Lincoln Kirstein's 1938 review in the *Nation* suggested that this episode contained a kind of "contemporary self-accusation, a praise of our rights, and a challenge to our own powers to persist as a democracy."[87] Yet it is likely the final episode of the 1938 presentation resolved these themes of injustice and repression, ending on a note of affirmation and hope, just as the 1942 version did.

American Document earned praise for its political relevance and gave Graham her first real exposure to a larger audience. Kirstein's review cited the presentation as the "most important extended dance creation by a living American."[88] Beiswanger praised the dance "for bring[ing] to bear upon today's perplexities all that was sturdy and upright and liberating in the American dream."[89] Ocko and Gilfond could finally agree on something. In *Dance Observer,* Gilfond concluded that the dance was a "testimonial to our love and loyalty to democracy in these trying and threatening days of 1938,"[90] while Ocko, writing in *TAC* (Theatre Arts Committee), which had taken up the leftist banner after the demise of *New Theatre* in 1937, pointed to it as one of Graham's "more significant works,"[91] an "affirmation of the American traditions of democracy and social justice."[92] The *New Masses* called the ballet a "testimony to the greatest of American traditions — democracy,"[93] and in *Dance Magazine,* Gervaise Butler characterized the dance as a "kind of Joycean manifestation of this land, this people whose history began, one stormy day with Plymouth Rock."[94]

American Document was critically acclaimed. It was uplifting. And it was popular. John Martin had reservations about the Bennington premiere, but when the dance was performed in New York in the fall, those misgivings disappeared. The Graham company received glowing reviews for its appearance at Carnegie Hall on October 9, 1938, in a benefit performance for the *New Masses.* In December the company appeared at the Alvin Theatre. In both cases *American Document* was the draw.[95] From February 23 to March 23, 1939, Graham toured the country to present it. *Dance Observer* reported enthusiastic audiences in Chicago, Los Angeles, and San Francisco, and the writer concluded that "at last the general American public welcomes, and is excited by, the American dance."[96]

In fact, *American Document* incorporated many elements that had proved popular in the revolutionary dance movement, including moral fervor, archetypal figures, pageantry, and text.

A close look at "Emancipation Episode" demonstrates just how much

Graham relied on the kind of techniques that characterized the earlier workers' dance movement. The Interlocutor began the section by asking a familiar question, "The United States of America—what is it?"

> A state—what is it?
> It is a unit in a nation of states
> *Group begins to enter singly.*
> One state has mountains
> One state has no mountains
> One state has sea
> One state has no sea
> One state has corn
> One state has gold
> One state has cotton
> Once, more than one state had slaves
> *The last dancer takes her place in the*
> *three lines that have formed center stage.*
> Now, no state has slaves
> Now every state has one deep word
> Here it comes:
> Emancipation!
> *Here follows the group in the dance*
> *Emancipation. Partway through the*
> *dance there is a pause. The Interlocutor*
> *speaks.*
> 1863—
> That government of the people, by the people, and for the people
> shall not perish from the earth.
> *The dance resumes. At the end, the group finishes in a semicircle,*
> *looking up in an ecstatic gesture, both arms spread to the side.*

Agnes de Mille recalled glory in the faces of the dancers. "They fell to their knees in lines, gazing in wonder and rapture on the incomparable vision of freedom and equality. The listeners went down in contrapuntal rows, their hands to their throats and when they came up in ranks they were shaken with ecstasy."[97]

> The Interlocutor continues:
> I, Abraham Lincoln, President of the United States, on this first day of January, in the year of our Lord one thousand, eight hundred and sixty-three, do order and declare: that all persons held as slaves shall be then, thenceforward and forever free.

*The group exits as Martha and Erick enter upstage opposite each other.
There is an ecstatic Duet and they exit centre back. Six dancers enter
in the Walk Around and exit.*[98]

Graham's dance had all the elements of pageantry, the idealized representation of the past, a transcendent vision of the future, the declamations, the poses, the dances interspersed with the spoken word. The Interlocutor speaks while the group is still; he falls silent and they dance; they pause and he speaks once again. But a lengthy description by Gilfond of Graham's newfound theatricality and accessibility leaves one wondering whether the critic had forgotten earlier efforts by revolutionary dancers or had never seen them:

> Martha Graham [is] breaking through the already stiffening form of modern concert dance. For the first time an actor is introduced into the dance as we know it today, an actor who announces the nature of the work, its characters, provides a setting the music cannot, sets a tone where it is necessary, makes clear to the audience whatever might need additional clarity, assures a complete rapport between the dancer and her audience. And why not? If a dancer wants to keep her audience in the dark why dance? *The wonder of it is that dancers have not done it before, made sure that their audiences understood completely what it was they were intending.* (Italics mine)[99]

It had been done before—*The Belt Goes Red, Van der Lubbe's Head, Strange American Funeral*—but not by Graham. Probably nobody had integrated the text with the dance in the way that Graham did. The revolutionary experiments with text had usually placed the speaker to one side, or even offstage. But Graham's Interlocutor was part of the action, as essential to the performance as any of the dancers. Graham's unusual intelligence had woven diverse texts together, juxtaposing them to create suspense and tension, ordering them to produce conflict and resolution. In the end, however, the effect on the audience must have produced results similar to the earlier creations. Graham's use of the spoken word and elements borrowed from pageantry produced a sociability and a dialogue between herself and the audience that had not existed before.

American Document was popular, and it was nationalistic. In a time when American solidarity was essential, Graham's work confirmed the uniqueness of the American experience; in this sense she was a political choreographer, though not a revolutionary one. Perhaps as Dane Rudhyar suggested, this was impossible, given her background.

Graham produced herself as a universal American body, traversing the limits of time, space, and race, bringing working America, Indian America, black America, colonial America, and contemporary America together on a single stage. The threads of American experience were united in one tapestry, and it was not defined by race, class, or eth-nicity—although Graham's universal body was almost certainly assumed to be a white Protestant body that somehow could subsume every other identity.[100] For the first time in her work, however, the dancing body was distinctly formulated in terms of gender. The presence of a male on stage, in the midst of what had previously been a bastion of female power and independence, occasioned considerable tension within the company, but undoubtedly Erick Hawkins's inclusion made Graham's work more ac-cessible. Critics such as Kirstein seemed relieved, noting that Hawkins had "acquitted himself ably . . . in support of Miss Graham," [101] as if Miss Graham were in need of support!

Graham's ability to enlarge the parameters of her performance by iden-tifying herself with historical and universal forces has been noted by other writers.[102] In *American Document* Graham stood not just for her-self, but for America, for all people in all times, the oppressed and the repressed, the enslaved and the liberated, the beggars, the workers, the fighters, the idealists. The Morgan photographs of the "AfterPiece" epi-sode show a series of images, superimposed, so that it is impossible to discern what movement or pose is meant to be central. Who is speaking, and at what moment? Are the photographs Morgan's vision, but perhaps Graham's as well? In the dance, Graham represents the working class as a part of a universal class; the women represent not one woman, but a million women.

At the 1938 preview pageant for the New York World's Fair Graham had represented American dance, and in 1939 she was asked to partici-pate in the official opening ceremonies. Graham's *Tribute to Peace* fol-lowed Roosevelt's dedication of the fair (figure 44): "On a wide platform, built as an altar to peace and which stood halfway between the Presi-dent's reviewing stand and the first row of an audience of 60,000 people, Martha Graham's company of twenty danced a solemn impressive trib-ute, to the music of Handel's 'See, the Conquering Hero Comes,' sung by the Westminster Choir." [103]

Earlier in the decade Graham had eschewed propaganda, but the ter-ritory was different now. The agenda of Roosevelt's New Deal at times softened the left's harshest criticism of American social policies, the Communist Party endorsed some parts of the New Deal, the Party's chair-man having proclaimed in 1935 that communism was twentieth-century Americanism, and many revolutionary dancers went to work for the gov-

44. The Martha Graham company in *Tribute to Peace,* 1939. (Wide World Photos, reproduced from *Dance Observer,* May 1939.)

ernment. The movement among dancers, as defined in terms of work issues, was over, and onto that empty stage stepped American interests, American dance, and American patriotism. This role fit Graham naturally.

Graham, suddenly at the forefront of politics and dance, acted as a spokeswoman for a reenergized nation. Whether this role was partially opportunism on her part or the result of deeply held convictions will never be known. Probably both opportunism and conviction were involved. The American dream of pulling oneself up by one's bootstraps, of riding bravely into the West, of each citizen's chance to become president, all would have fit nicely with her own fierce belief in individual potential.

In 1955 Graham became an ambassador of culture for the United States when she and her company were sponsored by the State Department on a tour of the Far East.

S I X

The People's Culture: Folklore
on the Urban Stage

An America existed that was not expressed in sophisticated documents or educated prose. Songs and dances, homemade instruments, homilies and folk sayings were the currency of this culture, and in the late 1930s it became a source of material for many artists on the left.

Sonny Terry was a blind Negro musician from the South who played the harmonica. In December 1938 the *New Masses* had sponsored a "From Spirituals to Swing" concert at Carnegie Hall, featuring Count Basie, many well-known or rising jazz and blues figures, and Sonny Terry.[1] Jane Dudley, who was in the audience, recalled her first impressions of Terry: "Sonny had the harmonica. All I remember was his look when he played. He'd take it away from his mouth and sing, alternating with singing that had no words that I could distinguish—a curious kind of animal wailing, or hooting, almost like flamenco: not the trill, but the high falsetto that a flamenco singer has, which is this thing of being connected to oneself."[2]

In the 1920s and 1930s so-called race records featuring black musicians were aimed specifically at black audiences. Outside black neighborhoods they were stocked only by specialty stores. Dudley found a place in Greenwich Village that carried Terry's "Harmonica and Washboard Breakdown," and she set about choreographing her signature piece, *Harmonica Breakdown,* to the recording (figures 45 and 46). The dance was structured in rondo form, with Dudley repeatedly returning to a singular theme, a strange, disjointed walk performed on a long diagonal from upstage right to downstage left.[3] Lois Balcolm, reviewing the premiere in *Dance Observer,* called it a "queer stiff-legged, flat-footed progression, like nothing on earth, unless one of Steig's Small Fry came to life and stalked out of the pages of the *New Yorker.*"[4]

Dudley drew on various impressions to express the eccentric and haunting quality of Terry's music in her walk. She remembered a skinny black man struggling to stand up after being shot in the leg by a white vigilante, a scene that she had witnessed in a film called *Native Land* by Paul Strand and her husband, Leo Hurwitz. She thought of an old hound dog scratching its leg, tail hidden between its legs. Then she recalled a curious shuffling step she had seen in a piece by the African American dancer Katherine Dunham, and she put that in as well. Performing the dance, she felt that "Ol' Mister Woe" was right behind her, waiting to grab her if she did not continue moving. That is what the queer walk meant to her, she said. If you were poor and Negro you had to keep on going.[5]

Musicians like Sonny Terry—blind, black, poorly educated—seemed living symbols of what the left was fighting for. Like most of the musicians in the "From Spirituals to Swing" concert, Terry had no formal musical training, could not read musical notation, and had not played in front of a mostly white audience before. John Hammond, who promoted the concert, argued that white American music lovers were ignorant of the "authentic music of the American Negro." To show both the general public and the serious musician what was going on outside the big cities and established centers of culture, Hammond had organized the concert "to present the unlettered Negro musicians of the South and the Southwest."[6]

For a New York audience, Terry's performance would have seemed as wonderful and strange as a journey to a foreign land except that it really was America. Intellectuals and avant-gardists, radicals and leftists, writers, composers, and modern dancers were discovering the enormous richness of the country's folk culture.

Initially, leftist artists were slow to grasp the ideological advantage that might be gained by incorporating folk material into their work. Historically, the term "folk" had applied to the peasant class of a feudal society.[7] Not surprisingly, the Soviet Union rejected such forms as decadent remnants of oppressed and enslaved people.[8] In the United States, too, folk dances and songs were initially considered a pre-revolutionary "badge of servitude."[9]

With the adoption of socialist realism, however, attitudes toward folk culture began to change. In the Soviet Union folk dance was promoted as a means of enlivening the new Soviet ballet, creating themes derived from the life of the people. A State Folk Dance Ensemble was established with Igor Moiseyev, formerly ballet master of the Bolshoi Theater, as its director. Returning from Moscow in 1938, Edna Ocko reported on the new folk ensemble and on Moiseyev's plans for creating a vital new form

45, 46. Jane Dudley in *Harmonica Breakdown*. (Photographs by Gerda Peterich. Courtesy of the Dance Collection, New York Public Library for the Performing Arts, Astor, Lenox and Tilden Foundations.)

of expression in Soviet dance. Igor Moiseyev was convinced that folk dance could represent the changing life of the people.[10]

In the United States two things had to happen for folk culture to become a source of inspiration to urban artists. First, folk art, folk music, folk dance had to be recognized as contemporary cultural expressions of the masses, urban as well as rural; and second, the idea of an American

folk culture had to be articulated. Many American intellectuals and artists were biased against American culture. Consequently, folk culture at first meant derivations of European folk culture, especially Russian.[11]

In fact, organizations for American folk dance were nothing new, and as early as 1931 John Martin wrote about folk dance in the *New York Times,* arguing for its place as a kind of lay dance that could increase the aesthetic awareness of the average citizen at the same time that it created a larger audience for the new modern dance.[12] But artists allied with working-class interests did not immediately perceive American folk and popular culture as comrades in the political struggle.

In an article, "The Folk Dance," Sophia Delza began to articulate a way for the left to embrace folk forms that otherwise would be suspect because of their association with the past. Delza, a dancer herself, considered the dancer's experience. She argued that folk dance had a place in contemporary society, not because of its historical traditions or because of a pleasing aesthetic, but because of its ability to unite the members of a community. It was a form of mass dance, like that advocated by Dudley and Edith Segal.

Delza's idea seems to have been to apply these communal ideals to the new art dance forms in the United States, although she was unclear on how it might happen. "The modern dance in order to thrive needs . . . mass sympathy," she wrote, "the communality (either in direct dancing participation or in understanding the audience['s] relation to dance), and the fruitful direction that has sustained the folk dance for so long." [13] While Delza argued for the integration of folk dance and modern dance, she made it clear that she considered popular social dances in the United States trivial and unworthy of honor. A rural folk culture seems to have been beyond her and others' imagining. So while a people's culture thrived among blacks and whites in urban and rural parts of the country, it was not yet called art. This blind spot regarding indigenous American culture was common among artists of radical bent.

When the Composers Collective was formed in 1931, it set out to engage and educate the masses musically and to create revolutionary songs, but it failed to give American folk music a passing glance. The Collective counted among its composer-members Henry Cowell, Elie Siegmeister, Charles Seeger, Wallingford Riegger, Earl Robinson, and Alex North, all of them busy collaborating with the new modern dancers. Many members of the Collective had trained in distinguished music schools in the United States and in Europe; as a group, they represented the most promising young composers in the country.

Looking for a model for proletarian song, the Collective kept running into roadblocks. They thought progressive political ideology demanded progressive music,[14] but privately they worried whether their compositions would be simple enough for a proletarian chorus. They balked at popular music, as Delza had balked at popular social dance. Though they were undoubtedly surrounded by American folk culture, they did not see it, or if they did, they felt that the material was musically illiterate. Folk music was simply not high-class. According to Charles Seeger, "members of the Collective wouldn't listen to folk music. We were professional musicians, unconcerned with that low-grade stuff." [15]

Ironically, the Collective admired Russian composers such as Borodin, Rimsky-Korsakov, and Moussorgsky who had been influenced by Russian and European folk material. As David Dunaway points out in his history of the Composers Collective, "this music had an unexpected effect on the transmission of native American folk music. Instead of learning from these composers and delving into their own folk melodies, they tried to write Russian folk tunes into American protest song."[16]

But thanks to John Hammond and others like him, the imaginative possibilities of an American folk culture had been widely recognized by the end of the 1930s, and, with the blessings of the Communist Party, artists on the political left now mined the rich lode. The flirtation with Russian folk culture was basically over. Seeger reversed his earlier prejudice against his country's folk music:

> Gather together a dozen average people from various parts of the country, people who are not too ingrained with the prejudices of music-professionalism, great wealth or smartness, add a guitar or banjo (no piano), and see how many songs you can get out of them —"folk-songs" if you're a sophisticate, "old songs" or mere "songs," if you are nice and common. Will there not be "Down in the Valley," and "Careless Love"? And how about "Frankie and Johnnie," "Wreck of the Old Ninety-Seven," "Red River Valley," "John Henry," "Shortnin' Bread," "Cripple Creek," "Maple on the Hill," "Buffalo Gals," "Barbara Allen"? Perhaps there will be "Jesse James," "Sam Bass," "Old Joe Clark," or even "The Golden Vanity," "Pretty Saro," "Lord Love". . . . The professional composer must get away from cities, suburbs, summer colonies, large estates and the sweet solitude of little retreats where urban atmosphere, ignorance and prejudice cling ever so easily.[17]

Cultural historian Warren I. Susman points out that the symbol of "the people," the common folk—that amorphous, all-enveloping entity—was the most pervasive image of this era.[18] Still reeling from the depression, American artists, revolutionary and bourgeois, joined in the search for a new set of American symbols and myths based on the "people."

The Federal Music Project collected American folk music, while the Federal Writers Project gathered reminiscences of former slaves and life histories of regular folk. American folk dance forms, including square dance, ballroom dance, jazz dance, tap, and clog began to insinuate themselves into concert dance programs. *Dance Observer,* always afraid that the modern dance would be left out, argued that American modern dance, the only dance form "created in America, by Americans, for Americans," was really the creative folk dance of Americans,[19] but that publication's pages, too, began to reflect the new interest in popular dance culture.

The romance with Americana and American folk culture yielded Martha Graham's *American Document* (1938), Agnes de Mille's *American Suite* (1939), featuring dances set to folk tunes and cowboy songs, and Doris Humphrey's *Square Dances* (1939), which incorporated social and ballroom styles.[20] A concert by Blanche Evan called "From Reels to Shag" was based on "social dances of the American people,"[21] and the October 1939 cover of *Dance Observer* featured a cowboy dance by a group from the Cheyenne Mountain School in Colorado Springs. For balletomanes, Lincoln Kirstein established Ballet Caravan to create American-style ballets. In its brief life (1936–1941) Ballet Caravan produced Eugene Loring's *Billy the Kid* and *Yankee Clipper* as well as Lew Christensen's *Pocahontas* and *Filling Station*. Radical dancer Sophie Maslow made *American Folk Suite* (1938), a group work in two sections, "I Had an Ol' Paint" (after a Western country song), and "Running Set" (after a Southern square dance).[22]

Like those of many other revolutionary artists, Maslow's early choreographic efforts were often sparked by Russian folk themes. Of Russian descent, she was born in Brooklyn and was steeped in Russian and Jewish folk culture from an early age. She learned about radical politics at home; her father had been a revolutionary in Russia and a political prisoner before he came to the United States, where he met and married her mother, also from Russia. Maslow describes her childhood as working class; her father was a dental technician, her mother had been a seamstress. But her parents were actually relatively sophisticated, members of a circle of Russian Jewish intelligentsia interested in art, theater, and literature, and passionate about exposing their children to the arts. Maslow's mother had friends who were actresses in the Jewish theater and was an admirer of Isadora Duncan. She took young Sophie to see Duncan dance.[23]

Drawing on a deep love for the "people" and upon her sense of Russian identity, Maslow composed *Themes from a Slavic People* in 1934 to the music of Béla Bartók, eliciting praise from one reviewer for the manner in which she "gracefully captured the spirit of the folk dance."[24] In 1935 she made *Two Songs About Lenin,* a dance inspired by the Soviet film by Dziga Vertov, *Three Songs of Lenin* (1934).

Reviewing the film in *New Theatre,* a writer described how folk songs structured the film: "From the mass of folklore born out of the revolution, Vertov chose three Eastern songs. These songs show us Lenin as he was seen by the formerly oppressed races of Middle Asia. For them Lenin meant freedom. His death a dreadful blow. His teachings the basis of their future life. These subjects make up the structural form for the film."[25]

Maslow composed a solo for herself, in two sections, based on the verse lines: "In January he died, and in April he was born." Alex North of the Composers Collective had brought back some Soviet songs from a trip to the Soviet Orient, and in the first performance Simon Rady, husband of the dancer Lily Mehlman, sang the songs while North beat an accompanying drum.[26] Despite the literalness of the title, Maslow remembers that the dance was basically a lyrical composition.[27] After all, she had been Louis Horst's student at the Neighborhood Playhouse.

As the decade drew to a close, Maslow began to turn from Russian folk themes, in their place discovering American folksinger Woody Guthrie. In two signature works, *Dust Bowl Ballads* and *Folksay*, Maslow created a kind of revisionist account of American history in which she placed herself on the plains of the Southwest.

It was an audacious move for Maslow—modern, urban, Jewish, and radical—to adopt the identity of an Oklahoma migrant farmer in *Dust Bowl Ballads*. Dancing to the words of Carl Sandburg, the "poet of the Prairies," in *Folksay* was equally bold. Seen as a response to the 1930s' yearning for community and for new American myths that would include not only the descendants of the Mayflower but all the tired, hungry, and poor who had arrived since then, Maslow's dances were powerful precisely because she was such an improbable representative of rural America.

"When I heard [Guthrie's] songs," Maslow said, "it was that special way of looking at a tragic situation in a humorous way that made it livable. . . . That seemed to me peculiarly American."[28] By "tragic situation," Maslow referred to the dust storms that swept through the Southwestern Plains during the 1930s. The storms had rolled in, darkening streets at midday, and distributing drifts of sand so high that they blocked doorways.[29] Thousands of farmers, soon widely known as "Okies," migrated to what they hoped would be a promised land in California.[30]

Maslow learned about the conditions of the migrant workers in California, probably from reading a government report called "Their Blood Is Strong" by John Steinbeck.[31] Published originally in the *San Francisco News* in 1936, it was reprinted two years later by the Simon J. Lubin Society in an attempt to create support for the problems of these agri-

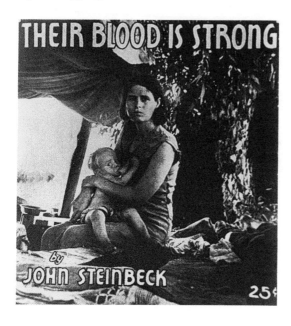

47. Cover of *Their Blood Is Strong,* a government report written by John Steinbeck on the conditions of migrant workers in California. Published by the Simon J. Lubin Society, 1938. (Photograph by Dorothea Lange.)

cultural workers. On the cover is the since well-known photograph by Dorothea Lange of a young migrant woman holding a small child who nurses at her breast (figure 47).

In 1939 Steinbeck's report became the partial basis for *The Grapes of Wrath,* his fictionalized account of a single Okie family driven off their land and trekking to the West. The impact of Steinbeck's novel was immense. It won the Pulitzer Prize, and only *Gone With the Wind* sold more copies that year. One year later, John Ford's motion picture was released.[32]

Woody Guthrie saw the film. In "Woody Sez," a column he wrote for the *Daily Worker* and one that Maslow followed, he called it:

> the best cussed picture I ever seen. *The Grapes of Wrath* you know is about us pullin out of Oklahoma and Arkansas, and down South, and a driftin' around over the state of California, busted, disgusted, down and out and a lookin for work.
>
> Shows you how come us to be that way. Shows the damn bankers, men that broke us and the dust that choked us, and comes right out in plain English, and says what to do about it.
>
> It says you got to get together and have some meetins, and stick together and raise old billy hell till you get your job, and get your farm back, and your house and your chickens, and your groceries and your clothes, and your money back.

Go to see *Grapes of Wrath*, pardner, go to see it and don't miss it. You was the star in that picture. Go and see your own self, and hear your own words and your own song.[33]

Guthrie knew who the villain was, and he did not hesitate to sing it out loud and clear. "The rich man took my home," he twanged, "and drove me from my door." His style was simple and folksy, inviting easy camaraderie, and when he sang, people listened, especially those on the left. Woody was the genuine article. He knew about driftin' and a lookin' for work and the damn bankers because he was an Okie himself, and he had suffered just as the Dust Bowl refugees he sang about had suffered.[34]

But while his songs documented the twin horrors of natural disaster and human greed, he was celebrating the spirit of the American farmer all the time, and Maslow liked that. She admired his attitude toward these catastrophic events and his refusal to portray the people he sang about as downtrodden. They were tough, they were Americans, and a little bit of hard luck was not enough to keep them down.

A photograph of *Dust Bowl Ballads* shows Maslow gazing across an imaginary Oklahoma plain (figure 48). Her blouse is open at the throat, a cowboy hat is plunked on her head; she waits, and she watches. For what? For a cloud of dust to roll from off the horizon and suffocate her newly planted crops? For the return of the enormous bulldozer that leveled the neighbor's tenant shack yesterday? For the passage of a stream of Okies making their way toward California, their cache of belongings piled atop a sagging wagon? Whatever it is, she is not moving. She leans forward and juts her chin out, as if daring anyone to challenge her. This is her space; she may be tossed about by the whims of nature, beleaguered by big business, but she is determined, and she has a few tricks up her sleeve.

Maslow is an unlikely cowgirl, with her Jewish background, her urban roots, and her socialist values, but in attitude, as well as in stance and pose, the figure she cuts bears similarity to the photographic portraits recorded by Walker Evans for the Farm Security Administration and popularized in his collaboration with James Agee, *Let Us Now Praise Famous Men*. In one photograph a farmer in a battered hat stares outward, arms akimbo and feet spread wide. Positioned in front of his field, he seems to be defending his territory in much the way Maslow laid claim to her space (figure 49). Another photograph, by Dorothea Lange, "Farmer Who Left Nebraska," could be the mirror image of Maslow's pose. The farmer is planted in front of the camera, hand on hip, one knee drawn

48. Gazing across an imaginary plain. Sophie Maslow in *Dust Bowl Ballads*. (Photograph by Marcus Blechman. Courtesy of the Dance Collection, New York Public Library for the Performing Arts, Astor, Lenox and Tilden Foundations.)

up, staring out impassively. Lange called her published work *An American Exodus* (figure 50).

Maslow's *Dust Bowl Ballads* premiered May 11, 1941, on a program entitled "America Dances," which included Jane Dudley's *Harmonica Breakdown*. Presented by the New Dance Group at the Heckscher Theatre, the program was billed as an arrangement of "authentic Folk, Social, and Jazz dances and their influence on the Modern Concert Dance." Featured were performances by the American Square Dance Group and the Lindy

49. Sharecropper. (Photograph by Walker Evans.
© Walker Evans Archive, The Metropolitan Museum of Art.)

Hoppers, as well as what reviewer Lois Balcolm referred to as dances by the "professional" side of the program.

> Sophie Maslow's *Dust Bowl Ballads*, done to two plaintive songs, "I Aint Got No Home in This World Anymore," and "Dusty Ol' Dust," were in a genre which Miss Maslow has often employed before but these dances seem to far surpass her earlier ones. Simple and crystal clear in pattern, never too sophisticated in movement or "technique," for the style of the music to which they were set, they were infused by deep feeling, tenderness and humor by turns.[35]

50. "Farmer Who Left Nebraska," Calpatria, California, February 1939. From *An American Exodus*. (Photograph by Dorothea Lange. Reproduced from the Collections of the Library of Congress, USF34-21058-c.)

The genre that Balcolm referred to derived from the fusion of elements of American folk culture—in this case, clogging and tap steps—with the percussive angularity of the Graham movement vocabulary in which Maslow was trained. The songs were Guthrie's.

Guthrie had recorded some of his tunes and palaver in Library of Congress recordings collected by Alan Lomax.[36] Maslow heard the recordings and initially made up her dances to this music, previewing the *Dust Bowl Ballads* as part of a 1941 revue by the Almanac Players, which included a troupe of left-wing dancers and theater people. Soon after that performance, Guthrie came to New York. Maslow, after talking with him at the loft where he was staying with other Almanac members, suggested they might perform together. Probably Guthrie was as taken with Maslow, with her forthright energy, her irrepressible spirit, and her absolute command of the medium of movement as she had been with his recordings. At any rate, they agreed to work together. The path was not to be smooth.

An account by Guthrie in *Dance Observer* describes his reaction to a rehearsal with Maslow: "After she got done with her dances she tried to teach me how to sing these same two songs like they was on the phonograph record. You'd be surprised how hard it was to sing a song the same way twice. Especially when you can't read music notes. I never could. I always just run my bluff, and sung them how I felt them."[37]

51. She thrust her hand into her pocket and it came out empty, but she was not defeated. Sophie Maslow in *Dust Bowl Ballads*. (Photograph by Gerda Peterich. Courtesy of the Dance Collection, New York Public Library for the Performing Arts, Astor, Lenox and Tilden Foundations.)

Maslow saw it differently. How could a dancer possibly deliver a precise choreographic thrust if the singer was taking a couple of deep breaths whenever he felt like it? Guthrie was used to clearing his throat when he wanted to, to strumming away for as long as it took him to remember whatever verse he was singing at the moment, but Maslow needed to know where the count of "1" was. After much frustration she thanked Woody and said goodbye. They never did perform *Dust Bowl Ballads* together.[38]

Still, Maslow liked the way he sang—plain. "He didn't do anything curly or interpret it his own way. His whole point was to tell a story, which he did. Very straightforward."[39] So, finally, she performed her dance to the recordings.

Over the phonograph Woody's voice rasped, "this dusty ol' dust is a gettin my home, and I've got to be drifting along," and on stage Maslow rolled on the floor, a clump of tumbleweed buffeted about by the winds. She got up and grabbed her hat, slapped it against her foot, her knee, her hip, and shook off the accumulated dust. She thrust her hand into her pocket, and it came out empty (figure 51). But she was not defeated. She still was out there fighting. Maslow danced plain, just the way Woody sang. The movements were literal, easy for anyone to understand.[40]

With *Dust Bowl Ballads,* Maslow created a new mythic American— poor, battered, always on the move, yet tough and plucky. The images of struggle alternate with bursts of energy signaling the indomitable spirit of America; the characters are never really defeated. Yet the dance is not without its sadness. It is the story of domestic refugees, disenfranchised from their land, banished from their homes, and through this theme echoes the experience of the forced migrations of Russian and European Jews. In this sense it is Maslow's story. At the same time, however, dancing the part of an Okie farmer linked Maslow to a larger American experience. When she danced, she could be not only a New York Jewish woman of immigrant parentage, but a country farmer, a third- or fourth-generation American, even Sweet Betsy from Pike. Making a place for herself within the country's heartland, Sophie Maslow effectively reconstructed historical America. Warren Susman has argued that the fascination with folk culture evidenced in all the arts at this time transcended individual historical experience and helped create a collective identification with American traditions; a sense of participation and belonging was crucial to the era.

On the political front the Communist Party also made efforts to create a space for itself within the American imagination: "[It] linked its movement to historic American tradition: it rewrote our history to find a place for itself so that the socialist movement would no longer be alienated from American life."[41] Appropriating the folklore of rural culture, artists on the left demonstrated their kinship with the historic Americans who also had been left out of the American dream. Performing the experience of Okie farmers, or untutored country musicians, dancers located an urban—and essentially foreign and socialist—vision within the larger American experience at the same time that they awakened their audience to a powerfully real present situation.

In 1942 Maslow worked with Guthrie again. This time she devised a way to bring him onto the stage. In *Folksay*, dancers break "into jig time and tap dancing nohow classical,"[42] while two guitarists (originally Guthrie and folksinger Earl Robinson, a former member of the Composers Collective) strum away, occasionally putting down their instruments to exchange pleasantries and jokes, like a couple of farmers hanging out at a country store. The dance was performed for the first time at the Humphrey-Weidman Studio Theatre in New York and genially introduced its audience to another time and place where "the goodnatured quality of a Saturday evening get-together" still prevailed.[43] Once again the urban sophistication of modern dance was infused with simple down-home folksiness. Robert Sabin, reviewing the concert in *Dance Observer*, noted: "Miss Maslow has kept the tart and humorous flavor of the songs, using modern dance technique, in a popular style, to splendid effect."[44]

The text for the dance, which runs throughout its ten sections, is a combination of Carl Sandburg's words from his long, rambling poem, *The People, Yes* (1936), and a book called *Folksay*, a collection of sayings handed down from generation to generation and scattered through Sandburg's verse.[45] Sandburg, like Guthrie, might be considered an authentic voice. Born in the Midwest, he had been a hobo, a journalist, and a socialist. *The People, Yes* was his paean to the common man.

Sandburg's poem touches on such traditional socialist issues as unemployment and hunger, but on a deeper level, like Whitman's *Leaves of Grass*, it celebrates the vitality and diversity of the American people, the country folk and the city folk rubbing elbows in verse. This fascination with people's small tragedies and triumphs, with their scrappiness and ordinariness, informs *Folksay*.

The dance is composed in the form of solos, duets, and small groups as well as sections for the entire company. Sometimes the musicians sing, while at other times dancers perform to the poet's words. In the introductory section, for example, the musicians recite,

> The people is Everyman, everybody.
> Everybody is you and me and all others.
> What everybody says is what we all say.
> And what is it we all say?[46]

As they speak, dancers casually wander on stage, as if to affirm that, yes, they are the people, the ordinary people who make up America.

This section is followed by "Dodgers," a dance for all nine performers, which resembles a square dance with its simple motifs of walking and circling oneself. Here, the dancers call out to each other, giving the impression of a spontaneous gathering, while the musicians sing, "Yes we're all dodgin' dodgin' dodgin' dodgin'. We're all a dodgin' out a way through the world." Other sections act out the small vignettes and folksy sayings sprinkled through Sandburg's poem. "Come on Superstition and get my goat," or "Blue eyes say love me or I'll die. Black eyes say love me or I'll kill you," or "Aw nuts! Aw go peddle your papers," a dance in which two men vie for territorial rights in a game of one-upmanship.[47]

In two spoken interludes the musicians banter back and forth, a technique Maslow may have borrowed from Guthrie, whose performance repertory often included anecdotes and humorous phrases.[48] "You live here all your life?" asks one. "Not yet," answers the other. Later, "Do you know what Paul Revere said to his horse after he made his famous ride?" "What?" "Whoa."[49] We seem to be eavesdropping on a conversation between characters who have known each other all their lives; they have sat here and exchanged greetings before, and very likely they will be back again tomorrow night with a new set of one-liners. The scene is familiar, the pace is unhurried, nobody is going anywhere. When they break into tunes like "On Top of Old Smoky" and "Sweet Betsy from Pike," every member of the audience could join in (figure 52).

In the New York Times, John Martin summed up the appeal of Maslow's creative use of American popular culture. "Unless you are pretty insensitive to the people that are America it [Folksay] is guaranteed to leave you with a lump in your throat."[50] Ironically, it was not Maslow's America, and it probably was not the America of her urban audience. The dance took place in an idealized, homogenized space, where troubles were simple and everybody shared the same values. The clamor of the urban metropolis, the dirty subways, the immigrant life, the working-class traditions were absent from these streets. But Folksay satisfied a certain longing for closeness, a desire for identity that permeated the later years of the decade. One of the least likely representatives of rural American culture had succeeded in staking a claim.

Although it is easy to categorize Maslow's works as variations of New Deal nationalism, it is harder to credit the political implications of performing folk material on the proscenium stage. Yet folklore is intrinsically radical because it exists on the margins of society, apart from an

52. Sophie Maslow and Bill Bales in "Sweet Betsy from Pike" from *Folksay*. (Photograph by David Linton. Courtesy of the Dance Collection, New York Public Library for the Performing Arts, Astor, Lenox and Tilden Foundations.)

economy of consumption.[51] Folk songs are usually anonymous—that is, they belong to no one, and since they are authorless, no one earns royalties.[52] Guthrie considered the folk song by definition a revolutionary force. Parallel to statements issued by workers' theater and dance groups, he had the words, "This machine kills fascists," emblazoned on his guitar.[53]

As soon as the folksinger came on stage, however, he shed his anonymity. The voice belonged to Guthrie, just as the wailing sounds belonged to Sonny Terry. When Guthrie played the guitar, or when Terry mouthed the harmonica, the music was their own. Guthrie at that time had a substantial following. He had had a radio show in California, his column had appeared in the *Daily Worker*, his songs had been recorded, he was beloved by the radical left. Terry had his following as well. He had wowed a Carnegie Hall audience. Whatever the genesis of their talent, these artists were certainly not anonymous.

Neither could the folk dance that Maslow presented on stage be called authorless. She included American folk dance styles in her compositions, liberally sprinkling clogs, grapevines, and hoedowns throughout the choreography, but all the while she was busy arranging and rearranging the steps in a manner to suit Louis Horst. John Martin correctly observed that Maslow did not incorporate actual folk dances in her compositions.[54] The people's culture, if its measure was anonymity, was doomed the minute it stepped on stage.

What the romance with folk culture did was to elevate the arts of rural and mostly poor folk, and this was consistent with the goals of the revolutionary dance movement. The appeal of the folk movement to leftists at that time partly grew from the way in which folk art seemed to empower the ordinary man,[55] and the extent to which Maslow blurred distinctions between her staged choreography and Guthrie's authentic rural voice is what had political implications. Guthrie may not have been an anonymous voice—and he probably was more calculated in his artistry than he was willing to admit—but he was a bona fide voice of the people, as was Terry. Their presences on stage as living incarnations of another culture were as important as the music they performed. Played by someone else, the message would not have been the same. By deflecting attention from her role as a conscious and technically skilled artist, letting Guthrie's style as an untutored, unrehearsed, "natural" musician shape the work, Maslow could bring the "people" on stage. A homey feeling was created through the homilies and vernacular speech exchanged by dancers and musicians. Seemingly spontaneous interchanges, both spoken and moved, between one dancer and another, between musician and dancer, and between musicians contributed to the unrehearsed atmosphere.

Guthrie's voice helped make *Folksay* an authentic expression of the "people," but Maslow's choreography gave that expression status in the world of culture and art. In fact, Maslow and Guthrie were mutually beholden. As Guthrie put it, they might belong to the same union. In "People Dancing" in *Dance Observer*, he wrote:

> Garment workers sew for a living and dance for a rest, and dancers sew so that they can look right; they could almost belong to the same Union—The Before and After Sewers Garment Workers Local. At least there's plenty in a big factory trotting full blast to dance

about. Make your audience see the factory full of people, and make the factory know the audience, and you got the world by the tail on a downhill pull.[56]

Because the staged people's culture blended differences between audience and performer, the performance itself carried the message of egalitarianism.[57] Maslow's deceptively simple choreography appealed to members of the audience, in part, because they could imagine themselves performing the infectious moves. It was a way for audience members to be participants as well as spectators, joined in the kind of communal movement experience that Delza had imagined. At the same time, the hoedowns and grapevines became "art" when performed on a proscenium stage and framed within a section of choreography, making the performance simultaneously an expression of the "people" and a professional artistic effort.[58]

In 1936 Dane Rudhyar questioned whether educated artists could dance out a proletarian message, but now, six years later, no one questioned whether Maslow could cast herself as the inhabitant of a sleepy town and cast her dancers as the "people." Susman points out the irony of middle-class Americans adopting as part of their own culture songs and expressions that were basically alien to them, and he notes the sentimentality of the vision of all Americans united under the umbrella of the "people." For an urban working class it must have been even stranger, and ultimately such visions would divert sympathies and energy from radical causes:

> The search for some transcendent identification with a mythic America led Americans in a few short years from the deep concern for the Okies of the Dust Bowl as a profound social and human problem to the joyous "Oh! What a Beautiful Morning" with the "corn as high as an elephant's eye" of Rodgers and Hammerstein's *Oklahoma!* (1943), a hugely successful, if sentimental, effort to recapture the innocent vitality of the historic American folk.[59]

Ten years after the formation of the Workers Dance League, the abrasive voice and body of the striking worker was replaced by country banter. The real presence of the worker on stage was replaced by an artistic representation of the "people." The "Internationale" was replaced by folk tunes strummed on the guitar or banged out on homemade instruments. Earl Robinson wrote "Ballad for Americans" for the WPA revue *Sing for Your Supper,* and it became the theme song for the 1940 Republican convention.

The revolutionary dance movement began with fierce involvement in working-class issues, and now, with the exception of the New Dance Group, all the working-class dance groups were gone. In 1942 Horst's *Dance Observer,* a leading critic of the Workers Dance League, sponsored a concert by League dancers Sophie Maslow, Jane Dudley, and William Bales, who was now working with them. In what was probably the considered opinion of the dance press, John Martin wrote, "the children have grown up." [60]

S E V E N

Dance and Politics

By the 1950s "new" dance was firmly cast as American, and the revolutionary call of the 1930s was framed as an artistic rebellion "by individuals against schools of dance and dance conventions"[1] rather than against schools of political thought. The vision of working-class art, of movement forms inextricably joined to social and political reality, was considered at best an embarrassment and at worst a form of treason. Why?

The answer is certainly not simple, although it would be hard to approach a response without considering American Communists' relationship to both the Soviet Union and their own government. For some, communism became the God that failed; first, the Russo-German nonagression pact of 1939, later the revelation of Stalin's atrocities, the millions murdered in purges, necessarily tarnished Lenin's vision of a socialist future and the promise of Soviet ideology. Many American Communists no longer could or would give their allegiance to the cause, although many of them, probably most, continued to value the ideals of social justice that had attracted them to the Soviet experiment. That is one part of the story. The other has to do with how the United States treated those individuals who openly embraced socialist goals during the 1930s. At the time of the Nazi-Soviet pact the New York State legislature began an inquiry into alleged Communist Party affiliations within New York City's school system. The Rapp-Coudert Committee, as it was called, created front-page news with its investigations of radicalism within the city schools, prefiguring events of the postwar period. Ultimately, the committee was responsible for the dismissal of more than a dozen faculty and staff members at CCNY. In 1950 Senator Joseph McCarthy first accused alleged Communists within the U.S. State Department of controlling American foreign policy, and over the next four years McCarthy, his subcommittee, and his allies effectively succeeded in terrorizing the American left.[2] To what extent did cold war ideology influence new academic systems of patronage and federal support of dancers and dance companies when government sponsorship of the arts blossomed forth once again?

In these pages I trace some of the events of the 1940s and 1950s in hopes of better understanding the virtual exclusion of left-wing dancers from the increasingly prestigious and stable venues for modern dance that gradually replaced working-class and union patronage and the construction of an American dance history that largely ignored their contributions.[3] This history is tied to the emergence of the United States as a world power and to notions of what the American "people" represented as an imagined cultural entity. In 1938 Martha Graham's *American Document* had posed the question, "What is an American?" During the cold war it became increasingly complicated to construct an identity as an artist and as an American, particularly for the outspoken rebels of the 1930s. Neither straightforward nor simple, the disappearance of the vociferous left from the modern dance scene is the result of a complex interweaving of social and political history with developments, both artistic and personal, in the lives of dance practitioners. While former revolutionaries continued, however elliptically, to explore themes related to the idea of the "people," the modern dance establishment of the 1950s, with Graham and Doris Humphrey at the helm, embraced a more universal concept of art that effectively divorced their work from contemporary realities.

Dancers continued to operate in the political arena with relative openness until the onset of the cold war. Throughout the 1930s, for example, a collective spirit remained more or less intact and was particularly apparent in lobbying by periodicals such as *Dance Observer* for continued subsidies for the arts. Shortly after the demise of the independent dance project under the WPA, dancers were urged to support federal arts bill H.R. 8239, which would create permanent government sponsorship for the arts. Among dance supporters were Graham, Humphrey, Charles Weidman, and Helen Tamiris.[4] By June 1938 Marjorie Church could write that approximately thirty different federal arts committees existed in metropolitan centers throughout the country, working in cooperation with other cultural and union organizations for passage of the bill.[5]

While dancers lobbied for a federal arts bill, forces in the government, fueled by congressional investigations of "subversive activities," conspired to mount an attack on current federal sponsorship of the arts. Beginning with the Fish Committee (1930–1932), and the McCormack–Dickstein Committee (1934–1935), the House Committee on Un-American Activities (commonly referred to as HUAC) rose to prominence under the leadership of Texas congressman Martin Dies in 1938. The Federal Theatre Project proved especially vulnerable to the committee's assaults. Charging incompetence on the part of project workers and the general irrelevance of the arts to the nation's health, HUAC gathered evidence that would help dismantle the FTP. In 1939 the conservative *Washington Post* editorialized on the hearings:

> Testimony provides critics of the so-called white collar projects with deadly ammunition for continuing their attacks. For it strongly indicates that efforts to combine relief for the unemployed with public patronage of the arts results not merely in waste of funds but also in degradation of the standards by which artistic competence would ordinarily be measured. . . . With millions of idle able-bodied workers in need of aid it ought to be evident that this nation cannot afford to finance costly theatrical rehearsals at the taxpayers' expense.[6]

Variety, the entertainment industry chronicle, had reported on charges leveled against employment practices in the FTP, during the late 1930s. Unskilled workers who were members of the Communist-dominated Workers Alliance allegedly were given preference over professionals who refused to sign up with that group. One committee investigator insinuated that the CP was receiving financial support from Hollywood, although this innuendo was hotly denied by W. S. Van Dyke, president of the Academy of Motion Picture Arts and Sciences and vice president of the Screen Directors Guild.

Calling the theater project a "cesspool of un-Americanism," *Variety's* reporter described an incident that had taken place during rehearsals of *Sing for Your Supper.*

> [Charles] Walton[7] told of attending party, largely attended by Theatre project and Workers' Alliance members, at which white girls danced with colored men. Sally Saunders, Vienna-born member of the cast of "Sing for Your Supper," in New York, testified a Negro youth tried to date her at a rehearsal, and that others in production, including producer Harold Hecht, deprecated the incident. She applied for and got a transfer.[8]

Probably this incident of racial mixing was taken by the Dies Committee as proof of Communist Party involvement; the Party did, after all, have a long history of support for the rights of American blacks and for social interaction among blacks and whites.

The truth was that many of these "costly theatrical rehearsals" dealt with sensitive social and political issues that almost certainly would have been considered subversive by the committee. Arnold Sundgaard's *Spirochete* (1938), for example, was created in response to the deadly threat of venereal disease and the U.S. surgeon general's "war on syphilis," while Arthur Arent's Living Newspaper, *One Third of a Nation* (1938), exposed the evils of tenement life. Marc Blitzstein's controversial folk opera *The Cradle Will Rock* was an account of a steel strike with a pro-union bias. Blitzstein's opera, incidentally, proved so controversial that Hallie Flanagan canceled the scheduled premiere in June 1937, forcing the production to open outside WPA auspices.

The FTP seemed to seek out controversial subject matter, and the Dies Committee was convinced that the project was dominated by Communists who were using federal funds to advance their propaganda:

> The revelations of Communist activities in the writers' projects throws light on another fundamental evil of the arts projects. This is the virtual impossibility of subjecting them to adequate supervision. Members of the Communist Party, quick to take advantage of this lack of effective oversight, have evidently managed to secure strategic positions which are much more useful in spreading propaganda than in relieving unemployment.[9]

Despite the best efforts of Flanagan to convince the committee otherwise, funds for the project were withdrawn in June 1939.

Outright suspicion and open criticism of the Communist Party declined as the United States geared up for World War II, making the United States and the Soviet Union temporary allies. Renewed prosperity, full employment, and a decline in tensions between labor and management accompanied war efforts. A General Motors industrial film featured singing and dancing workers joyously caroling, "This Is Your War," as they performed assembly-line tasks.[10]

Revolutionary dancers waved the flag. Maslow danced on a program with Woody Guthrie, the blues singer Leadbelly, and the Almanac Singers that was advertised as "New in form, new in material, with a large cast of singers and dancers—and a WIN–THE–WAR spirit and theme."[11] Lily Mann, formerly of the WPA, was featured in "Kickin' the Panzer," part of an International Workers Order revue, *Red White and Blues*.[12] The New Dance Group sponsored a panel discussion, which included Valerie Bettis, Eugene Loring, Pearl Primus, Anna Sokolow, and Sophie Maslow, on the place of the dancer in the war effort.[13]

In *It's Up to You,* Helen Tamiris made an appearance as Black Market Lucy the Porterhouse Steak. Staged as a prologue to the feature film in movie theaters, the skit was produced in cooperation with the U.S. Department of Agriculture and was designed to popularize wartime meat rationing. The revue, directed by Elia Kazan, with book by Arthur Arent, music by Earl Robinson, and lyrics by Lewis Allan, Alfred Hayes, and Hi Zaret, provided Tamiris with an opportunity to display the sensuous side of modern dance once again:

> Temptation looks around to see if Uncle Sam's eagle is watching, then whispers, "Porterhouse? Ain't you illegal?"
> "Illegal, Ilshmegal," says Porterhouse Lucy.
> "The point is I'm rare and I'm thick and I'm juicy!" [14]

Perhaps it was simpler in the midst of the war effort to feel certain about what an American was—and therefore what American dance was—and to feel a sense of community with other Americans. Martha Graham's *Appalachian Spring,* premiering on the eve of the U.S. victory in Europe, looked hopefully to a prosperous future where men and women would be united again. [15] Graham's script also played nicely into expectations that, with the war almost over, women would return to the home. When American men went off to fight, women had taken their places in factories and offices across the country, a situation that now needed to be reversed.

Graham's dance, with its promise of open space and, by association, open opportunity, was an idealization of the American dream, but it was, in fact, derived from the experience of Americans like Graham. This contrasted sharply with the experiences of Japanese Americans who found themselves interned in camps during the war, of German Americans harassed in places like New York City's Yorkville, and of African Americans who performed military service, but in segregated units. Still, the Japanese American dancer Yuriko made her first appearance with the Martha Graham company as one of the followers in *Appalachian Spring.* It is tempting to speculate on how deliberately Graham may have acted in this case. She had, after all, been outspoken in her defense of Jewish members of her company when she was invited to Germany in 1936.

The temporary truce that existed between the United States and the Soviet Union, as well as between American leftists and conservatives, slowly unraveled after the war, and an atmosphere of suspicion and distrust toward all things Russian settled in once again. Many conservatives believed that Roosevelt had been duped by Stalin at the Yalta Conference of the "Big Three" powers and that American interests had been betrayed. During the late 1940s and early 1950s, loyalty checks and deportation campaigns were instituted, and federal indictments were brought against American Communists. Soviet activities were suspect. Could those who had supported the Soviet Union still be considered American? the question seemed to be.

When the Soviet Union exploded an atom bomb in 1949, many Americans were convinced that nuclear secrets had been leaked to the Soviets. Ultimately, Julius and Ethel Rosenberg were tried for conspiracy to commit espionage, found guilty in a court case that has been generally discredited, and executed in 1953, the first Americans to be put to death for spying during peacetime. Demonstrations in major cities around the world urged clemency, but President Dwight D. Eisenhower denied the plea, claiming that by their actions the Rosenbergs had increased the chance of atomic warfare and "may have condemned to death tens of millions of innocent people all over the world."[16] Dancer Edith Segal wrote a book of poems, *Give Us Your Hand: Poems and Songs for Ethel and Julius Rosenberg in the Death House at Sing Sing,* but no mention of the cause célèbre appeared in *Dance Observer.* It seems inconceivable that the dance periodicals of the 1930s would have been silent on such an event, but by the 1950s Americans were reluctant to speak out on controversial issues that could leave them open to accusations of disloyalty or even treason. Where was there room for a dance like Edith Segal's *Scrubwomen,* which critiqued the class system in the United States, or Sophie Maslow's *Two Songs About Lenin,* which celebrated a foreign vision, or the New Dance Group's *Charity,* which pointed an accusing finger at the practices of some religious institutions? Grassroots Bible and prayer movements were sweeping the country, and evangelist Billy Graham declared that God was against communism. "Religion was virtually synonymous with American nationalism in the 1950s," according to one respected historian.[17]

By the early 1950s the cold war in the United States was in full force, and McCarthyism was a household word. The Hollywood Ten— seven screenwriters, two directors, and one producer—refused to declare their political affiliations before HUAC. Blacklisted by the motion picture industry, all of them served federal prison terms of a year or less. They were among only the earliest of literally thousands of actors, writers, directors, technicians, and other skilled professionals in entertainment and the arts who were barred by blacklisting from pursuing their livelihoods and careers. NBC and CBS required loyalty oaths of new employees, who were forced to answer, in effect, the infamous question, "Are you now or have you ever been a member of the Communist Party?" A group called American Business Consultants established a publication,

Red Channels, for the purpose of identifying entertainers and artists as subversives. Television variety show host Ed Sullivan apologized to a sponsor after the celebrated tap dancer Paul Draper appeared on his program; Draper had been accused of procommunist sympathies.[18]

In retrospect, it is surprising that activists in the leftist dance movement survived the 1950s at all. Anyone who had been associated with the leftist movement in the 1930s was suspect, and revolutionary dancers had a long history of questioning government policy. Repercussions occurred. Government investigators came to Anna Sokolow's door;[19] Edna Ocko was called to testify before HUAC;[20] in 1955 the workers' camps that had been so hospitable to revolutionary theater and dance artists were investigated by a New York legislative committee, and Edith Segal was subpoenaed:

> When they asked me whether I taught dances with content, I said absolutely, and I gave as an example the dance that I had made to the lovely Yiddish song, "Hob Ich Mir a Mantle," which means "I have an old coat." I told this committee that I had explained to the children that this was a story of an old man who was very poor, and he had an old coat from which he had to make a jacket, and then a vest, and then a pocket, and so forth, and then there was nothing left so out of his troubles he made a song. As I went through this explanation, they tried to stop me. They said, "That's not what we mean." I said, "But this is what I teach the children to show them that this man could rise to such heights that he made a song out of his troubles."[21]

Of all the revolutionary groups that had flourished at the beginning of the 1930s, only the New Dance Group had a continuous history through the 1940s and 1950s, functioning as a school for educational and recreational students as well as for professionals and as a producing agent for choreographers committed to dancemaking with a social and political conscience. In 1942 Sophie Maslow, Jane Dudley, and William Bales formed a trio, giving their first performance at the Studio Theatre loft belonging to Charles Weidman and Doris Humphrey on West 16th Street. During the next decade the trio appeared under the auspices of the New Dance Group in concerts at the 92nd Street YMHA, at summer festivals in Connecticut, and in Broadway theaters, attracting diverse audiences with a style that retained links to the "people."

The New Dance Group's school from its beginnings in the 1930s was beset by financial problems, its ongoing struggle to meet the rent leading to frequent moves. The school rarely advertised in *Dance Observer,* perhaps because of its many relocations. A notice about summer classes in the June–July 1938 issue placed the school in a studio that occupied the parlor floor of a tenement building at 26 West 18th Street. Judith Delman, who directed the studio from 1939 until 1966, recalled that Jane Dudley was then serving as director. The rent was $45.00 a month, which had to be paid in installments—presumably because money was never sufficient to make the entire payment at any one time.[22]

Classes were inexpensive, and the curriculum varied. According to Delman, students in 1938 could purchase four one-hour classes for $1.50 (one class a week for four weeks); two classes a week for the same period cost $2.50. Class offerings included ballet and modern (by exponents of the Holm, Humphrey, and Graham techniques), composition taught by Bessie Schoenberg, and folk dance. Philosophically, the New Dance Group continued to emphasize the idea that dance belonged to everybody. Pragmatically, its members never exclusively associated themselves with any one style. At one point, for example, an association with the American Square Dance Group proved helpful in attracting young men as potential students.

In August 1939 the New Dance Group's school moved to a loft at 17 West 24th Street. Finances were slightly better, and enough money was available to have a telephone installed and to purchase a typewriter. The dancers also constructed a stage. From this relatively stable base, the group continued its operations, occasionally producing evenings on the concert stage but more importantly taking dance to new audiences in trade union settings, presenting technique demonstrations in settlement houses in the Bronx, and attracting a varied student body. When the first scholarship auditions were held, the African American dancer Pearl Primus was chosen to receive one. Primus went on to dance in group productions and to teach at the school, promoting black-white solidarity through her dancing. Appearing on a benefit sponsored by the International Workers Order for camp Wo-Chi-Ca (short for Workers Childrens Camp) in 1944, Primus expressed her hopes for a future free of racism.

> As children we carry deep in our hearts the richest of human affections, free from bigotry and hate. We must help our children grow up with this affection strengthened. We owe it to them. And that is why we must be generous when it comes to helping organizations that help children. That is why I will dance for camp Wo-Chi-Ca and that is why you should come to see me dance.[23]

The New Dance Group occupied its large studio until 1944 when circumstances again forced it to move. Delman found a studio on West

48th Street and there was a flurry of renovations that surely were costly on their limited budget, but the building was sold shortly thereafter and once again Delman was in search of inexpensive space suitable for dance. The group finally settled into a studio on East 59th Street, which became its home for the next ten years. Pavlova supposedly had once studied in the building, which was full of dance studios, and it was clearly a step up for the group. There were good wooden floors, even dressing rooms, and two mirrors were purchased. But fees, as always, were kept low to make dance available to working-class students and a work scholarship program was instituted (scholarship students ran errands, did general office work, and assisted at studio programs in return for their classes). The general student body included artists, teachers, musicians, and factory workers, some of whom came year after year, even though they never progressed past the fundamentals, because they felt they had a place within the communal dance atmosphere. Many students considered their reception at the studio as an education in life as well as in dance.[24]

The distinctive atmosphere of the New Dance Group, which somehow blurred lines between life and art, which emphasized collective structures, and which created a sense of family within the studio's walls, challenged the independent "frontier" spirit increasingly associated with American dance. The New Dance Group has no place in the neat genealogical pattern of extended choreographic families in Don McDonagh's *The Complete Guide to Modern Dance*.[25] In this hereditary structure, dancers are all descended from one or another of the "Founders." Students at the New Dance Group School, however, might well have considered themselves descendents of Graham, Humphrey, and Holm in terms of the technical education they received. But the group's collective structure and the emphasis on dance as a social activity as well as an artistic pursuit was the students' true heritage.

During the 1950s the New Dance Group was probably best-known for Sophie Maslow's *The Village I Knew,* a dance suite based on the tales of Sholom Aleichem (figures 53 and 54). Aleichem's humor would have appealed to Maslow in much the same way that Woody Guthrie's had, celebrating the human ability to confront misfortune with an undefeated spirit.

The first section of *The Village I Knew* (initially titled *Festival*) was performed at Connecticut College in 1949 during the American Dance Festival's second season, and the nearly complete suite was presented the following year. Writing in *Dance Observer,* Nik Krevitsky cited *The Village I Knew* as the festival season's most popular presentation. Composed of seven vignettes, the dance explored experiences in a Jewish

53. Sophie Maslow's *The Village I Knew.* From left, Muriel Manings, Normand Maxon (in air), Nina Caiserman, Billie Kirpich. (Photographer unknown. Courtesy of the Dance Collection, New York Public Library for the Performing Arts, Astor, Lenox and Tilden Foundations.)

shetl: Sabbath; It's Good to Be an Orphan; A Point of Doctrine; Festival; The Fiddler; Why Is It Thus?; Exodus. While the opening segments were praised for their humor, for the "lighthearted reflection of the lives of simple happy people," Exodus depicted a pogrom, and the dark vision that it presented made some reviewers uneasy. Krevitsky wrote, "it [was] out of keeping with the spirit of the rest of the dance." [26]

What had happened to Jews during the war could not be expressed lightheartedly.

Jewish themes had been part of the workers' dance movement from the beginning, particularly in the work of Miriam Blecher, Anna Sokolow, and Lillian Shapero. Many revolutionary choreographers now made new attempts to explore their identities as Jews. Surely, the grim statistics that accompanied the end of World War II, the almost unbearable news of Hitler's program of genocide, made Jews in the United States acutely conscious of their heritage. Among active choreographers during the postwar years, some seemed specifically and exclusively tied to working with the traditions of Jewish life and within a folk genre, while others trans-

formed such events into narratives to be explored within the wider modern dance idiom. A concert by Katya Delakova and Fred Berk at the 92nd
Street YMHA in 1947, for example, was composed entirely from aspects of
the Jewish experience, from biblical stories to contemporary Palestinian
life.[27] At the Yiddish Art Theatre, Lillian Shapero, active since the 1930s,
performed in *Palestinian Suite* that same year,[28] and at Hunter College a
Jewish dance festival sponsored by the School of Jewish Studies featured
works by Delakova and Berk, Shapero, and the Jerusalem-born Hadassah,
who was now teaching ethnic dance at the New Dance Group studio.[29]

Maslow, Sokolow, and other Jewish dancers who had more or less
sided with the revolutionary dance movement also were concerned with
themes of Jewish life, but they worked more straightforwardly within a
modern dance idiom. Maslow's *The Village I Knew,* for example, is tech-

54. Jane Dudley, Sophie Maslow, and Ronne Aul in *The Village I Knew.* (Photograph by Walter Owen. Courtesy of the Dance Collection, New York Public
Library for the Performing Arts, Astor, Lenox and Tilden Foundations.)

55. Anna Sokolow in *Exile*. © Barbara Morgan.

nically grounded in Graham technique. The formal base of contraction
and release governs almost every interaction between performers within
the dance, although the representation also succeeds on the level of mimetic gesture. Sokolow's *The Exile* (1939), which she performed as part
of the Jewish dance festival at Hunter, depicted the Nazi regime as a beast
within the garden of Jewish life (figure 55). Set to Palestinian folk music
arranged by composer Alex North and accompanied by the words of Sol
Funaroff, *The Exile* was modern dance, not folk dance.[30]

Although Sokolow probably did not consider herself to be a religious
Jew, her Jewish heritage was clearly a source of pride and inspiration.
The Bride (1945), set to traditional folk music, portrayed a young Ortho-
dox woman on the eve of her wedding, while *Kaddish*, to music by Ravel,
took the Jewish ritual of mourning as its subject.[31] In 1951 Sokolow combined words, music, and movement into a dance drama based on *The
Dybbuk*, a play by S. Ansky. Supported by a cast composed mainly of
Actors Studio members, Sokolow danced the part of Leah, a young Jewish girl possessed by the spirit of her dead lover. While the presentation
did not prove entirely successful, Sokolow earned praise for her performance and for her discovery of new movement patterns.[32]

The emphasis on a "people's" tradition—based on rural American traditions in dances such as Dudley's *Harmonica Breakdown* and Maslow's
Dust Bowl Ballads, but also on religious and ethnic traditions—was central to the New Dance Group's identity and an antidote to the more
homogenized American experience that Martha Graham's choreography
presented in works such as *Appalachian Spring.* By the late 1940s a number of works created by African American choreographers also continued
a people's tradition. Sympathetic whites had assumed black identities on
the stage during the 1930s, demonstrating links between blacks, immigrants, and workers based on class identity, and the African Americans
Asadata Dafora Horton and Hemsley Winfield had explored African
themes, performing infrequently on such stages as the 92nd Street YMHA.
Black Americans now produced a new canon of social protest dances on
concert stages previously dominated by whites; many of these choreographers and performers, including Pearl Primus, Donald McKayle, Talley
Beatty, and Ronne Aul, found a home within the New Dance Group.

Talley Beatty's *Southern Landscape* (1947), to music by Elie Siegmeister,
depicted events in Southern black life during Reconstruction. Beatty had
trained and worked with Katherine Dunham in Chicago before embark-
ing on his career. *The Negro Speaks of Rivers* (1944), by Pearl Primus, was
set to a poem by Langston Hughes and fused African-based movement
elements with modern dance technique. Donald McKayle's *Games* (1951)
explored street life in the urban ghetto, using songs and games popular
in black culture; his 1959 *Rainbow 'Round My Shoulder,* set to traditional
black folk music, depicted a chain gang in the South.

The first legitimately interracial casts appeared in New Dance Group
productions, many choreographed by Sophie Maslow.[33] Primus performed in a 1946 production of *Folksay;*[34] McKayle in *Champion* (1948),
based on a Ring Lardner story about a boxer (figure 56); and Ronne Aul
in the premiere production of *The Village I Knew* (1949). McKayle also
appeared in *Village.*[35] Maslow had an absolute loyalty to her dancers—
black or white—and more than likely, her integrated casts cost her performing opportunities in the South.[36]

On two successive weekends in the winter of 1953, New Dance Group
Presentations produced a festival of works at the Ziegfeld Theatre on
West 54th Street, featuring dances by Charles Weidman, Sophie Maslow,
Jane Dudley, and the young choreographers active in the New Dance
Group, including Daniel Nagrin, Donald McKayle, Ronne Aul, and
Hadassah. While Anna Sokolow was scheduled to perform, she never
appeared.

The same spring a season of American modern dance, produced by

56. Mark Ryder, Donald McKayle, and Bill Bales in *Champion*. (Photographer unknown. Courtesy of the Dance Collection, New York Public Library for the Performing Arts, Astor, Lenox and Tilden Foundations.)

the Bethsabee de Rothschild Foundation, was being presented at the Alvin Theatre. De Rothschild was a patron of Graham's and had recently bought her a small house on East 63rd Street to be used for her school — quite a gift considering the price of New York City real estate. (Ironically, the New Dance Group was just about to enter the real estate market. In

1954, forced to move yet again, the group purchased a building on West 47th Street; ownership was placed in a corporation of the group's faculty members.) The season at the Alvin featured the work of Graham, Doris Humphrey, and José Limón, as well as works by younger choreographers who only recently had entered the dance scene. The way the choreographers lined up reflected a division between "high" art and a more populist approach. Curiously, Weidman was now appearing with the New Dance Group Presentations. (Humphrey-Weidman as a repertory company had ended in the mid-1940s, and he had always shown a predeliction for social commentary in his work.)

For the 1953 New Dance Group Festival Weidman contributed *Fables for Our Times* (1947); Maslow, *The Village I Knew* and *Champion;* Dudley, *Family Portraits* (1953), a psychological study based on the character of a childish brat. Donald McKayle created a stir with his new group work, *Games,* and Daniel Nagrin's *Strange Hero* (1948), based on the urban nightlife "hipster" character, received bravos from a packed house. A reviewer worried about the "strong Hollywood influence" and "quality of night club theatrical dancing"[37] in Nagrin's movement, drawing attention once again to the presumed austerity of modern dance (and perhaps also the events at the Alvin Theatre?). Why couldn't a dance be popular and artistic at the same time? In all, the New Dance Group Festival showcased diverse choreographers and a collection of thematic materials that likely attracted a more populist audience than most modern dance offerings.

In 1948 *Dance Observer* published one of its increasingly rare editorials. In it, Gertrude Lippincott argued that art was essentially nonpolitical. She was objecting to recent actions by the Soviet Union where charges had been brought against three of its most celebrated musical artists, Shostakovich, Prokofiev, and Khachaturian, for writing "decadent, bourgeois, and anti-democratic" music; in defense of the artists, Lippincott argued that great music transcended political boundaries, that its appeal was universal and not nationalistic. Commenting on the public confessions wrested from the artists on this occasion, she wrote, "it is difficult for us to understand how men of such stature in the arts can ascribe political characteristics to what in essence is an aesthetic activity."[38] Clearly, Lippincott meant to defend artistic independence by implying that art was — or should be — independent of social and political prohibitions. "No artist," she wrote, "can serve any master other than himself."

A second article by Lippincott later the same year is more problematic. In it, Lippincott accused artists of "mistak[ing] their particular function, that of creating works of art, for something else, in this case—

politics. . . . Artists as artists, cannot be primarily concerned with the state of humanity."[39] Despite the debates swirling around Marxist versus "bourgeois" approaches to art throughout the 1930s, the idea had been generally accepted that art could, and indeed should, reflect contemporary human concerns. Artists of all kinds had joined the Popular Front, creating literature, music, paintings, and dances in support of the Loyalist cause in the Spanish Civil War. Critics like Henry Gilfond and Ralph Taylor may have had trouble with the agitprop styles of some of the most explicitly Marxist compositions, but they too argued for the social relevance of dance. Now, little more than a decade later, the ideological assumptions that had proved vital to early modern dance were under attack; not only the socialist vision that had seemed to promise such hope, but also the definition of the artist's role in relation to contemporary society were open to question. Lippincott's article presaged the debates about art-for-art's-sake and formalist approaches that emerged in the 1950s and that effectively made the issue of content irrelevant.

The cold war historian Stephen Whitfield points out that during the height of Senator McCarthy's influence, dissent in the United States became practically synonymous with disloyalty, that for many the right to speak freely was severely restricted.[40] While the live theater escaped the most restrictive measures that shaped employment practices in both the television and film industries, most writers still did not openly object to the climate of fear in the United States, adopting instead forms of code to protest the loss of freedom. Arthur Miller's *The Crucible* (1953), for example, while set in seventeenth-century Massachusetts, was unmistakably a protest against the bullying tactics employed by Senator McCarthy's subcommittee and HUAC as well as the treachery of people one thought one could trust; it was also, of course, a play about the witchcraft trials in Salem.

Choreographers played with themes of deception and treachery, making similar allusions to the witchcraft trials of Salem. Mary Anthony, who taught at the New Dance Group as well as at the Holm studio, made a piece called *The Devil in Massachusetts,* which was presented at a 92nd Street YMHA concert in 1952. Louis Horst wrote that "it objectively portrays a horrifying climax of the witch-hunting mania of 17th century New England," but he failed to point out any connections to the witch-hunting taking place in Washington, D.C.[41] *Salem Witch Hunt* by Miriam Pandor of the Humphrey-Limón Company was performed on a program at the Brooklyn Museum of Art that same year. In Pandor's dance drama an innocent young girl was betrayed by the testimony of an "Addled Girl" and branded as a witch, a clear parallel to the kind of "naming" taking place before HUAC. [42]

José Limón made a dance called *The Traitor* (1954). Limón had danced in New Dance League concerts and in the Federal Dance Theatre, but he probably was best-known for his roles in the Humphrey-Weidman company throughout the 1940s. He now headed his own company with Doris Humphrey as artistic director. Working with an all-male group, Limón's dance told the story of Jesus' betrayal at the hands of Judas. But it was the plight of Judas that most interested him (figure 57). In an article in the *Juilliard Review,* Limón quoted V. S. Pritchett, "the truly symbolic figure of our time is the traitor or divided man — it is Judas." Limón specifically related the impulse for his dance to contemporary events. "My intent," he wrote, "[was] to use this only as it pertained to our own time." [43]

> The tragedy of Judas Iscariot has been very close to me during the last few years, for the reason that there has been so many traitors around us, on both sides of the titanic antagonism. I have been affected by their accounts of treachery, and their confessions and self-justifications. I have great pity for these unhappy human beings and for the anguish of spirit which they must experience and the torment in which they must live. [44]

In the dance, Limón played Judas, who after betraying Christ, hanged himself.

It must have been hard to know how to respond to the perfidy of the times. Pauline Koner, a colleague and partner of Limón's, made *Cassandra* (1953), based on the Greek tragedy of Cassandra who, destined to forecast the future, is rendered mute, unable to communicate what she knows.

Yet evidence also shows that even before Senator Joseph McCarthy's rise to power (a circumstance that caused many Americans to assume a mute posture) and before Soviet policies disillusioned so many American Communists and fellow travelers, "new" dance — American modern dance — had already separated itself from the working-class movement, from an explicitly political agenda, and from the structures of social activism within urban communities.

Beginning with summer sessions at Bennington College in the 1930s, a network of dedicated teachers created centers of modern dance education in the Midwest and South as well as the Far West, and as modern dance spread beyond its urban origins and became established within the academic community, the populist and working-class elements that had helped define early modern dance declined.

57. "There have been so many traitors around us, on both sides of the titanic antagonism." José Limón (right) and Lucas Hoving in *The Traitor*. (Photograph by Arnold Eagle. Courtesy of Dorothy Eagle and the Dance Collection, New York Public Library for the Performing Arts, Astor, Lenox and Tilden Foundations.)

By the 1950s American modern dance was an art receiving support from colleges and universities nationwide. Even a cursory glance through *Dance Observer* and other dance periodicals demonstrates the extent to which academic institutions replaced the old networks of unions and immigrant recreational clubs that had been central to the dissemination of techniques and information about dance in the 1930s. Universities and colleges were now providing teaching jobs for dancers, a constant stream of new students, and opportunities for performance. A section devoted to college correspondence was placed just inside the front cover of *Dance*

Observer most months, following the teaching directory—more or less where the editorial page had been. An editorial rarely appeared these days. In the column news about various college activities was published. In 1950 readers learned one month about a summer program at Stanford University, part of a workshop in physical education; another month saw a report on the undertakings at the University of Kentucky; also featured were activities and performances at the University of New Hampshire, the University of Georgia, the Boston Conservatory, Reed College, and a consortium of colleges in the Philadelphia area including Bryn Mawr, Temple, Swarthmore, and the University of Pennsylvania. Summer programs were advertised at Connecticut College, at Reed College in Oregon, at Black Mountain College in North Carolina, at Mills College in California, at the Perry-Mansfield School of Dance and Theatre in Steamboat Springs, Colorado, at the University of Wisconsin, and at the University of Wyoming. In New York City the High School of Performing Arts was established in 1948 on West 46th Street to provide professional training for students in music, theater, and dance, and Juilliard, the prestigious musical school, opened its doors to college-age dancers in 1952.[45]

Throughout the 1950s the Connecticut College summer program was the place for a young dancer to be; for six weeks aspiring dancers immersed themselves in classes taught by the most prominent names in American modern dance. The first summer the teaching staff included Graham, Erick Hawkins, Humphrey, and Limón as well as leading members of their companies. The New Dance Group was also in residence, with the Dudley-Maslow-Bales trio, and an end-of-summer festival featured performances by the trio and by the Graham and Limón companies.[46] In 1935 at the Bennington Summer School of Dance, "An Evening of Revolutionary Dance" had featured members of the New Dance League, including Anna Sokolow, Miriam Blecher, Sophie Maslow, Merle Hirsh, Jane Dudley, Lily Mehlman, Marie Marchowsky, and Lil Liandre,[47] but of those artists explicitly associated with working-class groups, only the New Dance Group earned a regular place at the festival in Connecticut.

Clearly, the academic establishment was now central to the health of modern dance, and the dancers who established themselves most prominently and securely within the new system of educational and academic patronage were those who had been least concerned with political activism during the 1930s. Just as clearly, the eager new students filling classes across the country were by and large college-educated, middle-class women (also white, Nordic, and Protestant) and not working-class women. There were exceptions, of course. African American dancers

Mary Hinkson and Matt Turney, who went on to distinguished performing careers with the Martha Graham company, emerged from the dance
program at the University of Wisconsin.

At the same time, the growing association with liberal centers of education created an estrangement between modern dance and a grassroots
popular audience. In 1938, *Dance Observer* had lobbied for the humanitarian role of dance: "The dance is a people's art. If participation in its
many forms were made available to all the people, not only would the life
of the people be enriched, but the art forms of the dance would undergo
a veritable renaissance through this contact with native sources."[48] Analyzing two recent trends in American dance, the critic Henry Gilfond had
come down squarely in support of a populist tradition. The one trend,
he said, approached "the people," and here he cited Eugene Loring's recent ballet, *Billy the Kid* (1938). The other he claimed reflected an inward
turn, "back to the abstract pattern, the precious audience, and away from
the people."[49]

But by the 1950s, modern dance could not be referred to, even nostal-
gically, as a "people's" art. It was now "high" art.

To what extent did former revolutionaries and activists pay for their
earlier idealism in the chilly climate of the 1950s? The Dudley-Maslow-
Bales trio did not appear at Connecticut after 1953. Dudley suffered from
an arthritic hip, and the trio disbanded, but the political climate at the
time also may have made the trio's employment difficult. Neither Sokolow nor Tamiris taught at Connecticut College or at the 92nd Street
YMHA, which had become an increasingly important center for dance activity in New York in the 1940s and 1950s. Ironically, William Kolodny,
who built the arts program there, was deeply committed to a vision of
Jewish culture, yet he made no attempt to hire either Maslow or Sokolow—who by this time had created repertory specifically dealing with
Jewish themes—to head the influential dance program that he instituted
in the 1940s. With John Martin as his adviser, Kolodny instead elected to
appoint Doris Humphrey as its head; later, Bonnie Bird, who had danced
with Graham early on, took over.[50] At Juilliard, Graham, Humphrey, and
Limón were the principal architects of the modern dance program; Sokolow did not join the faculty until 1958, and Tamiris had to wait until
1959 to be invited to choreograph for the Juilliard Dance Theatre, the
company created by Doris Humphrey to showcase talented Juilliard students as well as other young professionals.

Deprived of the most prestigious teaching positions during these
years, Tamiris[51] as well as Sokolow found support from the Broadway

theater. Coincidentally, this Broadway alternative may have given them the opportunity to connect once again with the popular audiences that had applauded their efforts in the Federal Theatre and Dance Projects. In the 1940s, for example, Sokolow choreographed one musical after another, frequently casting members of her own company as dancers in the productions. *Street Scene* (1946) with a book by Langston Hughes and music by Kurt Weill was set in a tenement on the Lower East Side. The *Great Campaign* (1947), which Helen Tamiris also worked on, was followed by *Sleepy Hollow* (1948) and *Regina* (1949), a musical based on Lillian Hellman's *The Little Foxes,* with a score by Marc Blitzstein. In 1950, Sokolow made the dances for *Happy as Larry.*

Intermittently, Sokolow returned to Mexico, where she had been working since the late 1930s, and she produced pageants at Madison Square Garden to aid the Israeli cause; she also continued to work with her own company. Sandwiched between *The Great Dreamer* (1954), a pageant produced for the Chanukah Festival for Israel, and *Red Roses for Me* (1955), a musical by Sean O'Casey, Sokolow premiered *Rooms* (1955), a study of urban alienation.[52] If *Case History #* was considered to be a sociological study, *Rooms,* which had grown out of a workshop at the Actors Studio, was a study in the psychological and the personal rather than the sociological and the political; the origins of human misery were situated within the individual psyche rather than within the social contract. Many artists in the 1950s adopted this position. Using elements of natural movement and gesture, distorted, then honed through timing and breath, Sokolow explored the internal dialogues that obsessed the eight characters in her dance. Hidden conflicts became embodied in danced behavior, the internal became external and observable in much the same way that an actor's craft might render it. Sokolow, remember, had been exposed to the work of Konstantin Stanislavsky at the Theatre Union.

Like Sokolow, Tamiris continued to work with actors and to be involved with Method training (she had conducted summer sessions for the Group Theatre in the 1930s). After the demise of the Federal Dance Project, she turned to Broadway musical comedy as a way to continue to speak to a popular audience and also as a way to employ those dancers with whom she had worked. From 1943 until 1957 she choreographed eighteen musicals, including *Annie Get Your Gun* (1946), *Show Boat* (1946), *Inside U.S.A.* (1948), *Carnival in Flanders* (1953), *Fanny* (1954), and *Plain and Fancy* (1955).[53]

Artistic response to social and political realities of the postwar period became increasingly dangerous and, therefore, coded and elliptically expressed. Nonrepresentational art, on the other hand, was exempt by definition from such political risks; abstract forms simply had no observable relation to contemporary life and issues. They had no content. In *Benton, Pollock and the Politics of Modernism* art historian Erika Doss traces in cold war culture the relationship between individualism, freedom, and abstract art that emerged at the same time that regionalist art, with its populist appeal and links to New Deal politics, became passé and associated with deviant mass politics.[54] Abstract expressionism, an art movement supported by avant-gardists at its inception in the mid-1940s, received more U.S. critical praise and patronage during this period, first from the U.S. State Department, next from the Museum of Modern Art, and finally from corporate America. It was pointed to as visible proof of the American ideal of freedom of the individual.

As always, the relationship between modern dance and other contemporary art forms is problematic, although there are certainly clear parallels. At the time that abstract expressionism was being promoted as "American," the abstract work of Merce Cunningham, Alwin Nikolais, and a young Paul Taylor were gaining their first recognition in the modern dance world. In ballet, Balanchine had been experimenting with abstraction since the 1940s, creating a more obvious parallel to experiments in other art forms during that period, but the prevailing "American" dance form was modern dance. When the State Department decided to export American culture as an expression of the country's good-will, Martha Graham was chosen as the ambassador of dance.

Describing her work in *The Dance in America,* initially published in 1956, Walter Terry wrote:

> The blood of ten generations of Americans is her bodily heritage, the "bone of the land in which she lives provides the skeleton of her dances; inseparable, they live in Martha Graham. Features may change, surface characteristics may vary in different dances, themes may be foreign or universal, but the Puritan blood and the American bone are as irremovable from her dances as they are from her own being.[55]

Terry, in the grip of 1950s paranoia, simultaneously declared modern dance to be American dance, and he designated Graham, a tenth-generation American (he claimed), as its principal spokesperson. What could have seemed more logical than to promote Graham and modern dance as a cultural weapon in the cold war, as a living demonstration of the role of the individual in a free society? Assisted by the State Department's international exchange program, Graham and her company left for an extended tour of the Far East in late 1955. Newspaper articles in Calcutta attributed improved relations in Indo-U.S. policies to her visit. A letter from the USIS office in Colombo, Ceylon, after noting the packed houses and good press that Graham enjoyed, concluded "she's great, superb, wonderful — we're so proud that she's an American." In a lengthy article a visiting lecturer at the University of Ceylon rhapsodized: "The Graham dance is the clearest incarnation of that inner often unrevealed to the rest of the world American spirit that has shaped the core of my country."[56]

In 1957 Graham received the annual *Dance Magazine* Award for her role in promoting relations with the Orient through the dance medium and Paul Grey Hoffman, director of the United Nations Special Fund, called her "the greatest single ambassador we have ever sent to Asia."[57] The repertory that Graham took with her on this lengthy tour included *Appalachian Spring,* her ode to the American frontier family, but also *Night Journey* (1947), her treatment of the Oedipus myth. Graham by this time was noted for her Greek cycle, which included *Dark Meadow* (1946), *Cave of the Heart* (1946), and *Errand into the Maze* (1947); the full-length, gorgeously decadent *Clytemnestra* (1958), based on the *Oresteia,* was the next major work she made after she returned to the United States. While it is ironic that an American cultural ambassador should be renowned for works derived from classical Greek literature, the link to high art and ancient culture still appeared to be necessary to legitimize American dance.

Epilogue

My first dance teacher was Fé Alf, a German modern dancer who had assisted Hanya Holm in the newly established Mary Wigman School in the 1930s, before she retired to my working-class community at the northern tip of Manhattan.

By 1950 Fé was married and had two small children. Opening a studio to teach neighborhood children must have seemed one way for her to continue her intense involvement with dance, yet still stay near home. She was a tall, handsome woman, with close-cropped reddish-brown hair and a long stride, and she managed to imbue her students with her own passion for dance.

Her studio was located in a basement on Seaman Avenue. To get to class, I walked through a long, dark alleyway, then past boilers, stored bicycles, and baby carriages to the very back. Off to the right was the studio. The room was perhaps twenty by thirty feet with a small dressing room just inside the entrance. Mirrors lined one end of the studio, and

58. Fé Alf. (Reproduced
from *Dance Observer,*
April 1937.)

I remember a smooth wooden floor. A barre ran along the wall opposite
the entrance.

Fé taught us modern dance (almost certainly based on Wigman techniques, although I did not know that then) and ballet. She found opportunities for us to perform in neighborhood institutions. (I remember
particularly doing the holiday polka at the Episcopalian church at the
corner of Seaman Avenue and Cummings Street.) She made sure that
we choreographed our own studies, and at the end of each year she had
conferences with our parents about our futures and wrote reports on our
strengths and weaknesses. I was always praised for my big movements
and encouraged to explore the world of small gesture. When she thought
we were old enough, she insisted that we go downtown to study with
May O'Donnell and Gertrude Shurr, who were then teaching in a small

studio on West 56th Street. Fé had been her first teacher when O'Donnell came to New York from the West Coast, and it must have seemed natural to Fé to send us to her former student. But it was Fé who coached us for our auditions at New York City's newly established High School of Performing Arts (now the Fiorello H. La Guardia High School of Music and Art and Performing Arts).

Growing up in the 1950s, I found that my sense of dance history was shaped by John Martin and Louis Horst. Art was art and politics were politics, and the two were best experienced separately. It was not until I became a graduate student that I learned more about Fé's background and my own brief intersection with the socialist roots of modern dance. Besides assisting Holm, Fé had performed, making her New York debut with a solo recital at the Little Theatre on West 44th Street in 1935. But she also had appeared in concerts sponsored by the Workers Dance League and the New Dance League (figure 58). In "The Problem and Scope of the Amateur Work in the German Dance Movement," Fé argued that large cultural and political movements could be expressed in amateur dance activities, presumably using movements of a pedestrian type. Some of her notes for a lecture she may have given for Nadia Chilkovsky posit "an unorganized dance proletariat in New York City which calls for leadership, clarification and mutual understanding." The dance proletariat, as Fé imagined it, was composed of schoolteachers, politically radical young Jews, and trained ballet dancers, and she set out organizational strategies to deal with these diverse groups. Handwritten at the bottom of the last page in her own bold script are the words: "Result: The New Dance Group." Indeed, several dancers active during this period mention Fé's name in conjunction with the founding of the New Dance Group.[58]

It is not so surprising that the moment joining art and politics in "new" dance proved fleeting, but it is striking how completely this history was forgotten as modern dance became institutionalized in subsequent decades.[59]

Coventry University

Partial Chronology of Dance Events Sponsored By
The Communist Party, the Workers Dance League,
the New Dance League, and the American Dance
Association (1928–1940)

January 21, 1928. Lenin Memorial Pageant at Madison Square Garden
   Director: Edward Massey; Lighting: John Dos Passos; Script: Adolf Wolf; Dances by
   Edith Segal: (1) Under the Tsars (mass pageant scene), (2) Russia in Revolt (bal-
   let), (3) The Workers Take Power, (4) Reconstruction (dance, ballet), (5) Lenin Is
   Dead, (6) Carry On! (ballet), (7) "1928" (pageant and mass scene).
January 22, 1930. "The Belt Goes Red": Lenin Memorial Pageant at Madison Square Garden
   Director: Emjo Basshe; Conceived by Edith Segal; Musical direction: Paul Ketler;
   Dances by Edith Segal: (1) The Belt (dance group), (2) American Federation of the
   Convention, (3) Revolt, (4) Organization, (5) Strike (dance group), (6) From the
   USSR, (7) Memorial March (dance), (8) Toward Struggle.
February 23, 1930. Art and dance evening at Unity Cooperative Auditorium, sponsored by
   Workers International Relief (WIR) culture and chess club. Dances by Edith Segal.
March 8, 1930. International Womens Day mass meeting at Irving Plaza. Edith Segal and
   Allison Burroughs perform Dance of Solidarity.
March 15, 1930. Daily Worker costume ball at Rockland Palace. Red Dancers perform
   American and Russian folk dances.
March 16, 1930. "The Soviet Union Forges Ahead," mass pageant presented by the depart-
   ment of cultural activities of the Workers International Relief at Bronx Coliseum.
   Red Dancers perform.
March 22, 1930. "Harlem Revels," second annual interracial dance at Rockland Palace.
   Allison Burroughs and Edith Segal perform Black and White.
April 1, 1930. Gastonia strike anniversary at Manhattan Lyceum. Edith Segal and Allison
   Burroughs do Dance of Solidarity.
April 13, 1930. Bronx Coliseum. Edith Segal directs Red Workers Ballet.
May 1, 1930. May Day celebration at Coney Island Stadium after Union Square demon-
   stration. Red Dancers perform.
September 16, 1930. Workers International Relief announces the opening of a Workers
   School of Music and the Dance. Edith Segal is on the faculty, along with Lily Mehl-
   man and Nadia Chilkovsky. Classes to begin October 15, 1930.
September 28, 1930. "A Night in Russia," a pageant for working women at Irving Plaza. Red
   Dancers perform.
October 25, 1930. Cartoonists and wrestling match and music program for Office Workers
   Union at New Harlem Casino. Red Dancers appear.

November 7, 1930. "Turn the Guns," mass pageant at Bronx Coliseum, directed by Workers Laboratory Theater for Russian Revolution's 13th anniversary. Red Dancers perform.

November 15, 1930. International photo exhibition and dance at Irving Plaza. Red Dancers appear.

November 22, 1930. 75th jubilee of Comrade Morris at Madison Square Garden. Red Dancers appear, along with Artef and the Freiheit Singing Society.

November 29, 1930. Concert and dance at the New Harlem Casino, sponsored by Metal Workers Industrial League and Jewelry Workers Industrial Union. Red Dancers appear in a program that includes Creole and Negro work songs, with John C. Smith's Negro Band.

January 2, 3, 4, 1931. Three-day joint bazaar at New Star Casino, 107th Street and Park Avenue. Red Dancers appear, with Edith Segal performing on Friday night. The Film and Photo League is also on the program, which is under the auspices of the Workers International Relief, the Needle Trades Workers Industrial Union, and the United Council of Working Class Women, to benefit the Needle Trades strike fund, the unemployed hunger marches, and children's camps of the Workers International Relief.

January 11, 1931. Concert and dance sponsored by *Empros*, a Greek Communist weekly, at Park Palace, Fifth Avenue and West 110th Street. Dancing until 3 A.M. Edith Segal performs along with the Freiheit Singing Society.

February 28, 1931. "3rd Arbeiter Festival" at the New York Labor Temple. Edith Segal performs Revolutionary Dances.

March 13, 1931. "First Festival of Proletarian Culture," sponsored by the cultural department of the Workers International Relief, held at Webster Hall. Edith Segal dances with the Junior and Senior Red Dancers. Nadia Chilkovsky is on the program with the Pioneer Dancers. WIR chorus also appears.

Edith Segal makes a trip to the Soviet Union as representative of New York City's John Reed Club. At the International Conference for Proletarian Culture, ways to overthrow "bourgeois" technique and create new revolutionary art are discussed.

New Dance Group is formed in 1932.

May 1, 1932. "Recognition Rally" of the Friends of the Soviet Union at Bronx Coliseum, sponsored by the *Daily Worker*. Workers Dance League is formed by Edith Segal, Nadia Chilkovsky, Anna Sokolow, and Miriam Blecher.

January 29, 1933. "Toward a New Theatre," New School for Social Research program. Red Dancers take part.

February 25, 1933. Costume ball sponsored by New York district of the International Labor Defense at Manhattan Lyceum. Red Dancers perform.

March 26, 1933. New Dance Group's first annual recital, "A Group of Folk Dances," is held at Heckscher Theater. Satires: Parasite, Charity, Jingoisms—traffic, politicians, peace conferences; Strike: Uprisings, Hunger, War Trilogy—breadlines, war, on the barricades; Final March.

June 1933. New Dance Group gives studio recitals.

June 4, 1933. First Workers Dance Spartakiade sponsored by Workers Dance League.
Artef Dance Group. Director: Lillian Shapero
Dance prologue to a play *The Steppe in Flames*.
Lillian Shapero
Good Morning Revolution
IWO High School Dance group and Junior Red Dancers. Director: Edith Segal
Dance of Victory (music: Red Army March, Song of the Red Fleet).

Two Children's Dance Group. Director: Edith Segal
> There Stands a Prisoner (song with action words by Segal).
>> 1 and 2 and 3 and 4 (Pioneer song).

Nature Friends Dance Group. Director: Edith Segal
> Dance of Today (music: Lahn Adohmyon): In the Shop, Unemployed, Hunger March; Red Front (music: Hans Eisler).

Nell Anyon
> Youth and War (music: Paula Halpern): Song of the Machine, Unemployed, At Reforestation Camps.

Needle Trades Workers Industrial Union Dance Group. Director: Edith Segal
> Revolutionary Funeral March; Practice for the Picket Line—adaptation of the Oxen Dance.

New Dance Group
> Awake (music: Estelle Parnas), directed by Miriam Blecher; Charity (music: Parnas), directed by Edith Langbert; Hunger (music: Parnas), directed by Grace Wylie.

Rebel Arts Dance Group. Director: Frances Leber
> Round of Labor, Strike.

Edith Segal
> Third Degree (Negro spiritual, new words by V. I. Jerome).

Rebel Dancers (Newark). Director: Fanya Chochem
> War—A Trilogy.

Red Dancers. Director: Edith Segal
> Southern Holiday (music: Murray Chase), Dance of the Scrubwomen (music: Chase), Red Cavalry (music: Russian folk song).

August 29, 1933. Anti-War Congress, sponsored by American League Against War and Fascism, at St. Nicholas Arena. Theatre Union Dance Group performs Anti-War Trilogy (Sokolow).

October 21, 1933. Opening of Harlem Workers School. New Dance Group appears at Harlem Casino, 116th Street and Lenox Avenue.

January 7, 1934. Workers Dance League Benefit for the *Daily Worker* at the City College Auditorium.

Theatre Union Dance Group
> Anti-War Cycle.

New Duncan Dancers
> Soviet Folk Dances; In Memoriam; If Need Be, We Give Our Youth.

Red Dancers
> Southern Holiday, Scottsboro, Red Cavalry.

Jack London Rebel Dancers
> War Trilogy—Depression, War, and Disillusionment and Revolt.

New Dance Group
> Blue Eagle, Charity, Workers' Dance Song.

April 20, 1934. Workers Dance League recital at Brooklyn Academy. Presented by United Front Supporters for the benefit of the *Labor Defender.*

New Dance Group
> Van der Lubbe's Head; Uprising.

New Duncan Dancers
> In Memoriam.

Theatre Union Dance Group

Depression-Starvation (music: Alex Soifer), March of the Pioneers (music: Sergei Prokofiev).

Edith Segal
  Black and White.
Charles Weidman
  Gymnopédies (music: Erik Satie).
Modern Negro Group
  Black Hands, Black Feet; Life and Death.
Fé Alf
  Summer Witchery.

June 2, 1934. Workers Dance League competition, Town Hall.
New Dance Group
  Van der Lubbe's Head (first prize); Uprising.
Theatre Union Dance Group
  Anti-War Cycle (second prize).
Nature Friends Dance Group
  Kinder, Kuche, and Kirche (third prize).
American Revolutionary Dancers
  Dirge, Red Tide.
Rebel Dance Group of Newark
  Contempo.
Red Dancers
  Comintern, Scottsboro.
New Duncan Dancers
  Bruno Tesch Memorial, Upsurge.

June 3, 1934. First Workers Dance League convention.
June 23, 1934. New Dance Group recital at 11 East 14th Street, with Jane Dudley and Miriam Blecher.
June 26, 1934. National Negro Theatre midnight show. Two male dancers, Add Bates and Irving Lansky, perform Black and White.
September 21, 1934. New Dance Group in Eastern Theatre festival at Civic Repertory Theatre performs New Theatre Skit.
November 25, 1934. Workers Dance League solo dance concert at Civic Repertory Theatre.
Anna Sokolow
  Illusion, Desire, Histrionics, Death of Tradition (with Mehlman and Maslow).
Lily Mehlman
  Defiance (music: Arthur Honegger), Death of Tradition (with Sokolow and Maslow).
Sophie Maslow
  Themes from a Slavic People, Death of Tradition (with Sokolow and Mehlman).
Jane Dudley
  Time Is Money, Life of a Worker, The Dream Ends.
Edith Segal
  Tom Mooney
Miriam Blecher
  The Disinherited (suite including the Woman), Awake, Three Negro Songs.
Nadia Chilkovsky
  March, Song of the Machine, Homeless Girl, Parasite.

December 1, 1934. Repeat performance of November 25 concert at Ambassador Theatre.
December 23, 1934. Workers Dance League Group program at Town Hall.
New Dance Group
Van der Lubbe's Head, Charity, We Remember (music: Parnas).
Theatre Union Dance Group
Anti-War Cycle, Forces in Opposition (to poem by Sergei Essenin, music: Swift), Two Pioneer Marches (music: Sergei Prokofiev).
Nature Friends Dance Group
Kinder, Kuche, and Kirche, Red Workers Machine, Cause I'm a Nigger.
Red Dancers
Black and White, Sell Out.
February 15-25, 1935. International Theatre Week, sponsored by International Union of the Revolutionary Theatre, includes performances by Workers Dance League, League of Workers Theatres, and Workers Music League.
February 16-17, 1935. Eastern conference of Workers Dance League.
February 17, 1935. Workers Dance League concert at Center Theatre as part of international theater week.
The Dance Unit
Anti-War Cycle.
New Dance Group
Van der Lubbe's Head, Charity.
Miriam Blecher
Woman.
April 7, 1935. New Dance League solo concert at the Civic Repertory Theatre.
Ernestine Henoch
Waltz, Mother of Vengeance, Action.
Marie Marchowsky
Agitation.
Bill Matons
Demagog.
Fé Alf
Girls in Conflict, Degradation, Slavery.
Rose Crystal
Despair, Invictus.
Lil Liandre
Call.
Eleanor King
Song of Earth, Mother of Tears.
April 10, 1935. At New School for Social Research, works by Lil Liandre, Hilda Hoppe, Elsa Findlay, Marie Marchowsky, Lydia Balsam, and New Dance Group.
April 21, 1935. New Dance League recital of solo and group performances at Mecca Temple. Solo works by Marchowsky, King, Henoch, Alf, Dudley, Matons, and group works by Dance Players, the New Dance Group, and a group led by Blanche Evan.
May 3, 4, 1935. New Theatre Magazine and New Dance League present "Men in the Modern Dance" at Park Theatre. Performances by Weidman and Group, George Groke, Gene Martel and Group, Roger Pryor Dodge, William Dollar, Eugene Von Grona, Bill Matons, Add Bates, and Irving Lansky.

June 9, 1935. "New Dance League Third Festival," for American League Against War and
Fascism, at Park Theatre. The afternoon was devoted to competition among amateur
groups, the evening to professional groups. Evening program:
Dance Unit
Strange American Funeral.
New Dance Group
Ah, Peace.
Ruth Allerhand
Strike.
Helen Tamiris
Escape, Flight, Individual and the Mass.
Charles Weidman
Tradition.
June 16, 1935. New Dance League Conference.
November 2, 1935. New Dance League sponsors Tamiris at Venice Theatre.
December 15, 1935. International Labor Defense Concert at Carnegie Hall.
Martha Graham
Celebration, Imperial Gesture, Course.
Doris Humphrey
New Dance.
Charles Weidman
Stock Exchange.
Helen Tamiris
Harvest, Work and Play.
The Dance Unit (Anna Sokolow)
Strange American Funeral.
December 22, 1935. New Dance League Concert at Adelphi Theatre.
The Dance Unit
Impressions of a Dance Hall.
Merle Hirsch
Valse Sentimentale (music: Ravel), Georgia Prisoner.
Letitia Ide and José Limón
Greeting, Nostalgic Fragments.
Jane Dudley
Middle-Class Portraits.
Lily Mehlman
Defiance (music: Arthur Honegger), Heil (Honegger), Song of Affirmation (music:
Alex North).
Sophie Maslow
Two Songs About Lenin, Prelude to a May First Suite (North).
Bill Matons
Escape (from a poem by Kenneth Fearing).
Marie Marchowsky
Conflict (music: Robert Branch).
February 14, 1936. Fé Alf, Jane Dudley, Blanche Evan perform with Prospect Dance Group
at Prospect Workers Center, Southern Boulevard, the Bronx.
March 15, 1936. New Dance League presents "Men in the Dance" at Majestic Theatre. Per-

formances by African Dancers, Saki, Roger Pryor Dodge, Vladimir Valentinoff, John Bovington, José Limón, Charles Weidman, and Bill Matons.

March 22, 1936. The Dance Guild presents Miriam Blecher, Jane Dudley, Blanche Evan, Eleanor King, and Mary Radin at Vanderbilt Theatre.

April 5, 1936. Anna Sokolow and Dance Unit at Kaufmann Auditorium.

Opening Dance (music: Vissarion Shebalin); Ballad (in a popular style) (music: Alex North); Romantic Dances, Illusions and Desire (music: Scriabin); Histrionics (music: Hindemith); Speaker (North); Four Little Salon Pieces (music: Shostakovich): Debut, Élan, Rêverie, Entr'acte; Strange American Funeral; Inquisition 1936, Provocateur and Vigilante (North); Suite of Soviet Songs.

May 18-25, 1936. National Dance Congress.

July 25, 1936. New Dance League at Bennington, Vermont, performances by Anna Sokolow, Bill Matons, Fara Lynn, and Eva Desca.

November 8, 1936. New Dance League presents Helen Tamiris at Guild Theatre.

Momentum (music: Herbert Haufreucht).

Unemployed, SH! SH!, Legion, Nightriders, Diversion, Disclosure.

Dance of Escape (music: Elie Siegmeister).

Composition for Group (music: J. Slavenski).

Flight (music: A. Mossolow).

Middle Ground (music: Shostakovich).

Manoeuvres (music: Debussy, Hindemith).

Impressions of the Bull Ring (music: R. Calleja).

December 20, 1936. Martha Graham premieres Chronicle.

January 17, 1937. New Dance Group at Grand Street Playhouse.

Jane Dudley

Four Middle Class Portraits, Ma Body's No Carcass (Folk, arranged by Lawrence Gellert), Life Is Joyous—a song for Soviet Youth Day (music: Bohuslav Martinů).

Miriam Blecher

Two Jewish Songs—Poland: In the Shop (music: Ernest Bloch), Biro Bidjan: In the Field (folk); Letter to the President (music: Moross); The Village Without Men (music: Estelle Parnas).

Bea Parris

Holiday (music: Norman Cazden), Death House Blues (folk).

April 25, 1937. New Dance League presents "Dances of Today" at St. James Theatre.

Jane Dudley

Songs of Protest—Lay Down Late and Sistern and Brethren (music: Lawrence Gellert); Song for Soviet Youth Day; Under the Swastika: "Germans Think with Your Blood," Though We Be Flogged (music: Alex North).

Lily Mehlman

Spanish Woman (music: Paul Creston), Lullaby for a Dead Child, No Pasarán, Harvest Song (Creston), Song of Affirmation (music: North).

Bill Matons

Letter to a Policeman in Kansas City (music: Menk).

Malvena Fried

Portrait of an American Lady (music: Bacon).

Blanche Evan

An Office Girl Dreams (music: Roy Harris), An Opportunist (Harris).

Miriam Blecher

Advance Scout—Lincoln Battalion (music: Ravel), Two Jewish Songs, Me and Robert Taylor and The Bum from East Side Sketches (music: Parnas).

May 6, 1937. How Long Brethren? opens at Nora Bayes Theatre.

May 14–16, 1937. American Dance Association Convention.

May 23, 1937. American Dance Association sponsors "Dances for Spain." Proceeds go to Medical Committee to Aid Spanish Democracy.

Ruthanna Boris

Gitanerías (popular), La Garterana (popular).

Polanco

Cape Dance (traditional), Farucca (traditional).

Helen Tamiris

South American Dance (popular air), Impressions of the Bull Ring (music: A. Rodríguez).

Sophia Delza

Renaissance Figure (music: Lieberson), We Weep for Spain (music: De Falla), We March for Spain (music: Chopin).

Lazar Galpern

War to the End (music: Isaac Albéniz), Farucca (music: De Falla).

Lily Mehlman

Spanish Woman (music: Paul Creston).

New Dance Group

Flower festival—Madrid, 1937 (music: Tolbie Sacher).

Anna Sokolow

Excerpts from a War Poem (F. T. Martinetti, music: Alex North).

November 21, 1937. American Dance Association Concert at 92nd Street YMHA.

Lily Mehlman

Lullaby for a Dead Child, Harvest Song, Girl.

Jane Dudley

Four Portraits, Fantasy—after images of a movie.

Sophie Maslow

Two Songs for Lenin, Ragged Hungry Blues, Runaway Rag, Evacuación (with Dudley).

José Limón

Danza de la Muerte, Hymn.

December 19, 26, 1937. Martha Graham performs Immediate Tragedy (music: Henry Cowell) and Deep Song (Cowell) at the Guild Theatre in New York.

January 19, 1938. Anna Sokolow does Dance of All Nations for Lenin Pageant at Madison Square Garden.

February 5, 1938. The Brooklyn Museum Dance Center presents Miriam Blecher.

Folk Dance; Mask Dances (music: Estelle Parnas): Daughter of the "60 Families" (Masque at the Waldorf), School Days, For Americans Only; Letter to the President (music: Moross); Three Negro Poems (Frank Home, Langston Hughes, folk poem); East Side Sketches: On Second Avenue—Me and Robert Taylor, On the Bowery—The Bum; The Woman, from The Disinherited (music: Parnas); Two Jewish Songs: From Poland—In the Shop (music: Bloch), From Biri Bidjan—In the Field (folk tune).

April 24, 1938. Guild Theatre, American Dance Association presents Miriam Blecher, Dorothy Bird, and Si-lan Chen.

Blecher:

> East Side Sketches (music: Parnas and folk), Mask Dances (Parnas), Three Jewish Songs (music: Joseph Achron, Bloch, folk), Opening Dance (music: Lev Knipper), Nostalgic Portrait (music: Alexander Tansman), Credo ("There is a tide in the affairs of men") (music: Alex North).

Bird:

> The World Owes Me a Living (music: Harold Arlen).

Si-lan Chen

> Chinese Boxer (music: Georges Auric), Boat Girl (music: Moussorgsky), National Dances of the Soviet East (folk).

January 15, 1939. Dave Doran memorial at Mecca Temple. Dudley, Maslow, Matons, Blecher, Sokolow, Ailes Gilmour, Mira Slavonica, Limón, Katherine Litz, Juan Martinez and Antonita, and Theatre Dance Company appear.

February 4, 5, 1939. American Dance Association conference at Mecca Temple.

February 4, 5, 1939. Second annual dance for Spain sponsored by American Dance Association for the Medical Bureau and North American Committee to Aid Spanish Democracy. Performances by Graham, Humphrey, Weidman, Tamiris, Sokolow, Arthur Mahoney, Thalia Mara, Martinez and Antonita, and Felicia Sorel's dancers from *Everywhere I Roam.*

March 5, 1939. Lily Mehlman and Si-lan Chen appear at Guild Theatre under the auspices of American Committee for Chinese War Orphans.

July 1939. Edith Segal does Immigrants All, Americans All at Camp Kinderland.

February 9, 1940. New Dance Group performs at Grand Street Playhouse.

Compiled from accounts in the *Daily Worker, New Theatre, Theatre Arts Committee (TAC), Dance Observer,* and the *New York Times,* and from programs and clippings in the Dance Collection of the New York Public Library for the Performing Arts.

A P P E N D I X   I I

Chronology of the Federal Dance Project
(January 1936–December 1937)

January 14, 1936. The Dancers Association telegraphs Hallie Flanagan, director of the Federal Theatre, requesting formation of an independent Dance Project with its own administrative staff and a permanent theater.

January 15, 1936. Elmer Rice, regional director for New York Federal Theatre Project, sends a telegram to Flanagan after consulting with his assistant, Philip Barber, and playwright Stephen Karnot. Rice suggests that an independent Dance Project be set up within the Theatre Project. Don Oscar Becque is recommended as supervisor by Rice and his colleagues.

January 29, 1936. Flanagan meets with Becque, head of the Dance Group, to discuss plans. Flanagan suggests that both modern dance and ballet be a part of the Project and that new dancers and choreographers be encouraged. Possible appointments are discussed, such as Doris Humphrey, Helen Tamiris, and Claire Leonard. Tamiris is described as "left-wing" in the Record of Appointments.

February 1936. Dance Observer announces the Dance Project and attributes its formation to the efforts of the Dancers Association. The Project will employ 185 dancers presently on relief and is budgeted for $155,000 until June 1, 1936.

March 5, 1936. All registrations for the Project are stopped in order to comply with a WPA ruling forbidding further requisitioning of personnel on the four arts projects, leaving the dance group with only 85 of the promised 185 dancers registered.

March 15, 1936. New York Times publishes details of the Dance Project, including the appointments of choreographers Humphrey, Charles Weidman, Tamiris, Felicia Sorel, and Gluck Sandor; musical director Donald Pond; associate musical directors Genevieve Pitot and Wallingford Riegger; and personnel director Grace Duncan Hopper.

April 6, 1936. Dancers are arrested for picketing Philip Barber's office to protest the hiring stoppage.

April 20, 1936. The Unemployed Group of the Dancers Association petitions Becque for (1) fulfillment of the dance quota, (2) the establishment of a 25 percent nonrelief quota, (3) the employment of all unemployed dancers.

April 22, 1936. Trial of dancers arrested on April 6, 1936, takes place; the case is dismissed. Becque writes to Flanagan, advising her of the dancers' demands, and he asks Flanagan to meet with members of the City Projects Council and the Dancers Association. He expresses sympathy for some of their demands.

June 17, 1936. Flanagan replies to demands by John Connolly of the Unemployed Section of the Dancers Association that an additional three hundred dancers be put on the project. She insists that no additions can be made.

Undated memo. Connolly claims that William Farnsworth, national administrator for the Federal Theatre Project, has agreed to remediate the unfair distribution of personnel between the Theatre Project and the Dance Project by July 1, 1936.

June 25, June 30, 1936. Candide (Weidman) plays at the Henry Street Playhouse and at the Majestic Theatre on Fulton Street in Brooklyn.

July 23, July 29, August 5, 1936. Salut au Monde (Tamiris) plays at the Henry Street Playhouse, at New York University, and at the McMillan Theatre at Columbia University.

August 6, 7, 8, 1936. Young Tramps (Becque) plays at the Majestic Theatre on Fulton Street in Brooklyn.

August 11, 1936. Becque in a memo to Barber, complaining of trouble with the unemployed dancers, refers to an additional hundred dancers who are to be put on the Project. First mention of audition and medical boards.

August 12, 1936. Press release by Becque, approved by Flanagan, states that an additional hundred dancers will be employed to fill the original dance quota. Dancers are to be employed on the basis of need *and* professional ability. They no longer have to be on relief, but they must be certified as needy by an emergency relief bureau. Two auditions boards—ballet and nonballet—are set up, "consisting of prominent people in the dance world, who are not associated with the project." Dancers applying will receive physical examinations at WPA clinics.

August 19, 1936. Auditions begin.

August 20, 1936. New York World-Telegram features photographs of dancers Susanne Remos and Lulu Morris before the auditions board.

August 24, 1936. Becque writes to Barber and tries to get Gluck Sandor fired for failing to cooperate.

September 9, 1936. Report of the Federal Dance Theatre on the continuing auditions at the Artef Theatre lists board members. Nonballet board includes Nadia Chilkovsky, Esther Junger, Gene Martel, Edwin Strawbridge, Lucile Marsh; ballet board consists of Enrico Zanfretta, Constantin Kobeloff, Hilda Butsova. Sixty dancers have been "requisitioned," but only two are on the payroll at this time. Nonrelief status of many applicants holding up requisitions. Reports of sentiment against Becque by the City Projects Council local and the circulation of petitions for his removal.

Sometime before the next events Becque probably heard about the charges being circulated against him.

September 15, 1936. Paula Katz, Ruth Firestone, Carmen Clifton, Edward Murray, Ruth Rand, Ruth Hoffman, and Albert Grant, all of the Bovington Group—now headed by Ruth Allerhand—are asked to reaudition. Only Grant and Murray comply. In a letter to the auditions board, Allerhand protests the demand for members of her group to be reauditioned.

September 16, 1936. George Hexter, executive officer of the New York Theatre Project, describes the incident of September 15 in a memo to Barber. The dancers who did not comply with the reauditioning order were summoned to the personnel department. Allerhand, Add Bates, and Paula Bass accompanied them, but they were asked to wait outside. The dancers demanded CPC representation, and Hexter countered with notices for insubordination. Allerhand's letter to the auditions board was considered insubordination, and she also received an official form.

September 17, 1936. Hearings are held in Barber's office with a delegation from the Dance

Theatre to discuss the dismissals. Fuss of City Projects Council represents the dancers and argues that dancers are being transferred because they have brought charges against Becque; he protests the policy of reauditioning. Fanya Geltman threatens that the dancers are prepared to walk out in protest over Becque.

September 18, 1936. Hexter writes to Becque and advises him that it is Flanagan's desire to have all members of the Dance Project reauditioned.

September 22, 1936. Becque writes Barber discussing conditions for the return of Humphrey and Weidman to the Project. There is agitation on the project for their return.

September 23, 1936. Hexter writes Flanagan to explain the situation on the Dance Project regarding reauditioning policy. He urges Flanagan to continue the reauditioning policy as a matter of disciplinary control. He admits that he advised Becque on September 18 that it was Flanagan's desire to see all dancers reauditioned. The policy is continuing despite protest.

Sometime before October 3, a hearing takes place before Flanagan, Barber, and Farnsworth, and the charges against Becque are "disproved," according to a November 12 memo by Becque.

October 20, 1936. Becque memo to Hexter rebuts Tamiris's complaint that Humphrey-Weidman dancers received preferential treatment in an audition.

In preparation for the November hearing on Becque, Tamiris sent out notices, and Susanne Remos passed out mimeographed circulars from the City Projects Council.

November 1936. Dance Observer reports on a public hearing against Becque in which:

Chilkovsky charges that the auditions board was used as an instrument against the dancers.

Geltman charges that Becque was incompetent.

Connolly charges that Becque was unresponsive to the unemployed dancers.

Tamiris charges that Becque was uncooperative with the choreographers; that Becque was dictatorial; that he was acting selfishly in his espousal of a common denominator technique.

Gluck Sandor charges that Becque knew nothing about choreography or theater.

Lucile Marsh declares Becque incompetent.

Humphrey declares her sympathy for the dancers.

November 6, 1936. Hiram Motherwell, assistant director of the Federal Theatre Project, acknowledges Chilkovsky's resignation from the auditions board.

November 12, 1936. Becque protests the *Dance Observer* coverage of the hearing and declares it the result of professional agitators. He asks for Tamiris's dismissal.

November 16, 1936. Fuss writes Barber requesting that Becque be dropped from the Project and protesting Becque's proposed dismissal of Tamiris. He alludes to Hexter's dismissal of Chilkovsky, but it is more likely she resigned.

December 2, 1936. Becque memo to Barber tries to ameliorate the situation by proposing to reorganize the Dance Project.

Gluck Sandor's *Eternal Prodigal* opens in New York.

December 7, 1936. Sit-in strike to protest threatened dismissals by theater workers, includes Lily Mann and Susanne Remos.

December 8, 1936. Dismissal of those who took part in the strike.

December 9, 1936. Daily Worker reports mass firings of WPA workers. Pictures of sleeping workers at sit-in strike protesting layoffs, including Mann and Remos. This strike includes members of all five arts projects.

December 10, 1936. Demonstration and picketing protesting dismissals at 70 Columbus

Avenue (West 62nd Street), WPA office of a Colonel Sommervell, who is responsible for federal theater activity in New York City area. Arts Projects "shut down" for four hours by a parade of some two thousand WPA workers. Sommervell holds firm, proposing to dock demonstrators.

December 24, 1936. New York Times reports that Becque is replaced by Lincoln Kirstein.

January 13, 1937. Arthur Mahoney, Becque's assistant, resigns, charging that the new administration has not made assurances that it will keep political agitation in check.

January 16, 1937. Tamiris is part of a delegation that goes to Washington, D.C., to protest upcoming cuts in federal arts projects.

Young Choreographer's Laboratory debuts at the Brooklyn Museum of Art. The program includes a work by Chilkovsky, called "Auditioning in the Summer of 1936."

January 29, 1937. Memo from Karnot to Flanagan describes almost universal bitterness toward Becque by dancers and choreographers and suggests that Becque made efforts to turn the administrative staff against a new administration. Karnot advises against returning Becque to the New York Federal Dance Project in any capacity.

March 5, 1937. First mention of plans for *How Long Brethren?*.

May 6, 1937. How Long Brethren? opens in tandem with *Candide* at the Nora Bayes Theatre.

May 17, 1937. Sit-in strike at the Nora Bayes Theatre.

June 19, 1937. Dance Magazine award goes to *How Long Brethren?*.

June 19, 1937. Vassar Summer Theatre begins six-week session. Tamiris teaches movement.

July 10, 1937. How Long Brethren? performed at Vassar College.

December 21, 1937. How Long Brethren? revived at the 49th Street Theatre.

Compiled from documents at the Research Center for the Federal Theatre Project, George Mason University, Fairfax, Virginia (now held at the Library of Congress Research Center for the Federal Theatre Project), and from newspapers and journals, January 1936–December 1937.

A P P E N D I X   I I I

Selected Poems and Songs

Black Fists, White Fists
By J. C. Eden
(Commemorating the first mass meeting
of White and Negro workers
in Chester, Pa.)

Under sickle and hammer
Black and white hand welded
A steel embrace.

Black fists,
White fists.

No blood seeking horde
Unleashing dogs to hound.
No murder cry
No yelp of white savagery.

The black man equal,
The white man equal.

Black and white hand welded
A steel embrace.
Augury of a day
When black and white armies
Stream from one thousand foundries,
fields, shops.

To march singing
On bleeding gold ramparts.

Text of poem as printed in the *Daily Worker*, March 7, 1929
(courtesy *People's Weekly World*).

Van der Lubbe's Head
By Alfred Hayes

And it is done—
In secrecy—at dawn
While houses sleep
While thieves disband

In sawdust lies the head
The bloody trunk falls backward from the block
The eyeless eyes are staring at the sunless sun
And it is done!
The mouth is shut.
Who fears betrayal from the sun?
Or treachery from walls that cannot speak?

Herr Headman wipes his sweating brow under his silk tophat.
And they—the twelve cold Citizens—the State—the
Ministers—the Chancellor—feel safer now.
For Oberfahten's mouth was muzzled in his flat
And in an Austrian inn stiffened the corpse of Bell.
Now Van der Lubbe's ghost goes headless down to hell!
And all the tongues that could have told—are stopped.
After this morning seek among the dead
The fire's secret buries with this head.
You bloody fools!
If Van der Lubbe's head a hundred times
Under a hundred guillotines should fall
Still—would the secret not be dead,
But truth cry out the hundred mouths of time
Each stone you walk on shriek aloud your guilt
The very earth betray the criminals and the crime.

And here, within this somber prison yard
Before the Dutchman's corpse has time to rot
A Greater Headsman shall be seen—
O final dawn
O last
O last Great Guillotine.

Text of poem as it appeared in souvenir program of the
Workers Dance League Bulletin, festival issue, June 1934.

———

Time Is Money
By Sol Funaroff

Tick-tock. Time is money
Tick-tock. Safety First.
and Haste is Waste

and all the mangled limbs of Time,
charred bodies, slag in white-hot steel,
the rotting teeth, the T.B. faces,
the yellow-green decaying skins of Time!
Time is Money!

Tick-tock.
Skeleton crews in speed-up shifts
clang their iron deaths
and spin a wealth of misery.
Whose bones are clacking in the wind?
Whose grinding laughter whirls about?
A billboard bears the braggard sign.
A ragged suicide turns and twists.
A young woman weeps.

Tick-tock. Scabshops of starvation. . . .
Fear in the gloom and dusty corners . . . Lean
years cutting:
        Time! Time! Time!
the skin to bone of workers, wives and
kids.
Oh, we work, work work,
time, time and overtime,
until the dawn is feverish in our faces
like the flush of a consumptive;
and our thin fingers ache with needles
                stitching pain.
Tick-tock: bourgeois formulas for increased
                dividends.
Time is Money and tailors' shears become
                the whirring cutters'
gears of efficient engineers.
Tick-tock. Time is money and financiers.

Text of poem as it appeared in program copy for *Revolutionary
Solo Dances*, Civic Repertory Theatre, November 25, 1934.

———

A Strange Funeral in Braddock
By Michael Gold

Listen! Listen to the drums of a strange American funeral.
Listen to the story of a strange American funeral

In the town of Braddock, Pennsylvania,
Where the steel mills live like foul dragons, burning,
devouring man and earth and sky,
It is spring. Now the spring has wandered in, a frightened child
in the land of the steel ogres,

And Jan Clepak, the great grinning Bohemian, on his way to work
at six in the morning,
Sees buttons of bright grass on the hills across the river, and
plum trees hung with wild white blossoms,
And as he sweats half naked at his puddling trough, a fiend by
the lake of brimstone,
The plum trees soften his heart,
The green grass-memories return and soften his heart,
And he forgets to be hard as steel and he remembers only his
wife's breasts, his baby's little laughters and the way men sing
when they are drunk and happy,
He remembers cows and sheep and the grinning peasants, and the
villages and fields of sunny Bohemia.
Listen to the mournful drums of a strange funeral.
Listen to the story of a strange American funeral.

Wake up! Wake up! Jan Clepak, the furnaces are roaring like
tigers,
The flames are flinging themselves at the high roof, like mad,
yellow tigers at their cage,
Wake up! it is ten o'clock, and the next batch of mad,
flowing steel is to be poured in your puddling trough,
Wake up! Wake up! For a flawed lever is cracking in one of the
fiendish cauldrons,
Wake up! and wake up! for now the lever has cracked, and the
steel is raging and running down the floor like an escaped
madman,
Wake up! Oh, the dream is ended, and the steel has swallowed you
forever, Jan Clepak!
Listen to the mournful drums of a strange funeral.
Listen to the mournful drums of a strange American funeral.

Now three tons of hard steel hold at their heart the bones,
flesh, nerves, the muscles, brains and heart of Jan Clepak,
They hold memories of green grass and sheep, the plum trees, the
baby laughter and the sunny Bohemian villages.
And the directors of the steel mill present the great coffin of
steel and man memories to the widow of Jan Clepak,
And on the great truck it is borne now to the great trench in the
graveyard,
And Jan Clepak's widow and two friends ride in a carriage behind
the block of steel that holds Jan Clepak,
And they weep behind the carriage blinds, and mourn the soft man
who was slain by hard steel.
Listen to the mournful drums of a strange funeral
Listen to the story of a strange American funeral.

Now three thinkers are thinking strange thoughts in the
graveyard.
"O, I'll get drunk and stay drunk forever, I'll never marry

woman, or father laughing children.
I'll forget everything and be nothing from now on,
Life is a dirty joke, like Jan's funeral!"
One of the friends is thinking in the sweet smelling graveyard,
As a derrick lowers the three tons of steel that held Jan Clepak.
(LISTEN TO THE DRUMS OF THE STRANGE AMERICAN FUNERAL!)
"I'll wash clothes, I'll scrub floors, I'll be a fifty-cent
whore, but my children never will work in the steel-mill!"
Jan Clepak's wife is thinking as earth is shoveled over the great
steel coffin.
In the spring sunlight, in the soft April air,
(LISTEN TO THE DRUMS OF A STRANGE AMERICAN FUNERAL!)

"I'll make myself as hard as steel, harder,
I'll come some day and make bullets out of Jan's body, and shoot
them into a tyrant's heart!"
The other friend is thinking, the listener,
He who listened to the mournful drums of the strange funeral,
Who listened to the story of the strange American funeral,
And turned as mad as a fiendish cauldron with cracked lever.
LISTEN TO THE MOURNFUL DRUMS OF A STRANGE FUNERAL
LISTEN TO THE STORY OF A STRANGE AMERICAN FUNERAL.

From *Proletarian Literature in the United States: An Anthology,* ed.
Granville Hicks, Michael Gold, Isador Schneider, Joseph North, Paul Peters,
Alan Calmer (New York: International Publishers, 1935).

———

How Long Brethren?

"Pickin' Off de Cotton"

Pickin' off—de cotton. Hoein' up de corn,
I'm de lazies' Darkie, Sho'—, as yo' born.
Mmmm. Aint dat de truth.

If Darkie work hahd—He worked out—'fore long.
An Captain only want him when he stay strong.
Mmmm. Aint dat de truth.

He work so hahd—jes' fo gettin' ahead.
But he were crosseye, filled Captains pockets instead.
Mmmm. Aint dat de truth.

De hahdes' workin' Darkie I ever saw,
now goin' 'roun beggin' can't work no mo'.
Mmmm. Aint dat de truth.

Laborin fo' white folks. No matter what I'm doin'—
I'm de lazies' Darkie Sho' as yo' born.
Mmmm. Aint dat de truth.

Pickin' off de cotton. Hoein' up de corn.
I'm de lazies' Darkie, Sho' as yo' born.
Mmmm. Aint dat de truth.

"Up de Mountain"

Upon de mountain chillun call.
Cain't make a dollar save my soul.
Chillun hungry, nothin' to eat.
Git no money, walkin' de street.
Ast mah Cap'n cain he use a man.
Use a man not a skeleton.
How cain I make, Ah don't know.
Tired of starvin', won' starve no moah!

"How Long Brethren?"

How long brethren, how long mus' my people weep and mourn?
How long, how long brethren, how long?
So long—my people been asleep,
White folks plowin' darkies soul down deep.
How long, how long brethren, how long?
Too long, brethren too long—
We just barely miserin' 'long.
Too long, too long, brethren too long.
White folk he aint Jesus
He jes' a man grabbin' biscuit out of poor darkie's hand.
Too long, too long, brethren, too long.
So long—brethren.
So long—Darkie keep asingin' de same ol' song.
So long—, so long, brethren, so long.
Darkie he jes' patch black dirt,
De raisin' part of de white man's earth.—
So long, so long, brethren, so long.

"Workin' on de Railroad"

Workin' on de railroad—fifty cents a day.
De boss at de comp'ny sto' sign all I makes away.
Mammy po'ly write, "Please send some money, son."
But I aint got no ready made money.
But I aint got no ready made money.
My goddamn black soul I can't send he none.—

Trouble never layin' dead on de bottom dis here Worl'.
Evrythin' you can see shinin' ain't no gol'.
Railroad it completed, cars arunning on de track.
No mo' work for me here abouts,—
No mo' work for me—here abouts.
It's time for packing up de ol' raggedy gripsack.

Help to build dat railroad, can't afford no riding tag.
Money talks, but my bits aint bits enough to wag.
Walkin' 'long side de track—hungry, wantin' to eat.
Dog dead tired—Shoes wore out—Dog dead tired—
Shoes wore out and Lawd, burnin' blisters on my feet.

"Sistern an' Brethren"

Sistern and brethren, Stop foolin' wid pray. Sistern an' brethren
Stop foolin' wid pray. When black face is lifted, Lord turnin' way.

Heart filled wid sadness, Head bowed down wid woe. Heart filled wid sadness,
Head bowed down wid woe. In his hour of trouble Where's a black man to go?

We's buryin' a brudder De kill fo' de crime. We's buryin' a brudder
Dey kill fo' de crime. Tryin' to keep what was his al de time.

When we's tucked him on under, What you goin' to do? When we's tucked him on under
What you goin' to do? Wait till it come dey's arousin' fo' you?

Yo' head tain' no apple Fo danglin' from a tree, Yo'
head tain' no apple Fo danglin' from a tree, Yo'

Stand on yo' feet,—	Club gripped 'tween yo' hands.
Stand on yo' feet,—	Club gripped 'tween yo' hands.
Spill dere blood too, Show em	yo's a man's

"Scottsboro"

Paper—come out—Done strewed de news
Seven—po' chillun, Moan deat' house blues.
Seven—po' chillun moanin' deat' house blues.
Seven nappy head wit' big shiny eye
All boun' in jail and framed to die
All boun' in jail and framed to die.

Messin'—white woman Snakely—in' tale,
hang an' burn And jail wi' no bail
Dat hang an' burn—and—jail wit' no bail
Worse ol' crime in white folks lan'
Black skin coverin' po' workin' man
Black skin coverin' po' workin' man.

Judge—an jury All in—de stan'
Lawd, biggety name Fo' same lynchin' band.
White folks and Darkie in great Co't house
Like cat down cellar wit nohole mouse,
Like cat down cellar wit' nohole mouse.
Paper—come out, Done strewed de news.
Seven po' chillun Moan deat' house blues.
Seven—po' chillun moanin' deat' house blues—

"Lets Go to the Buryin'"

Come on,—come on,—let's go to de buryin'
Come on,—come on,—let's go to de buryin'
Come on,—come on,—let's go to de buryin'
Wayover in de new buryin' groun.'

Heah a mighty rumblin', let's go to de buryin'
Heah a mighty rumblin', let's go to de buryin'
Heah a mighty rumblin', let's go to de buryin'
Wayover in de new buryin' groun'

Cap'n kill my buddy, let's go to de buryin'
Cap'n kill my buddy, let's go to de buryin'
Cap'n kill my buddy, let's go to de buryin'
Wayover in de new buryin' groun.'

Song texts from *Negro Songs of Protest* (Lawrence Gellert and Elie Siegmeister)
as the songs appeared in the program for *How Long Brethren?* produced by
the Federal Dance Project at the Nora Bayes Theatre, New York, May 1937.

N O T E S

One. The Dance Is a Weapon

1   Harvey Klehr, *The Heyday of American Communism: The Depression Decade* (New York: Basic Books, 1984), pp. 33–34.

2   Ibid., p. 53.

3   Ibid., pp. 73–74.

4   *Daily Worker,* April 29, 1930.

5   Throughout, "working class" is used to refer to "all those whose primary means of making a living is through the sale of their labor power for wages or salaries and who, as a consequence, exert little or no control over the institutions in which they work." Bruce McConachie and Daniel Friedman, eds., *Theatre for Working-Class Audiences in the United States, 1830–1980* (Westport, Conn.: Greenwood Press, 1985), p. 4.

6   *Daily Worker,* April 27, 1932.

7   Stacey Prickett in "Dance and the Workers' Struggle" and the *Daily Worker* cite the 1932 date, but an editorial in *New Theatre* placed the date early in 1933. Prickett, *Dance Research* 8, no. 1 (Spring 1990): 52; *Daily Worker,* June 8, 1935; *New Theatre,* September–October 1933, p. 20.

8   "From Our Correspondence," *New Theatre,* September–October 1933 (unsigned), 23.

9   Grace Wylie, "A Reply from the New Dance Group," ibid., p. 22.

10 Michael Gold, "Change the World," *Daily Worker,* June 14, 1934.

11 Edna Ocko, "Reply to Michael Gold," *New Theatre,* July–August 1934, p. 28. Also Ezra Freeman, "Dance: Which Technique?" *New Theatre,* May 1934, pp. 17–18.

12 Douglas McDermott, "The Workers' Laboratory Theatre," in McConachie and Friedman, eds., *Theatre for Working-Class Audiences,* p. 124. Significantly, *Workers Theatre* changed its name to *New Theatre* around this time (September 1933).

13 John Martin, "The Dance: The Far East," *New York Times,* October 15, 1933.

14 John Martin, "Success Scored by Dance League," *New York Times,* November 26, 1934, p. 12.

15 John Martin, "Workers League in Group Dances," *New York Times,* December 24, 1934.

16 John Martin, "The Dance: To the NDL," *New York Times,* June 16, 1935, p. 4.

17 Edna Ocko, "The Revolutionary Dance Movement," *New Masses,* June 12, 1934, pp. 27–28.

18   Lincoln Kirstein, "Revolutionary Ballet Forms," *New Theatre,* October 1934, p. 14.

19   I have used the descriptive terms radical and revolutionary interchangeably.

20   See Stacey Prickett, "The People: Issues of Identity Within Revolutionary Dance," in *Of, By and For the People: Dancing on the Left in the 1930s,* ed. Lynn Garafola, *Studies in Dance History* 5, no. 1 (Spring 1994): 14. Prickett's dissertation, "Marxism, Modernism and Realism: Politics and Aesthetics in the Rise of Modern Dance," Laban Centre for Movement and Dance, London, 1992, locates the primary differences between revolutionary dance and the emerging modern dance in tensions between modernist tenets of art and Marxist realist aesthetics. Although both Prickett and I deal in detail with the same period in American dance, Prickett's research formally analyzes the Marxist aesthetics embedded in revolutionary dance, while my research is primarily concerned with how the dances provided a stage for negotiating tensions in American culture surrounding issues of Americanization.

21   Quoted in Klehr, *Heyday of American Communism,* p. 222.

22   Cultural historian Warren I. Susman points to the pervasiveness of the image of the "people" during this decade. See his *Culture as History: The Transformation of American Society in the Twentieth Century* (New York: Pantheon Books), 1984, p. 172.

23   But as Susan Manning points out in "American Document and American Minstrelsy," Graham staged the white body as the universally American body, a convention common to many choreographers of the 1930s. Manning, *Moving Words: Rewriting Dance,* ed. Gay Morris (London: Routledge, 1996), pp. 183–202.

24   Paul Veyne, *Writing History* (Middletown, Conn.: Wesleyan University Press, 1984 [1971]), p. 13.

25   See *Of, By and For the People.* Also see Mark Franco, *Dancing Modernism, Performing Politics* (Bloomington: Indiana University Press, 1995).

26   In *Benton, Pollock and the Politics of Modernism: From Regionalism to Abstract Expressionism,* Erica Doss argues that modern art was seen as a symbol of individualism within the noncommunist world during the cold war (Chicago: University of Chicago Press, 1991), pp. 370–372.

27   See Nancy Lee Ruyter, *Reformers and Visionaries: The Americanization of the Art of Dance* (New York: Dance Horizons, 1979), for an analysis of Delsarte's role in the development of American modern dance.

28   For an analysis of Duncan's use of the expressive body, see Ann Daly, *Done Into Dance: Isadora Duncan in America* (Bloomington: Indiana University Press, 1995), pp. 118–154.

29   Isadora Duncan, *The Art of the Dance,* ed. Sheldon Cheney (New York: Theatre Arts Books, 1969 [1928]), p. 54.

30   Suzanne Shelton. *Divine Dancer: A Biography of Ruth St. Denis* (New York: Doubleday, 1981), pp. 126–128. See also Jane Sherman, *The Drama of Denishawn Dance* (Middletown, Conn.: Wesleyan University Press, 1979).

31   Daly, *Done Into Dance,* p. 111.

32   See Linda J. Tomko's "The Settlement House and the Playhouse: Cultivating Expressive Dance in Early Twentieth Century New York" for a discussion of the role of the settlement house in the development of modern dance in the United States, in *Conference Papers,* 5th Hong Kong International Dance Conference (July 15–18, 1990), vol. 2, p. 277. Also Melanie Blood, "The Neighborhood Playhouse, 1915–1927," Ph.D. diss., Northwestern University, 1994.

33 "Tamiris in Her Own Voice: Draft of an Autobiography," *Studies in Dance History* 1, no. 1 (Fall/Winter 1989–90): 7.

34 Nancy Woloch, "The Founding of Hull House," in her *Women and the American Experience* (New York: Knopf, 1984), pp. 253–268.

35 Festivals staged at places like the Henry Street Settlement House also helped ease tensions between the Americanized immigrant children and their more traditional parents, while productions such as *Salut Au Monde* (1922) at the Neighborhood Playhouse promoted an expansive vision of American society and its distinctive nationalities. See Blood, "The Neighborhood Playhouse," pp. 156, 137.

36 See John Higham, *Strangers in the Land: Patterns of American Nativism, 1860–1925* (New Brunswick, N.J.: Rutgers University Press, 1955).

37 Doris Humphrey, *Doris Humphrey: An Artist First*, ed. and completed by Selma Jeanne Cohen (Middletown, Conn.: Wesleyan University Press, 1977), p. 62.

38 Don McDonagh, "Conversation with Gertrude Shurr," *Ballet Review* 4, no. 5 (1973): 19.

39 Thanks to Susan Manning for drawing my attention to this theme, which required explication.

40 See Paul Mishler's "The Littlest Proletariat: American Communists and Their Children, 1922–1950" for a discussion of the role of the Communist Party in children's cultural programs; Mishler also deals with the tensions between support of Americanization as a way to spread Communist values and support of ethnic identity among immigrants, particularly immigrant children. Ph.D. diss., Boston University, 1988, pp. 20–24.

41 For a discussion of the comradely union featured in so much New Deal art, see Barbara Melosh, *Engendering Culture: Manhood and Womanhood in New Deal Public Art and Theatre* (Washington, D.C.: Smithsonian Institution Press, 1991), pp. 1–3.

42 For a discussion of Duncan's use of the dancing body as "a site of cultural debate," see Daly, *Done Into Dance*, p. 220.

43 Ruth Allerhand, "The Lay Dance," *New Theatre*, April 1935, p. 26.

44 Elizabeth Gurley Flynn, quoted in Martin Green, *New York 1913: The Armory Show and the Paterson Strike Pageant* (New York: Collier Books, 1988), p. 6. Green argues that politics and art may be viewed as spiritual projects, a perspective that helps to explain the passion with which this group of New York City dancers embraced modern dance and the great social experiment.

45 Marie Marchowsky, interview with Laura Caplan, January–February 1979, Dance Collection, New York Public Library for the Performing Arts.

46 Jane Dudley was one revolutionary dancer who was inspired by William Gropper's cartoons for the *New Masses*. See my interview with Dudley, New York City, January 7, 1992.

Two. Proletarian Steps: Workers Dancing

1 "The Internationale."

2 "Lenin Memorial Program Ready," *Daily Worker*, January 14, 1928.

3 Moissaye Olgin, "M. Olgin Describes Lenin Pageant," *Daily Worker*, January 26, 1928.

4 Unless otherwise noted, information about Edith Segal and her choreography is compiled from interviews with Bea Lemisch, Oral History of the American Left,

Tamiment Library; Lesley Farlow, Dance Collection, New York Public Library for the Performing Arts; and mine, December 9, 1991.

5   In this regard, transformation through action is the core of ritual. In ritual, action and belief are fused; thus, to perform the action is to incorporate the belief, a procedure that cannot be done falsely. See Roy A. Rappaport, "The Obvious Aspects of Ritual," in *Ecology, Meaning, and Religion* (San Francisco: North Atlantic Books, 1979), p. 192. For an exploration of the role of ritual in performance, see Richard Schechner, *Between Theatre and Anthropology* (Philadelphia: University of Pennsylvania Press, 1985).

6   Segal interview with Bea Lemisch, Camp Midland Collection, Oral History of the American Left, Tamiment Library.

7   Olgin, "M. Olgin Describes Lenin Pageant."

8   Segal, interview with Farlow, p. 25.

9   Ibid.

10 See Mishler, "The Littlest Proletariat," for an examination of Party practices with youth organizations.

11 "Comrade" seems to have been used as a sympathetic term without regard to the recipient's gender, perhaps because the issue of class superseded all else. In Olgin's description, the figures draped in red and Segal as the Spirit of Lenin also seem curiously unsexed.

12 Olgin, "M. Olgin Describes Lenin Pageant."

13 Ibid.

14 As the published program, *Daily Worker,* January 22, 1930.

15 Segal, interview with Farlow, p. 56. Photograph from the collection of Edith Segal.

16 As advertised in the *Daily Worker,* January 27, 1928. See also Jay Williams, *Stage Left* (New York: Charles Scribner's Sons, 1974), p. 22.

17 *Daily Worker,* March 12, 1929.

18 Quoted in Segal, interview with Lemisch.

19 See David Glassberg, *American Historical Pageantry: The Uses of Tradition in the Early Twentieth Century* (Chapel Hill: University of North Carolina Press, 1990), p. 284. Glassberg's book is a fascinating study of the civic pageantry craze that peaked in the early twentieth century.

20 Ibid., pp. 178–180.

21 Linda Nochlin, "The Paterson Strike Pageant of 1913," in McConachie and Friedman, eds., *Theatre for Working-Class Audiences,* p. 91. See also Martin Green's *New York 1913* for an account of the artistic and political radicalism that shaped the event.

22 Frantisek Deak, "Russian Mass Spectacles," *Drama Review* 19, no. 2 (June 1975): 18. Not surprisingly, American civic pageantry and mass spectacle had a common ancestor: the revival of pageantry in England in the late nineteenth century.

23 Huntley Carter, quoted in ibid., p. 18.

24 Announcement in *Daily Worker,* February 20, 1928.

25 Announcement in *Daily Worker,* April 18, 1931.

26 Articles about this event appeared in *Daily Worker,* March 9, 27, and 31, 1928.

27 Announcements in *Daily Worker,* October 15 and 18, 1928, November 2, 1928. The event was scheduled for November 4, 1928, and a review was published November 5.

28 Announcement in *Daily Worker,* November 3, 1930. The event was scheduled to take place November 7, 1930.

29 Announcement in *Daily Worker*, November 11, 1930. The event was scheduled to take place November 22, 1930.

30 Announcement in *Daily Worker*, April 21, 1928. The event was scheduled for May 1, 1928.

31 From reports in *Daily Worker*, October 18, November 5, 1928.

32 Olgin, "M. Olgin Describes Lenin Pageant."

33 See Daniel Friedman's "The Workers' Theatre Movement" for a description of acting styles in workers' theater, in McConachie and Friedman, eds., *Theatre for Working-Class Audiences*, pp. 111–120.

34 This slogan appears on the souvenir program of the first annual recital of the New Dance Group. Clippings, Dance Collection, New York Public Library for the Performing Arts.

35 Advertisement in *Daily Worker*, February 21, 1930.

36 Advertisement in *Daily Worker*, March 6, 1930. The program was scheduled for March 8, 1930.

37 Advertisement in *Daily Worker*, March 14, 1930. The Red Dancers may have been in existence as early as 1928. See Stacey Prickett, "From Workers' Dance to New Dance," *Dance Research* 2, no. 1 (Spring 1989): 47.

38 Advertisement in *Daily Worker*, March 15, 1930.

39 Segal, interview with Farlow, p. 30.

40 Program notes from First Workers Dance Spartakiade, presented by the Workers Dance League, June 4, 1933. Dance Collection, New York Public Library for the Performing Arts.

41 *Daily Worker*, January 22, 1930.

42 *Daily Worker*, April 28, 1930.

43 *Daily Worker*, March 7, 1929.

44 Program copy, Edith Segal Archives.

45 The anniversary at the Manhattan Lyceum of the Gastonia strike was announced in the *Daily Worker*, March 31, 1930, and held on April 1.

46 *Daily Worker*, April 1, 1930.

47 Edna Ocko remembered that this slogan was used with the dance. See my interview with Ocko, June 14, 1989.

48 Ibid.

49 Segal, interview with Farlow, p. 145.

50 Quoted in *New Theatre*, October 1934, p. 3.

51 Sometimes spelled Ad Bates.

52 Segal, interview with Farlow, p. 60.

53 Segal, interview with Lemisch.

54 See Klehr, *Heyday of American Communism*, p. 227.

55 Ann Burlak, "Dance Notes," *New Theatre*, November 1934.

56 Segal's name appears as director of each of these groups in the program notes of the First Workers Dance Spartakiade, June 4, 1933.

57 Segal, interview with Lemisch.

58 See Mishler, "The Littlest Proletariat," pp. 128–168, for a discussion of radical summer camps.

59 "Dance Group in a Trade Union," *New Theatre*, January 1934.

60 Ibid.

61   Jane Dudley, "The Mass Dance," *New Theatre*, December 1934.

62   Ibid.

63   Dudley, my interview, January 5, 1992.

64   Dudley, "The Mass Dance."

65   Segal, my interview.

66   Segal, "Directing the New Dance," *New Theatre*, May 1935, p. 22.

67   Ruth Allerhand, "The Lay Dance," *New Theatre*, April 1935, p. 26.

68   Edith Segal Archives.

69   Segal, interview with Farlow, p. 65.

70   The title for this dance appears as either *Kinde, Kiche, and Kirche* or *Kinder, Kuche, and Kirche,* the first obviously containing typographical errors.

71   Two organizations grouped under the rubric of the Workers Dance League did escape this aesthetic critique: the New Dance Group and the Theatre Union. See chapter 3, below.

72   Edna Ocko, "The Dance League Recital," *New Theatre*, February 1935, p. 25.

73   I am grateful to Deborah Jowitt for pointing this out.

74   See George Szanto, "Three Theatres of Propaganda," for an analysis of different theaters of propaganda. In Szanto, *Theatre and Propaganda* (Austin: University of Texas Press, 1978).

75   Segal, interview with Farlow, p. 76.

76   According to Pavel Kerjensev, theorist of the agitprop theater in the Soviet Union: "the objective of the proletarian theatre is not to form good professional artists capable of performing in the pieces of the socialist repertory, but to permit the large masses to express their artistic instincts." Quoted in Hassan Tehranchian, "Agit-Prop Theatre: Germany and the Soviet Union," Ph.D. diss., New York University, 1982, p. 182.

77   This change in name was part of an attempt to broaden its influence. For further details, see chapter 5, below.

78   Mishler, "The Littlest Proletariat," p. 144.

79   Bob Heisler and Judee Rosenbaum, "Interview with Edith Segal," Kinderland Reunion Journal, Vertical Files, Tamiment Library.

80   "Volunteer Dancers, Singers, Actors Asked for May Day Pageant," *Daily Worker,* April 4, 1936.

81   *Daily Worker,* May 3, 1936.

82   Program notes, May Day Celebration, Vertical Files, Tamiment Library.

83   See Barbara Stratyner, " 'Significant Historical Events . . . Thrilling Dance Sequences': Communist Party Pageants in New York, 1937," for an account of events in 1937. *Of, By and For the People*, pp. 31–37.

84   Ibid.

85   *Daily Worker,* November 15, 1937.

86   Larry Warren, *Anna Sokolow: The Rebellious Spirit* (Princeton, N.J.: Dance Horizons, 1991), p. 305. Sokolow's group, however, probably did not contain any amateur dancers, as discussed in chapter 3, below.

87   Segal, interview with Farlow, p. 98.

88   *Be My Friend and other poems for boys and girls* (New York: Citadel Press, 1952), p. 11.

Three. Dancing Red

1   Jane Dudley, interview with Richard Wormser, p. 2, Oral History of the American Left, Tamiment Library.

2   For a discussion of the role of modernism in the new dance, see Deborah Jowitt, "The Created Self," in her *Time and the Dancing Image* (New York: William Morrow, 1988), pp. 151–177.

3   "A Letter to Blanche Evan: From the Workers Dance League," *New Theatre,* June 1934.

4   "New School Series. Nadia Chilkovsky of the Workers' Dance League." *Dance Observer,* August–September 1934, p. 68.

5   See Ann Betts, "An Historical Study of the New Dance Group of New York City." Master's thesis, New York University, 1945.

6   "A Letter to Blanche Evan: From the Workers Dance League," *New Theatre,* June 1934.

7   Nell Anyon, "The Tasks of the Revolutionary Dance," *New Theatre,* September–October 1933. Nell Anyon was a pseudonym used by dancer Nadia Chilkovsky.

8   Leonard Dal Negro, quoted in Warren, *Anna Sokolow,* p. 47. This dance was probably first performed as *Anti-War Trilogy* in a concert sponsored by the American League Against War and Fascism at St. Nicholas Arena in New York City. Warren, *Anna Sokolow,* pp. 299–300.

9   Ezra Freeman, "What to Dance About," *New Theatre,* March 1934.

10 Ibid.

11 Ralph Taylor, "Workers Dance League," *Dance Observer,* February 1935, p. 8.

12 Martin, "Workers League in Group Dances," *New York Times,* December 24, 1934.

13 "The Dance League Recital," *New Theatre,* February 1935.

14 The Wigman school opened in New York City in 1931 under the direction of Hanya Holm; in 1936 it officially became known as the Holm School.

15 Jane Dudley, my interview, January 7, 1992.

16 See "Reviewing on the Left: The Dance Criticism of Edna Ocko," selected and introduced by Stacey Prickett, for a lively collection of Ocko's reviews, *Of, By and For the People,* pp. 65–103.

17 "The Dance: The New Dance Group," *New Theatre,* March 1934.

18 Geltman (Del Bourgo), interview with Karen Wickre, December 16, 1977, p. 10, Research Center for the Federal Theatre Project, George Mason University.

19 Program for the First Workers Dance Spartakiade, June 4, 1933, Dance Collection, New York Public Library for the Performing Arts.

20 Dudley, my interview; Betts, "The New Dance Group," pp. 9–10.

21 First Workers Dance Spartakiade program, June 4, 1933.

22 "Workers Dance League," *New Theatre,* January 1934.

23 Dudley, interview with Wormser, p. 4.

24 Grace Wylie, "A Reply from the New Dance Group," *New Theatre,* September–October 1933.

25 "The Dance: The New Dance Group," *New Theatre,* March 1934.

26 Ibid.

27 For an account of the controversies surrounding the establishment of a national dance in the United States, see Susan Manning, *Ecstasy and the Demon: Feminism and Nationalism in the Dances of Mary Wigman* (Berkeley: University of California Press, 1993), pp. 255–285.

28   Edna Ocko, "New Dance Group," *New Theatre,* November 1934.

29   Douglas McDermott, "The Workers' Laboratory Theatre: Archetype and Example," in McConachie and Friedman, eds., *Theatre for Working-Class Audiences,* pp. 124–126.

30   New Dance Group First Annual Recital, Souvenir Program, Dance Collection, New York Public Library for the Performing Arts.

31   This was usually the case, although in the first Spartakiade, sponsored by the Workers Dance League in June 1933, directors' credits did appear beside three New Dance Group entries: *Awake* by Miriam Blecher, *Strike* by Grace Wylie, and *Charity* by dancer Edith Langbert.

32   "Dance Notes," *New Theatre,* November 1934.

33   *Daily Worker,* March 25, 1933.

34   Dudley, my interview.

35   Wylie, "A Reply from the New Dance Group," *New Theatre,* September–October 1933.

36   Wylie, "Dance Convention," *New Theatre,* July–August 1934.

37   Horst, "Workers Dance League," *Dance Observer,* March 1935.

38   Oakley Johnson, "The Dance," *New Theatre,* February 1934, p. 17.

39   Dudley, my interview.

40   Paul Love, "Workers Dance League," *Dance Observer,* May 1934, p. 43.

41   Edna Ocko, "The Revolutionary Dance Movement," *New Masses,* June 12, 1934.

42   For a detailed exploration of Marxist aesthetics as manifested in American modern dance, see Prickett, "Marxism, Modernism and Realism."

43   Ocko, my interview, June 14, 1989.

44   Blecher's family came from Austria-Hungary, however, and not from Russia.

45   Interview with Miriam Blecher. Courtesy of Daniel and Zachery Sklar.

46   Ellen Graff, interview with Zachery Sklar, May 16, 1996.

47   Ocko, my interview.

48   Mary Jo Shelley, "Workers Dance League," *Dance Observer,* January 1935.

49   Edna Ocko, "The Dance League Recital," *New Theatre,* February 1935.

50   Ocko, my interview.

51   "The Dance: Prize Winner," *New York Times,* July 1, 1934.

52   Ibid.

53   Dudley, interview with Wormser.

54   Eisler was admired by members of the Composers Collective, a revolutionary musical group that used his music as a model for the political songs they hoped to compose for American workers. See David King Dunaway, "Unsung Songs of Protest: The Composers Collective of New York," *New York Folklore* 5, nos. 1–2 (Summer 1979): 1–19. In chapter 6 I trace the history of the collective.

55   Dudley, my interview.

56   Steve Foster, "The Revolutionary Solo Dance," *New Theatre,* January 1935, p. 23.

57   Henry Gilfond, "Workers Dance League," *Dance Observer,* January 1935.

58   Ocko, my interview.

59   Ibid.

60   *Daily Worker,* March 25, 1933.

61   "New Dance Group," *Dance Observer,* February 1937, p. 18.

62   Dudley was influenced by Stanislavsky's work, which is examined later in this chapter.

63   In chapter 5 I deal with the transformation of the Workers Dance League into the American Dance League.

64   Si-lan Chen was married to radical filmmaker Jay Leyda.

65   "Choreographics," *Dance Observer*, April 1938, p. 58.

66   "New Dance Group," *Dance Observer*, March 1940, p. 38.

67   In 1942 the activities of the New Dance Group received a considerable boost when Maslow, Dudley, and William Bales formed a trio that proved both popular and successful.

68   See Warren, *Anna Sokolow*, p. 43. Warren's excellent biography provides extensive background on Sokolow's work with the Theatre Union, while an appendix documents her work, beginning with a student performance at the Neighborhood Playhouse in 1931.

69   Mark Wolf Weisstuch, "The Theatre Union, 1934–1937: A History," Ph.D. diss., City University of New York, 1982.

70   Warren, *Anna Sokolow*, pp. 43–45.

71   "Meet the Theatre Union," *New Theatre*, February 1934.

72   Millicent Green, quoted in ibid.

73   John Martin, "The Dance: Prize Winner," *New York Times*, July 1, 1934.

74   This was not Sokolow's only experiment with text and movement, although it is probably her best-known work from the mid-1930s. *Forces in Opposition* (1934) was based on a poem by the Russian Sergei Essenin; *Excerpts from a War Poem* (1937) included the words of Italian poet F. T. Marinetti; *The Exiles* (1939) was danced to the words of Sol Funaroff's poem by the same name.

75   Mike Gold, "Change the World," *Daily Worker*, June 5, 1934.

76   Muriel Rukeyser, "The Dance Festival," *New Theatre*, July 1935.

77   Gold, "Change the World."

78   Carl Sands, "Workers Audience Applauds Gold's Poem Set to Music," *Daily Worker*, June 26, 1934.

79   Ibid.

80   My impressions are gathered from a New Music recording (San Francisco) of *The Strange Funeral in Braddock*, performed by Elie Siegmeister and Mordecai Bauman around 1936 (Music Division, New York Public Library for the Performing Arts). Simon Rady, a frequent collaborator with the revolutionary dancers, who married Lily Mehlman, sang the text at the 1935 performance for the benefit of the International Labor Defense at Carnegie Hall. It is not clear whether he vocally accompanied the dance at other times. *Dance Observer*, January 1936, p. 6.

81   Martin, "New Dance League Holds 3d Festival," *New York Times*, June 10, 1935.

82   Quoted in Warren, *Anna Sokolow*, p. 70.

83   Anna Sokolow, interview with Barbara Newman, February 19/4, May 1975, Dance Collection, New York Public Library for the Performing Arts.

84   Warren, *Anna Sokolow*, pp. 9–10.

85   See William Stott for an analysis of documentary techniques and their importance during the 1930s in social science research. *Documentary Expression and Thirties America* (Chicago: University of Chicago Press, 1986 [1973]).

86   Warren, *Anna Sokolow*, p. 20.

87   Ruth Ann Heisey, "Anna Sokolow—Interview," in *Dance Observer*, August–September 1937, p. 77.

88   Dal Negro, *New Theatre*, August 1935.

89 See Warren, *Anna Sokolow,* pp. 41–50, for a discussion of Sokolow's early group.

90 See Janet Soares, *Louis Horst: Musician in a Dancer's World* (Durham, N.C.: Duke University Press, 1992), p. 69.

91 Margaret Lloyd, *The Borzoi Book of Modern Dance* (Brooklyn: Dance Horizons, 1974 [1949]), p. 215.

92 Sokolow, interview with Newman, p. 63.

93 Warren, *Anna Sokolow,* p. 71.

94 In describing herself, Sokolow admitted that she always had deep social feelings, but that those feelings had nothing to do with politics. Sokolow's interview with Newman, pp. 51–58.

95 Edith Segal ("Kurt Jooss," *New Theatre,* January 1934) once criticized Jooss's *The Green Table* (1932), because it failed to offer a solution to the problem of fascism and war, only stating the problem.

96 M. A. Chekhov, "Stanislavsky's Method of Acting," as arranged from Chekhov's notes by Molly Day Thatcher, *New Theatre,* December 1934, January 1935.

97 Douglas McDermott, "The Workers' Laboratory Theatre: Archetype and Example," in McConachie and Friedman, eds., *Theatre for Working-Class Audiences in the United States,* pp. 124–125.

98 *New Theatre* editorial, September–October, 1933.

99 According to McDermott, "The Workers' Laboratory Theatre," Group Theatre members such as Morris Carnovsky and Elia Kazan also worked with the Workers Laboratory Theatre.

100 "Meet the Theatre Union," *New Theatre,* February 1934.

101 Weisstuch, "The Theatre Union," pp. 178–186.

102 Harold Clurman, *The Fervent Years: The Group Theatre and the 30s* (New York: Da Capo, 1983 [1941]), p. 130.

103 Weisstuch, "The Theatre Union," pp. 178–186.

104 Warren, *Anna Sokolow,* pp. 51–60.

105 *Martha Graham: The Early Years,* ed. Merle Armitage (New York: Da Capo, 1978 [1937]), p. 97.

106 Valentina Litvinoff, "The Use of Stanislavsky for the Teacher of Modern Dance," *Dance Scope,* Fall–Winter 1971–1972.

107 Dudley, my interview.

108 Nell Anyon, "The Tasks of the Revolutionary Dance," *New Theatre Magazine,* September–October 1933. Here, the reference was pointedly to Humphrey's *Life of the Bee.* While the activity of the dance's beehive represents human social activity, this metaphor apparently was not literal enough to suit the radical press. See Marica B. Siegel's description of the dance in *Days on Earth: The Dance of Doris Humphrey* (New Haven, Conn.: Yale University Press, 1987, pp. 77–80.

Four. How Long, Brethren? Dancers Working

1 Robert S. McElvaine, *The Great Depression* (New York: Times Books, 1984), p. 271.

2 Hallie Flanagan, *Arena: The Story of the Federal Theatre* (New York: Limelight Edition, 1985 [1940]), pp. 333–373. Unless otherwise noted, references to the history of the Federal Theatre Project are drawn from this text.

3 *Dance Observer,* February 1936, p. 14.

4   Helen Tamiris, "Tamiris in Her Own Voice: Draft of an Autobiography," *Studies in Dance History* 1, no. 1 (Fall-Winter 1989): pp. 4–5.

5   Christena Schlundt, "Tamiris: A Chronicle of Her Dance Career, 1927–1955," *Studies in Dance History* 1, no. 1 (Fall-Winter, 1989): 74.

6   Mary F. Watkins, "Concert Dancers Unite in Battle-Array to Combat Lions in the Pathway of the Sunday Recital," *New York Herald Tribune,* March 16, 1930.

7   Schlundt, "Tamiris," p. 99.

8   *Dance Observer,* February 1936, p. 14.

9   The CWA was an early federal attempt at providing relief that had been dismantled by this time, according to Flanagan, *Arena,* p. 16.

10   I believe this reference is to the state school where such dancers as Susanne Remos and Paula Bass received their training. Initially, training was free, but later a fee of 10¢ per class was instituted. *New Theatre,* August 1935, p. 25.

11   "Dancers Union," *New Theatre,* January 1935, p. 29.

12   On December 20, 1934.

13   *New Theatre,* January 1935.

14   Nell Anyon, "The New Dance League," *New Theatre,* April 1935, p. 28.

15   Constitution of the Dancers Association, 1936, Clippings, Dance Collection, New York Public Library for the Performing Arts.

16   John Martin, "The Dance: Organization," *New York Times,* February 9, 1936.

17   "Dance Front," *New Theatre,* December 1935, p. 32.

18   Western Union telegram, January 14, 1936, Library of Congress Federal Theatre Project Collection.

19   Hallie Flanagan, Record of Appointments, January 29, 1936, Library of Congress Federal Theatre Project Collection.

20   WPA Sample Statement for Public Announcement, n.d., Library of Congress Federal Theatre Project Collection.

21   Schlundt, "Tamiris," p. 100.

22   Grant Code, "Dance Theatre of the WPA," *Dance Observer,* October 1939.

23   Flanagan, *Arena,* pp. 55–59.

24   I believe this is the Unemployed Section, also called the Unemployed Group, of the Dancers Association, which lobbied for including all unemployed dancers in the project. Unemployed Councils were part of a nationwide movement organized by the Communist Party. See Klehr, *Heyday of American Communism,* pp. 49–68.

25   Susanne Remos (Nadel), interview with Karen Wickre, October 23, 1977, p. 17, Library of Congress Research Center for the Federal Theatre Project, Oral History Program.

26   Mura Dehn, interview with Karen Wickre, April 20, 1978, p. 11, Library of Congress Research Center for the Federal Theatre Project, Oral History Program.

27   Anne Lief (Barlin), interview with Karen Wickre, October 25, 1977, p. 4, Library of Congress Research Center for the Federal Theatre Project, Oral History Program.

28   Fanya Geltman, a dancer in the Federal Dance Project, was extremely active in organizing the dancers.

29   Lili Mann (Laub), interview with Karen Wickre, May 24, 1978, p. 9, Library of Congress Research Center for the Federal Theatre Project, Oral History Program.

30   Fanya Geltman (Del Bourgo), interview with Karen Wickre, December 16, 1977, p. 2, Library of Congress Research Center for the Federal Theatre Project, Oral History Program.

31 Flanagan, letter to John Connolly, representative for the Unemployed Section of the Dancers Association, June 17, 1936, Library of Congress Federal Theatre Project Collection.

32 The Dancers Association, letter to Don Oscar Becque, April 20, 1936, Library of Congress Federal Theatre Project Collection.

33 Geltman, "Letters," *Dance Observer,* May 1936, pp. 57–58.

34 Pauline Tish (Bubrick), "Remembering Helen Tamiris," *Dance Chronicle* 17, no. 3 (1994): 343.

35 Code, "Dance Theatre of the WPA."

36 Grant Code Correspondence, Dance Collection, New York Public Library for the Performing Arts.

37 *New Theatre,* September 1935, p. 28, December 1935, p. 32.

38 Fanya Geltman (Del Bourgo), Karen Wickre's videotaped interview with eight dancers from the Federal Theatre Project, UCLA Studio, February 20, 1978, Library of Congress Federal Theatre Project Collection.

39 Lief (Barlin), interview with Karen Wickre, p. 15.

40 Dehn, interview with Karen Wickre, p. 10.

41 Mann (Laub), interview with Karen Wickre, p. 32.

42 Saida Gerrard, interview with Karen Wickre, February 21, 1978, p. 26, Library of Congress Research Center for the Federal Theatre Project, Oral History Program.

43 Remos (Nadel), interview with Karen Wickre, p. 17.

44 "Unemployed Section of the Dancers Association," Library of Congress Federal Theatre Project Collection.

45 Correspondence, Don Oscar Becque to Hallie Flanagan, April 22, 1936, Library of Congress Federal Theatre Project Collection.

46 Don Oscar Becque, interdepartmental memo to Mr. Barber, August 11, 1936, Library of Congress Federal Theatre Project Collection.

47 Ibid.

48 Federal Dance Project press release, August 12, 1936, Library of Congress Federal Theatre Project Collection.

49 "Great Victory for the Unemployed of the Dancers Association," Library of Congress Federal Theatre Project Collection.

50 "Minimum Requirements for Admission to the Federal Dance Theatre," Library of Congress Federal Theatre Project Collection.

51 Geltman must have been transferred back to the Dance Theatre sometime later since she appeared in the project's production of Tamiris's *How Long Brethren?* (1937).

52 Bovington had danced with the Workers Dance League, performing with a group called the Theatre Collective Dance Group.

53 Transcript of the September 17, 1936, hearings, Library of Congress Federal Theatre Project Collection.

54 Marion Sellars, "The Dance Project—WPA Stepchild," *New Theatre,* August 1936, p. 24.

55 *Dance Observer,* October 1936, p. 87.

56 Code, "Dance Theatre of the WPA," p. 264.

57 Petition for the removal of Don Oscar Becque, Library of Congress Federal Theatre Project Collection.

58 Becque, letter to Philip Barber, November 12, 1936, Library of Congress Federal Theatre Project Collection.

59   Fuss, letter to Philip Barber, November 16, 1936, Library of Congress Federal Theatre Project Collection.

60   Flanagan, *Arena,* pp. 199–200; Schlundt, "Tamiris," p. 98.

61   Flanagan, *Arena,* p. 327.

62   As quoted in a WPA report defending project guidelines against attacks by the National Dance League, "WPA Dance Director Refutes Charges of Dance League," Library of Congress Federal Theatre Project Collection.

63   Don Oscar Becque, memo to George Hexter (executive officer), October 20, 1936, Library of Congress Federal Theatre Project Collection.

64   Nadia Chilkovsky (Nahumck), interview with Karen Wickre, May 25, 1978, pp. 12–13, Library of Congress Research Center for the Federal Theatre Project, Oral History Program.

65   There is some suggestion that Chilkovsky was fired for her outspokenness, but a letter dated November 6, 1936, acknowledges receipt of a copy of her letter of resignation to Becque. Library of Congress Federal Theatre Project Collection.

66   John Martin, "The Dance: WPA Theatre," *New York Times,* May 16, 1937.

67   Schlundt, "Tamiris," pp. 106–107.

68   December 21, 1937, to January 15, 1938.

69   Schlundt, "Tamiris," pp. 70–71.

70   As listed in the original Federal Theatre program, Library of Congress Federal Theatre Project Collection.

71   Throughout this chapter I use the word Negro, instead of African American or black, because that term prevailed at the time.

72   Tish (Bubrick), "Remembering Helen Tamiris," pp. 347–350.

73   Press release from George Kondolf, New York City director of the Federal Theatre Project before the revival, December 10, 1937, Dance Collection, New York Public Library for the Performing Arts.

74   Production Notes, "How Long Brethren?" Library of Congress Federal Theatre Project Collection.

75   The lyrics that appeared in the program copy of the Federal Dance Project's production substitute the term "darkie" for "Nigger," which was used by Gellert in the published score. *Negro Songs of Protest,* collected by Lawrence Gellert (New York: American Music League, 1936). Clearly, the project was nervous about the insulting word.

76   *How Long Brethren?* was reconstructed by Dianne McIntyre in 1991 as part of the Federal Theatre Festival at George Mason University. Using dancers from the Washington, D.C., area, McIntyre's production featured an integrated cast. Her reconstruction also was restaged at the American Dance Festival in Durham, N.C., 1993 and 1995.

77   When *How Long Brethren?* was revived in December 1937, this oversight was rectified. That program lists all performers.

78   Martin, "The Dance: WPA Theatre."

79   Negro Theatre units were active in Boston, San Francisco, Los Angeles, Philadelphia, Cleveland, Chicago, and Seattle, as well as in New York. Flanagan, *Arena.*

80   Fanya Geltman recalled trying to get Negroes on the project; Add Bates, a Negro dancer who had worked in radical dance in New York City before the project began, was employed in the Dance Unit. Geltman, interview with Karen Wickre, p. 18. Bates was featured in Weidman's *Candide.*

81   John Perpener, "African American Dance and Sociological Positivism During the

1930s," *Of, By, and For the People,* p. 23. In 1996 the Dance Collection, New York Public Library for the Performing Arts, hosted a program called "Classic Black." Many panelists recounted difficulties they had experienced during their training.

82 Cited in "WPA Dance Director Refutes Charges of Dance League," Library of Congress Federal Theatre Project Collection.

83 Edna Ocko, my interview.

84 Dehn, interview with Karen Wickre, p. 8.

85 Marshall Stearns and Jean Stearns, *Jazz Dance: The Story of American Vernacular Dance* (New York: Schirmer Books, 1979 [1964]), p. 322.

86 Add Bates, formerly of Edith Segal's Red Dancers, was an exception.

87 Dehn, interview with Karen Wickre, pp. 6–8.

88 Quoted in Lynne Fauley Emery, *Black Dance: From 1619 to Today* (Princeton, N.J.: Dance Horizons, 1988 [1972]), p. 248.

89 Dehn, interview with Karen Wickre, pp. 5–6.

90 Flanagan, *Arena,* p. 74. See also John Houseman's account in *Run-Through* (New York: Simon and Schuster, 1972), pp. 173–210.

91 Tamiris, "Tamiris in Her Own Voice," pp. 40–41.

92 Stearns and Stearns, *Jazz Dance,* and Emery, *Black Dance,* both describe the characteristics of American minstrelsy in detail. Paul Draper, Fred Astaire, Ray Bolger, and other white tap dancers are more contemporary and more positive examples of the same phenomenon.

93 My impressions of this dance and of *Go Down, Moses* (see below) are taken from the 1959 film *Negro Spirituals,* produced by the William Skipper Corporation with an introduction by John Martin, and from the 1977 *Trailblazers of Modern Dance,* directed by Emile Ardolini for the PBS series, "Dance in America."

94 Tamiris, "Tamiris in Her Own Voice," pp. 40–41.

95 Schlundt ("Tamiris," p. 87) theorizes that Tamiris was unhappy with the esoteric atmosphere created by many of her contemporaries.

96 Martin, "The Dance: WPA Theatre."

97 Martin introducing the film *Negro Spirituals.*

98 Quoted in Schlundt, "Tamiris," p. 105.

99 Lloyd, *Borzoi Book of Modern Dance,* p. 133.

100 Quoted in Maxine Cushing, "The Precious Press," *Dance Observer,* October 1938, p. 117.

101 Tamiris, "Tamiris in Her Own Voice," p. 51.

102 Schlundt, "Tamiris," p. 76.

103 See Deborah Jowitt, "The Veils of Salome," in her *Time and the Dancing Image* (New York: William Morrow, 1988), pp. 105–123.

104 Quoted in Schlundt, "Tamiris," p. 71.

105 *New York World-Telegram,* August 20, 1936.

106 Unidentified press clipping, a gift of Susanne Remos Nadel, Library of Congress Federal Theatre Project Collection.

107 Ibid.

108 "Hundreds Sit-In at WPA Theatre," *New York Post,* May 20, 1937.

109 Ibid.

110 Flanagan, *Arena,* p. 201.

111 Louise Mitchell, "Note to Mr. Hopkins: 'Dancers Don't Think with Their Feet,'" *Daily Worker,* May 21, 1937.

112 Ibid.
113 Publicity release from Philip Barber, director of productions of the Federal Theatre Project in New York City, Helen Tamiris Clipping File, 1935–1939, Dance Collection, New York Public Library for the Performing Arts.
114 Geltman (Del Bourgo), interview with Karen Wickre, p. 4. Although Geltman's remark about sit-ins was well-meant, she was mistaken in her history. The sit-in had been used in earlier labor struggles, both in Europe and the United States, going back to the late nineteenth century.
115 "Hundreds Sit-In at WPA Theatre."
116 Paula Bass (Perlowin), videotaped interview with Karen Wickre, UCLA Studio, February 20, 1978, Library of Congress Research Center for the Federal Theatre Project.
117 John O'Conner and Lorraine Brown, eds., *Free, Adult, Uncensored: The Living History of the Federal Theatre Project* (Washington, D.C.: New Republic Books, 1978), p. 215.
118 See Flanagan, *Arena*, pp. 333–373.
119 Bass (Perlowin), interview with Karen Wickre, p. 27.
120 According to Paula Bass (ibid., p. 26), Tamiris poured the first bowl of soup. Dancer Mura Dehn was one of the waitresses. Dehn, interview with Karen Wickre, p. 14.

Five. Dances for Spain, Dances for America

1 Dane Rudhyar, "Art and Propaganda," *Dance Observer*, December 1936, p. 113.
2 Martha Graham, quoted in Agnes de Mille, *Martha: The Life and Work of Martha Graham* (New York: Random House, 1991), p. 15.
3 Rudhyar, "Art and Propaganda," p. 109.
4 De Mille, *Martha*, p. 81.
5 Although Graham was not considered a political revolutionary earlier in the decade, she had certainly earned a reputation as a radical artist. See Costonis, "Martha Graham's *American Document*: A Minstrel Show in Modern Dance Dress," *American Music* 9, no. 3 (Fall 1991): 299–310. Also see Mark Franko, "Emotivist Movement and Histories of Modernism," in *Dancing Modernism/Performing Politics*, pp. 38–74.
6 "We Visit Martha Graham," *Dynamics*, May 5, 1934. Graham Clippings, vol. 8, Dance Collection, New York Public Library for the Performing Arts.
7 De Mille, *Martha*, pp. 82–83.
8 Ernestine Stodelle, *Deep Song: The Dance of Martha Graham* (New York: Schirmer Books, 1984), p. 79; de Mille, *Martha*, p. 180.
9 De Mille, *Martha*, p. 90.
10 *Heretic*, Fox Movietone News, 1931, Dance Collection, New York Public Library for the Performing Arts.
11 John Martin, *New York Times*, April 15, 1929. Some years later, Henry Gilfond referred to the group as a multiplication of Graham (*Dance Observer*, March 1935, p. 30).
12 Agnes de Mille, interview with Clare Saperstein, November 27, 1991.
13 De Mille, speaking at the 1992 de la Torre Bueno Prize, Dance Perspectives Foundation, June 1, 1992, Bruno Walter Auditorium, New York Public Library for the Performing Arts.
14 Blanche Evan, "A Dancer's Notebook," *New Theatre*, April 1936, p. 31.
15 As advertised in *Dance Observer*, Summer 1935.
16 Edna Ocko, "Whither Martha Graham?" *New Theatre*, April 1934, p. 8.

17   Edna Ocko, "Martha Graham Dances in Two Worlds," *New Theatre,* July 1935.
18   Edna Ocko, my interview, June 14, 1989.
19   Ocko, "Whither Martha Graham?"
20   Edna Ocko, "Dance Reviews," *New Theatre,* December 1934, p. 28.
21   Marchowsky, interview with Laura Caplan, p. 10. Also Martha Graham, "Affirmations," in Merle Armitage, *Martha Graham: The Early Years* (New York: Da Capo Press, 1978 [1937]), p. 97.
22   Deborah Jowitt, *Time and the Dancing Image* (New York: William Morrow, 1988), pp. 171–172.
23   Ocko, "Dance Reviews."
24   Ocko, "Martha Graham Dances in Two Worlds."
25   Ibid.
26   Mignon Verne, "Observer or Partisan," *New Theatre,* November 1934, pp. 20–21.
27   Henry Gilfond, "Martha Graham and Dance Group," *Dance Observer,* March 1935 and January 1936.
28   Henry Gilfond, "Workers Dance League," *Dance Observer,* December 1934, p. 89.
29   Henry Gilfond, "Let Us Have Critics," *Dance Observer,* October–November 1934, p. 78.
30   Editorial, *Dance Observer,* January 1935.
31   Henry Gilfond, "Redder than the Rose," *New Theatre,* September 1935.
32   See Janet Soares, *Louis Horst: Musician in a Dancer's World* (Durham, N.C.: Duke University Press, 1992), p. 114.
33   Nell Anyon, "The New Dance League," *New Theatre,* April 1935.
34   Quoted in Henry Gilfond, "New Dance League," *Dance Observer,* May 1935.
35   Dance Guild flyer, Dance Collection, New York Public Library for the Performing Arts.
36   Eve Stebbins (Edna Ocko), "The Dance in America," *Dance Observer,* May 1936.
37   Lincoln Kirstein, "Revolutionary Ballet Forms," *New Theatre,* October 1934.
38   Editorial, *Dance Observer,* October 1937.
39   Henry Gilfond, "ILD Concert," *Dance Observer,* January 1936.
40   John Martin, "The Dance: To The NDL," *New York Times,* June 16, 1935.
41   Graham appeared on at least one other "revolutionary" program at this time, a New Year's Eve international celebration under the auspices of the Workers' Training School on December 31, 1935, at the Venice Theatre.
42   *Encyclopedia of the American Left,* ed. Mari Jo Buhle, Paul Buhle, and Dan Georgakas (Urbana: University of Illinois Press, 1992), pp. 146–158.
43   Klehr, *Heyday of American Communism,* p. 354.
44   Conversation with Lloyd Morgan, June 4, 1996, Dobbs Ferry, New York.
45   According to *Dance Observer* (January 1937), Graham was scheduled to speak before the Artists Congress in February 1937.
46   Nicholas Wirth, "Mary Wigman, Fascist," *New Theatre,* August 1935.
47   Advertisement in *Dance Observer,* April 1935.
48   Virginia Stewart and Merle Armitage, *Modern Dance* (New York: Dance Horizons, 1970 [1935]).
49   Virginia Stewart, "German Letter," *Dance Observer,* October 1935.
50   Ibid.
51   Edna Ocko, "Letters," *Dance Observer,* November 1935.

52   Edna Ocko, "The Swastika Is Dancing," *New Theatre,* November 1935, p. 17.

53   Ibid.

54   "Dance Front," *New Theatre,* December 1935, p. 32.

55   Although Dudley is listed as a member of the Graham company from 1935 on, she turned down Graham's offer to stay with the group after she had appeared as part of the augmented ensemble for *Panorama* at Bennington College during the summer. Not until the premiere of *Chronicle* in late 1936 did she make her official debut with the Graham company. How much contact she had with Graham in the Winter of 1935 and the Spring of 1936 is unclear.

56   Quoted in *Dance Observer,* April 1936, p. 38.

57   See Manning, *Ecstasy and the Demon,* pp. 275–279, for an account of this controversy within the dance world. Manning also provides documentation on the spectacle that Wigman mounted for the Berlin Olympics. Some 10,000 performers took part in this piece of pageantry celebrating the invincibility of the Nazi state before 100,000 spectators. "From Modernism to Fascism," *Ballet Review* 14, no. 4 (1986): p. 94.

58   Henry Gilfond, "Dance Congress and Festival," *Dance Observer,* June–July 1936, p. 61.

59   Henry Gilfond, "Demonstration Groups," ibid., p. 68.

60   Quoted in Edna Ocko, "The Dance Congress," *New Theatre,* July 1936.

61   Ibid.

62   *Dance Observer,* June–July 1936, p. 64.

63   See Barry Fischer, "Graham's Dance Steps in the Street and Selected Early Technique: Principles for Reconstructing Choreography from Video Tape," Ed.D. diss., New York University, 1986.

64   Program notes, Dance Collection, New York Public Library for the Performing Arts.

65   Gilfond, "Martha Graham and Dance Group," *Dance Observer,* April 1937, p. 42.

66   "Martha Graham and Group," *Dance Observer,* January 1937. The Graham company recently reconstructed sections of *Chronicle,* including "Spectre 1914." The manipulations of the soloist's red underskirt indeed suggest rivers of blood. In the final section of *Chronicle,* "Prelude to Action," the solo figure is all in red, and the dance activity clearly suggests a call to action. While the program notes indicate that Graham saw this act of unification as a pledge to the future, the movement is unmistakeably militaristic.

67   Gilfond, "Martha Graham and Dance Group," *Dance Observer,* April 1937.

68   Edna Ocko, "Artist and Audience," *New Theatre,* March 1937, p. 64.

69   My impressions are drawn from the revival of *Steps in the Street,* performed by the Martha Graham Dance Company at City Center in 1989, reconstructed by Yuriko from a film by Julien Bryan. See also Fischer, "Graham's Dance Steps in the Street."

70   Perhaps this dance language is what Martin was trying to define as metakinesis, "the thought-conveying quality of movement, especially of movement that is . . . non-representational." Martin, *The Modern Dance,* p. 85. It is also an example of Litvinoff's point about Graham's instinctive affinity with the Stanislavsky Method.

71   Gilfond, "Martha Graham and Group," *Dance Observer,* January 1937, p. 6.

72   "Dances for Spain," *Dance Observer,* June–July 1937, p. 69.

73   Gilfond, "Martha Graham and Group," *Dance Observer,* January 1937, p. 6.

74   Gilfond, "Martha Graham," *Dance Observer,* January 1938, p. 8.

75   This appearance occurred in February 1937. De Mille, *Martha,* p. 221.

76 "Modern Dance at the New York World's Fair," *Dance Observer,* May 1938, p. 67.

77 See "Affirmations," a collection of Graham's early writings published in Armitage, *Martha Graham,* p. 101.

78 Ibid.

79 Program notes, quoted in Barbara Morgan, *Martha Graham: Sixteen Dances* (New York: Duell, Sloan and Pierce, 1941). William Stott cites Graham's *American Document* as an example of the prevalence of documentary genres during the 1930s. See Stott, *Documentary Expression and Thirties America* (Chicago: University of Chicago Press, 1986 [1973]), pp. 123–128.

80 Costonis, "Martha Graham's *American Document.* Costonis concludes that Graham transformed the racist stereotypes of the classic minstrel show to create a sense of sympathy with the black Americans who had formerly been mocked in these forms. See also Susan Manning, "*American Document* and American Minstrelsy," in *Moving Words: Rewriting Dance,* ed. Gay Morris (London: Routledge, 1996).

81 My impressions of this dance are drawn from Barbara Morgan's well-known photographs and the descriptions and essays that accompany them, from the dance libretto written by Graham, "Dance Libretto," *Theatre Arts,* September 1942, pp. 565–574, and from accounts of the dance by Costonis, "Martha Graham's *American Document,*" and Manning, "*American Document* and American Minstrelsy."

82 Stevens is referring to Sophie Maslow and Erick Hawkins. Hawkins had just joined the company, becoming its first male member.

83 De Mille, *Martha,* p. 234.

84 May O'Donnell, speaking at Barbara Morgan's photography exhibition, "Shadows, Light, Movement: Moments in American History," Marymount College, Tarrytown, N.Y., December 2, 1990.

85 Ray Green recalled that this trio was performed separately at a 1938 Carnegie Hall performance sponsored by the Communist Party. However, I have been unable to find any other documentation of the event. Green, my conversation, December 2, 1990.

86 George Beiswanger, "The New Theatre Dance," *Theatre Arts,* January 1939, p. 54.

87 Lincoln Kirstein, "Martha Graham at Bennington," *Nation,* September 3, 1938.

88 Ibid.

89 George Beiswanger, "Martha Graham: A Perspective," in Morgan, *Martha Graham,* p. 145.

90 Henry Gilfond, "Bennington Festival," *Dance Observer,* August–September 1938, p. 101.

91 Edna Ocko, *TAC Magazine,* October 1938, p. 15.

92 Edna Ocko, *TAC Magazine,* December 1938, p. 2.

93 Owen Burke, *New Masses,* October 18, 1938, p. 29.

94 Gervaise Butler, "*American Document* Re-Viewed," *Dance Magazine,* November 1938, p. 129.

95 See advertisements in *Dance Observer,* October 1938 and December 1938.

96 Catherine Vickery, "*American Document* Tours America," *Dance Observer,* April 1939, pp. 205–206.

97 De Mille, *Martha,* p. 235.

98 Graham, "Dance Libretto," pp. 571–573.

99 Gilfond, "Bennington Festival."

100 Many thanks to Susan Manning for sharing this concept. American Studies Asso-

ciation Conference, October 28–November 1, 1994. See also Manning's "*American Document* and American Minstrelsy."

101 Kirstein, "Martha Graham at Bennington," p. 231.
102 See especially Jowitt, *Time and the Dancing Image,* p. 206.
103 Editorial, *Dance Observer,* May 1939.

Six. The People's Culture: Folklore on the Urban Stage

1 David Sears, "Breaking Down Harmonica Breakdown," *Ballet Review,* Winter 1984, p. 58.
2 Dudley, quoted in ibid., p. 59.
3 My impressions of the dance are gathered from a reconstruction performed by Nancy Colohan in New York City, May 25, 26, 27, 1988, and from the performance by Sheron Wray of the London Contemporary Dance Theatre for the New Dance Group Gala Retrospective, June 11, 1993.
4 Lois Balcolm, "America Dances," *Dance Observer,* June–July 1941. Steig was apparently a favorite of Dudley's. *The Lonely Ones* (1946) was based on Steig cartoons. Dudley, interview with author.
5 Dudley, quoted in Sears, "Breaking Down Harmonica Breakdown," pp. 60–61.
6 John Hammond, quoted in Sears, ibid., p. 60.
7 Willard Rhodes, "Folk Music Old and New," *Folklore and Society: Essays in Honor of Benj. A. Botkin,* ed. Bruce Jackson (Hatboro, Pa.: Folklore Associates, 1966), p. 10.
8 "Mass Dance in the Soviet Union," *New Theatre,* February 1934, p. 5.
9 Hans Eisler, a German composer much admired by American leftist composers for his revolutionary songs for the working class, is quoted as saying this. Apparently he believed that American folk music and popular music were unsuitable as a basis for creating songs of protest. See David King Dunaway's "Unsung Songs of Protest: The Composers Collective of New York," *New York Folklore* 5, no. 1–2 (Summer 1979): 7.
10 Edna Ocko, "Three Interviews with Russian Dancers," *Dance Observer,* January 1938, pp. 5–6.
11 Dunaway, "Unsung Songs of Protest," p. 3.
12 John Martin, "The Dance: Popularity of Folk Forms," *New York Times,* April 12, 1931.
13 Sophia Delza, "The Folk Dance," *New Theatre,* November 1934, p. 16.
14 Dunaway, "Unsung Songs of Protest," p. 7. This philosophy was developed by Eisler and adopted by the Composers Collective.
15 Quoted in ibid., p. 3.
16 Ibid., p. 8.
17 Charles Seeger, "Grass Roots for American Composers," *Modern Music* 16, no. 3 (March–April 1939): 146–147. Seeger sometimes wrote under the pseudonym Carl Sands.
18 Warren I. Susman, *Culture as History: The Transformation of American Society in the Twentieth Century* (New York: Pantheon Books, 1984), p. 178.
19 Editorial, *Dance Observer,* June–July 1940, p. 79.
20 In *Days on Earth* (New Haven, Conn.: Yale University Press, 1987), p. 172, Marcia B. Siegel quotes Humphrey's description of the dance as "social and ballroom dances done in a modern style."
21 Program note, April 8, 1939. Quoted in Henry Gilfond's review, "Blanche Evan," *Dance Observer,* May 1939, p. 219.

22 Another variation of this dance, performed as part of a lecture demonstration at the YMHA in 1939, had sections entitled "Off to Montan'" and "Running Set," while a study in 1940 listed sections entitled "Mountain Song" and "Kentucky Hill Tune."

23 Biographical material on Sophie Maslow is compiled from interviews by Elizabeth Kendall (1976), Dance Collection, New York Public Library for the Performing Arts; by Lucile Nathanson (1976), ibid.; and my own, June 16, 1989, New York City.

24 Steve Foster, "The Revolutionary Solo Dance," *New Theatre,* January 1935, p. 23.

25 *New Theatre,* November 1934, p. 10. Author not cited.

26 Maslow, interview with author; interview with Kendall, p. 114. A review in *Dance Observer* (January 1936), however, lists the composer as Gylzejnep.

27 Maslow, my interview.

28 Maslow, interview with Kendall, p. 198A.

29 A picture in Donald Worster's *Dust Bowl: The Southern Plains in the 1930s* (New York: Oxford University Press, 1979), p. 125, shows a small house with sand drifts piled so high that the doorway is blocked.

30 The New Deal's Federal Emergency Relief Administration financed a documentary by Pare Lorentz, *The Plow That Broke the Plains,* about the Dust Bowl and the problems of soil erosion. The score by Virgil Thomson was filled with folk melodies and remains popular in its own right. Originally, a working script was written by cameramen Leo Hurwitz, Ralph Steiner, and Paul Strand, all members of Nykino, a group devoted to progressive social films. But the scenario, which described the role of capitalism in the destruction of America's resources, proved too radical for the government. Last-minute rewrites softened the attack on capitalist ideology. Peter Ellis, "The Plow That Broke the Plains," *New Theatre,* July 1936, pp. 18–19.

31 Maslow, my interview.

32 Worster, *Dust Bowl,* pp. 54–55.

33 Guthrie, "Woody Sez," ed. John Dunston, *Mainstream,* August 1963, p. 21.

34 In "Woodie Guthrie and His Folk Tradition," Richard Reuss explains Guthrie's appeal to urban leftists, pointing out that Guthrie was "the living incarnation of social issues they had grappled with either in the abstract or at first hand." *Journal of American Folklore* 83, no. 329 (July–September 1970): 278.

35 Balcolm, "America Dances."

36 Library of Congress recording, c. 1936.

37 Woody Guthrie, "Singing, Dancing and Teamwork," *Dance Observer,* November 1943, p. 105.

38 Joe Klein, *Woody Guthrie: A Life* (New York: Alfred A. Knopf, 1980), pp. 223–224. See also Maslow, my interview.

39 My interview.

40 My impressions are based on a series of photographs by Gerda Pederich of Maslow dancing, and on a viewing of Ted Pollen in "I Ain't Got No Home" and Lyn Freilinghaus in "Dusty ol' Dust" performed at the American Dance Guild Association annual conference, June 15, 1991, and the video recording of the 1980 Maslow reconstruction of the dances as part of a longer work called *Woody Sez.* Dance Collection, New York Public Library for the Performing Arts.

41 Susman, *Culture as History,* p. 203. See also Klehr, *Heyday of American Communism,* pp. 365–385, for a discussion of the Party during this era.

42 These words are from the introduction to Carl Sandburg's poem, *The People, Yes* (New York: Harcourt Brace Jovanovich, 1990 [1936]).

43 Roberta Krugman, Dance Notation Score, 1951, Dance Collection, New York Public Library for the Performing Arts.

44 Robert Sabin, "Jane Dudley, Sophie Maslow, William Bales," *Dance Observer,* April 1942, p. 47.

45 Maslow, interview with Kendall, p. 210.

46 Sandburg, *The People, Yes,* p. 26.

47 My impressions are drawn from the 1976 video recording of a staged rehearsal by the Sophie Maslow Dance Company. Dance Collection, New York Public Library for the Performing Arts.

48 Reuss, "Woody Guthrie and His Folk Collection," p. 282.

49 These sayings are part of the script included in Krugman's 1951 Dance Notation Score.

50 John Martin, "The Dance: Gala Debut," *New York Times,* March 15, 1942.

51 José E. Limón, "Western Marxism and Folklore: A Critical Introduction," *Journal of American Folklore* 96, no. 379 (1983): 47–50.

52 In *American Folksongs of Protest* (Philadelphia: University of Pennsylvania Press, 1953), p. 5, John Greenway proposes that one of the qualifications of a genuine folksong is that "the song has lost its identity as a consciously composed piece."

53 Hampton, *Guerrilla Minstrels,* p. 117.

54 Martin, "The Dance: Americana," *New York Times,* January 28, 1945. In an interview, *Christian Science Monitor,* January 19, 1946, Maslow said, "We aren't presenting authentic folk material. It is the folk spirit we want and this colors the movement."

55 Barbara Kirshenblatt-Gimblett suggests a way to understand the implications of this kind of appropriation in "Authorizing Lives," *Journal of Folklore Research* 26, no. 2 (1989): 123–149. Pointing to the folk movement's appeal during this period, she cites "the political implications of a technique that ostensibly empowered the subject by letting him speak for himself" (p. 130).

56 Guthrie, "People Dancing," *Dance Observer,* December 1943, p. 115.

57 A "Concert of American Folk Dances" performed by Maslow and Dudley for the Rifle Range and Rexall Road USO Club, for example, was to be followed by an evening of square dancing for all. Sophie Maslow Clipping File, 1930–1939, Dance Collection, New York Public Library for the Performing Arts.

58 Kirshenblatt-Gimblett writes in "Authorizing Lives," p. 131: "Presenting the text as a quotation by a researcher is among other things a technique for lending to that text the imprimatur of scholarship. The text is thereby rendered authoritative simultaneously as a personal document and as a scientific document." I paraphrase: Presenting folk dances and songs as a quotation by the choreographer is, among other things, a technique for lending to that folk dance the imprimatur of artistry. The folk dance is thereby rendered credible as people's culture and as a professional work of art.

59 Susman, *Culture as History,* pp. 205–206.

60 Martin, "The Dance: Gala Debut."

Seven. Dance and Politics

1 Walter Terry, *The Dance in America* (New York: Harper and Row, 1971 [1956]), acknowledgment.

2 See David Halberstam, *The Fifties* (New York: Villard Books, 1993), p. 52. Also see

Mari Jo Buhle, Paul Buhle, and Dan Georgakas, eds., *Encyclopedia of the American Left* (Urbana: University of Illinois Press, 1992), p. 644.

3   See Lynn Garafola, "Toward an American Dance: Dance in the City 1940–1965," in *New York: Culture Capital of the World 1940–1965,* ed. Leonard Wallock (New York: Rizzoli, 1988), pp. 158–165.

4   "Federal Arts Bill," *Dance Observer,* January 1938, p. 3.

5   "Federal Arts Campaign," *Dance Observer,* June–July 1938, p. 85.

6   "WPA and the Arts," *Washington Post,* May 3, 1939.

7   Walton was the New York director of the Theatre Project at this time.

8   *Variety,* August 24, 1938, p. 2.

9   "WPA and the Arts."

10 *Are We Winning, Mommy? America and the Cold War,* produced and directed by Barbara Margolis, 1986.

11 Sophie Maslow Clipping File, 1940–1949, Dance Collection, New York Public Library for the Performing Arts.

12 Special Collections, Library of Congress Research Center for the Federal Theatre Project.

13 New Dance Group Programs, Dance Collection, New York Public Library for the Performing Arts.

14 *Life,* April 26, 1943, p. 28; cited in Schlundt, "Tamiris," pp. 126–127.

15 Thanks to Rebekah Kowal for pointing this out.

16 Quoted in Buhle, Buhle, Georgakas, eds., *Encyclopedia of the American Left,* p. 659.

17 Stephen J. Whitfield, *The Culture of the Cold War* (Baltimore: John Hopkins University Press, 1991), p. 87.

18 Ibid., pp. 166–167.

19 Warren, *Anna Sokolow,* p. 124.

20 Ocko, my interview.

21 Bob Heisler and Judee Rosenbaum, "Interview with Edith Segal," Kinderland Reunion Journal, n.d., p. 29. Vertical Files, Tamiment Library, New York University.

22 The history of the New Dance Group during this period is compiled from "Making the Dance Today." Judith Delman, interview with Lucile Nathanson, Nassau Community College, Dance Collection, New York Public Library for the Performing Arts.

23 Quoted in Mishler, "The Littlest Proletariat," p. 149.

24 Former New Dance Group student Marcia Bender. *Dance Magazine,* July 1958, quoted in souvenir program, "The New Dance Group Gala Concert," June 11, 1993.

25 Don McDonagh, *The Complete Guide to Modern Dance* (New York: Doubleday, 1976), inside cover. While McDonagh's brief biographies often cite the New Dance Group's role in the development of individual artists, the NDG does not appear as an entity within his tree of modern dance.

26 Krevitsky, "American Dance Festival," August–September 1950, p. 102.

27 Nik Krevitsky, "Delakova and Berk," *Dance Observer,* April 1947, p. 45. See Naomi Jackson, "Converging Movements: Modern Dance and Jewish Culture at the 92nd St. Y, 1930–1960" (Ph.D. diss., New York University, 1996), for an account of the intersection of the development of modern dance with themes of Jewish identity.

28 "Choreographics," *Dance Observer,* August–September 1947, p. 81.

29 Mildred Ackerman, "Jewish Dance Festival," *Dance Observer,* January 1948, p. 8.

30 See Warren, *Anna Sokolow,* for a more detailed description of the dance, p. 77.

31 Ibid., pp. 103–106.

32 Nik Krevitsky, "Anna Sokolow and Company," *Dance Observer*, May 1951, p. 71.

33 Graham's company, acknowledged for its interracial character during the 1950s, first included black dancers in 1952.

34 Primus appears in a photograph of *Folksay* taken during a 1946 performance for CBS Television. New Dance Group Programs, Dance Collection, New York Public Library for the Performing Arts.

35 New Dance Group Programs, Dance Collection, New York Public Library for the Performing Arts.

36 Maslow also recalled that at Connecticut College, black dancers had difficulties getting campus housing. Interview with author.

37 Nik Krevitsky, "New Dance Group Festival," *Dance Observer*, April 1953, p. 55.

38 Gertrude Lippincott, "Freedom and the Arts," *Dance Observer*, April 1948, p. 44.

39 Gertrude Lippincott, "No Compromise," *Dance Observer*, November 1948, pp. 117–119.

40 Whitfield, *Culture of the Cold War*, p. 203.

41 Louis Horst, "Theatre Dance Inc.," *Dance Observer*, May 1952, pp. 73–74.

42 Lucy Wilder, "Stage for Dancers," *Dance Observer*, April 1952, p. 58.

43 José Limón, "Composing a Dance," *Juilliard Review* 2, no. 1 (Winter 1955): 20.

44 Ibid., 18.

45 However, entries in *The Encyclopedia of New York City*, ed. Kenneth T. Jackson (New Haven: Yale University Press, 1995), cite 1947 as the opening of the High School of Performing Arts, and 1951 as the opening of the Juilliard Dance Program.

46 See Jack Anderson's *The American Dance Festival* (Durham, N.C.: Duke University Press, 1987) for a complete history of the program at Connecticut College.

47 Sali Ann Kriegsman, *Modern Dance in America: The Bennington Years* (Boston: G. K. Hall, 1981), p. 49.

48 "Five Arts Bill," *Dance Observer*, March 1938, p. 35.

49 Henry Gilfond, "Summing Up," *Dance Observer*, June–July 1939, p. 238.

50 Jackson, "Converging Movements," pp. 108–142.

51 Beginning in 1956, however, Tamiris was in residence most summers at Perry-Mansfield School of Theatre and Dance in Steamboat Springs, Colorado.

52 See Warren, *Anna Sokolow*, pp. 299–363.

53 See Schlundt, "Tamiris," pp. 128–154.

54 Doss, *Benton, Pollock and the Politics of Modernism*.

55 Terry, *Dance in America*, p. 83.

56 "More News Items From the Martha Graham 'ANTA' Tour," *Dance Observer*, March 1956, p. 41.

57 Quoted in "The Presentation of *Dance Magazine*'s 1957 Awards," *Dance Magazine*, April 1957, p. 19.

58 Fé Alf Papers, c. 1928–1933, Dance Collection, New York Public Library for the Performing Arts.

59 I first was made aware of this history through Deborah Jowitt's article on Edith Segal, "A Lifetime of Art on the Left," *Village Voice*, July 6, 1982.

Bibliography

Aaron, Daniel. *Writers on the Left.* New York: Avon Books, 1961.

Ackerman, Mildred. "Jewish Dance Festival." *Dance Observer,* January 1948.

"A Letter to Blanche Evan: From the Workers Dance League." *New Theatre,* June 1934.

Allerhand, Ruth. "The Lay Dance." *New Theatre,* April 1935, p. 26.

Anderson, Jack. *The American Dance Festival.* Durham, N.C.: Duke University Press, 1987.

Anyon, Nell (Nadia Chilkovsky). "The Tasks of the Revolutionary Dance." *New Theatre,* September–October 1933.

———. "The New Dance League." *New Theatre,* April 1935.

Appel, Benjamin. *The People Talk: American Voices from the Great Depression.* New York: Simon and Schuster Touchstone, 1982 [1940].

Armitage, Merle, ed. *Martha Graham: The Early Years.* New York: Da Capo Press, 1978 [1937].

Ashton, Dore. *The New York School: A Cultural Reckoning.* New York: Penguin Books, 1979.

Balcolm, Lois. "America Dances." *Dance Observer,* June–July 1941, p. 82.

Barlin, Anne Lief. Interview by Karen Wickre. Van Nuys, California, October 25, 1977. Library of Congress. Research Center for the Federal Theatre Project. Oral History Program.

Bass, Paula (Perlowin). Interview by Karen Wickre. Laguna Hills, California, October 23, 1977. Library of Congress. Research Center for the Federal Theatre Project. Oral History Program.

———. Videotaped interview by Karen Wickre. UCLA, February 20, 1978. Library of Congress. Research Center for the Federal Theatre Project.

Beard, Rick, ed. *On Being Homeless: Historical Perspectives.* New York: Museum of the City of New York, 1987.

Beiswanger, George. "Martha Graham: A Perspective." In Barbara Morgan, *Martha Graham: Sixteen Dances.* New York: Duell, Sloan and Pearce, 1941.

———. "The New Theatre Dance." *Theatre Arts,* January 1939.

Bentley, Toni. *Winter Season: A Dancer's Journal.* New York: Vintage Books, 1982.

Bergman, Andrew. *We're in the Money: Depression America and Its Films.* New York: Harper and Row, 1971.

Betts, Anne. "An Historical Study of the New Dance Group of New York City." Master's thesis, New York University, 1945.

Blood, Melanie. "The Neighborhood Playhouse 1915–1927." Ph.D. diss., Northwestern University, 1994.

Brinkley, Alan. *Voices of Protest: Huey Long, Father Coughlin and the Great Depression.* New York: Vintage Books, 1983.

Buhle, Mari Jo, Paul Buhle, and Dan Georgakas eds. *Encyclopedia of the American Left.* Urbana: University of Illinois Press, 1992.

Buhle, Paul. *Marxism in the USA.* London: Verso, 1987.

Burke, Owen. *New Masses.* October 18, 1938.

Burlak, Ann. "Dance Notes." *New Theatre,* November 1934.

Butler, Gervaise. "American Document Re-Viewed." *Dance Observer,* November 1938.

Buttita, Tony, and Barry Witham. *Uncle Sam Presents: A Memoir of the Federal Theatre Project, 1935–1939.* Philadelphia: University of Pennsylvania Press, 1982.

Carter, Dan T. *Scottsboro: A Tragedy of the American South.* Baton Rouge: Louisiana State University Press, 1979 [1969].

Chekhov, M. A., as arranged by Molly Day Thatcher. "Stanislavsky's Method of Acting." *New Theatre.* December 1934, January 1935.

Chilkovsky, Nadia (Nahumck). Transcript of interview by Karen Wickre. May 25, 1978. Library of Congress. Research Center for the Federal Theatre Project. Oral History Program.

Chipp, Herschel, B. *Theories of Modern Art.* Berkeley: University of California Press, 1968.

"Choreographics." *Dance Observer.* April 1938.

"Choreographics." *Dance Observer.* August–September 1947.

Citron, Atay. "Pageantry and Theatre in the Service of Jewish Nationalism." Ph.D. diss., New York University, 1989.

Clurman, Harold. *The Fervent Years: The Group Theatre and the 30's.* New York: Da Capo, 1983 [1941].

Code, Grant. "Dance Theatre of the WPA." *Dance Observer,* October 1939.

Costonis, Maureen Needham. "*American Document:* A Neglected Graham Work." *Proceedings of the Society of Dance History Scholars.* Twelfth Annual Conference, Arizona State University, February 17–19, 1989.

———. "Martha Graham's *American Document:* A Minstrel Show in Modern Dance Dress," *American Music* 9, no. 3 (Fall 1991).

Crowley, Alice Lewisohn. *The Neighborhood Playhouse.* New York: Theatre Arts Books, 1959.

Cushing, Maxine. "The Precious Press." *Dance Observer,* October 1938.

Daly, Ann. *Done into Dance: Isadora Duncan and America.* Bloomington: Indiana University Press, 1995.

"The Dance: The New Dance Group." *New Theatre,* March 1934.

"The Dance: Prize Winner." *New York Times,* July 1, 1934.

"Dance Front." *New Theatre,* December 1935.

"Dance Group in a Trade Union." *New Theatre,* January 1934.

"The Dance League Recital." *New Theatre,* February 1935.

"Dance Notes." *New Theatre,* November 1934.

"Dancer's Union." *New Theatre,* January 1935.

"Dances for Spain." *Dance Observer,* June–July 1937.

Deak, Frantisek. "Russian Mass Spectacles." *Drama Review,* June 1975.

Dehn, Mura. Interview with Karen Wickre. New York City, April 20, 1978. Library of Congress. Research Center for the Federal Theatre Project. Oral History Program.

Delza, Sophia. "The Folk Dance." *New Theatre,* November 1934.

De Mille, Agnes. *Dance to the Piper.* Boston: Little, Brown, 1952.

———. Interview with Clare Saperstein, November 27, 1991.

———. *The Life and Work of Martha Graham.* New York: Random House, 1991.

Doss, Erica. *Benton, Pollock and the Politics of Modernism: From Regionalism to Abstract Expressionism.* Chicago: University of Chicago Press, 1991.

Dudley, Jane. Interview with Ellen Graff. New York City, January 7, 1992.

———. Interview with Richard Wormser. Oral History of the American Left. Tamiment Library, New York University.

———. Interview with Tobi Tobias. Dance Collection. New York Public Library for the Performing Arts.

———. "The Mass Dance." *New Theatre.* December 1934.

Dunaway, David King. "Unsung Songs of Protest: The Composers Collective of New York." *New York Folklore* 5, no. 1-2 (Summer 1979): 1–19.

Duncan, Isadora. *The Art of the Dance,* ed. Sheldon Cheney. New York: Theatre Arts Books, 1969 [1928].

Eden, J. C. "Black Fists, White Fists." *Daily Worker,* March 7, 1929.

Elion, Harry. "Perspectives of the Dance." *New Theatre.* September 1934.

Ellis, Peter. "The Plow That Broke the Plains." *New Theatre,* July 1936.

Emery, Lynne Fauley. *Black Dance: From 1619 to Today.* Second Revised Edition. Princeton, N.J.: Dance Horizons, 1988 [1972].

Evan, Blanche. "A Dancer's Notebook." *New Theatre,* April 1936.

Ewen, Elizabeth. *Immigrant Women in the Land of Dollars: Life and Culture on the Lower East Side, 1890-1925.* New York: Monthly Review Press, 1985.

"Federal Arts Bill." *Dance Observer,* January 1938.

"Federal Arts Campaign." *Dance Observer,* June–July 1938.

First Annual Workers Dance League Spartakiade. Souvenir Program. Dance Collection. New York Public Library for the Performing Arts.

Fischer, Barry. "Graham's Dance Steps in the Street and Selected Early Technique: Principles for Reconstructing Choreography from Video Tape." Ed.D. diss., New York University, 1986.

"Five Arts Bill." *Dance Observer,* March 1938.

Flanagan, Hallie. *Arena: The Story of the Federal Theatre.* New York: Limelight Editions, 1985 [1940].

Foster, Steve. "The Revolutionary Solo Dance." *New Theatre,* January 1935.

Foster, William Z. *Toward Soviet America.* New York: International Publishers, 1932.

Franco, Mark. *Dancing Modernism/Performing Politics.* Bloomington: Indiana University Press, 1995.

Freeman, A. B. "What to Dance About." *New Theatre,* March 1934.

Freeman, Ezra. "Dance: Which Technique?" *New Theatre,* May 1934.

Friedman, Daniel. "A Brief Description of the Workers' Theatre Movement of the Thirties." *Theatre for Working-Class Audiences in the United States, 1830-1980,* ed. Bruce A. McConachie and Daniel Friedman. Westport, Conn.: Greenwood Press, 1985.

"From Our Correspondence." *New Theatre,* September–October 1933.

Funaroff, Sol. *Exile From A Future Time: Posthumous Poems of Sol Funaroff.* New York: Dynamo, 1943.

Garafola, Lynn, ed. *Of, By, and For the People: Dancing on the Left in the 1930s. Studies in Dance History* 5, no. 1 (1994).

Garafola, Lynn. "Toward an American Dance: Dance in the City." *New York: Culture Capital of the World, 1940–1965,* ed. Leonard Wallock. New York: Rizzoli, 1988.

Gellert, Lawrence. *Negro Songs of Protest.* Collected by Lawrence Gellert, arranged for voice and piano by Elie Siegmeister. New York: American Music League, 1936.

Geltman, Fanya (del Bourgo). Interview with Karen Wickre. New York City, December 16, 1977. Library of Congress. Research Center for the Federal Theatre Project. Oral History Program.

———. Videotaped interview with Karen Wickre. University of California at Los Angeles, February 20, 1978. Library of Congress. Research Center for the Federal Theatre Project.

———. "Letters." *Dance Observer,* May, 1936.

Gerrard, Saida. Interview by Karen Wickre. Hollywood, Calif., February 21, 1978. Library of Congress. Research Center for the Federal Theatre Project. Oral History Program.

Gilfond, Henry. "Bennington Festival." *Dance Observer,* August–September 1938.

———. "Blanche Evan." *Dance Observer,* May 1939.

———. "Dance Congress and Festival" and "Demonstration Groups." *Dance Observer,* June–July 1936.

———. "The ILD Concert." *Dance Observer,* January 1936.

———. "Let Us Have Critics." *Dance Observer,* October–November 1934.

———. "Martha Graham." *Dance Observer,* January 1938.

———. "Martha Graham and Dance Group." *Dance Observer,* January 1936.

———. "Martha Graham and Dance Group." *Dance Observer,* April 1937.

———. "New Dance League." *Dance Observer,* May 1935.

———. "Redder Than the Rose." *New Theatre,* September 1935.

———. "Summing Up." *Dance Observer,* June–July 1939.

———. "Workers Dance League." *Dance Observer,* December 1934.

Glassberg, David. *American Historical Pageantry: The Uses of Tradition in the Early Twentieth Century.* Chapel Hill: The University of North Carolina Press, 1990.

Gold, Michael. "Change the World." *Daily Worker,* June 5, 1934, June 14, 1934.

———. "Strange Funeral in Braddock." With musical score by Elie Siegmeister. New Music, c. 1936. Music Collection. New York Public Library for the Performing Arts.

Graff, Ellen. "Dancing Red: Art and Politics," in *Of, By, and For the People: Dancing on the Left in the 1930s,* ed. Lynn Garafola, *Studies in Dance History* 5, no. 1 (Spring 1994): 1–13.

Graham, Martha. "Affirmations." In *Martha Graham: The Early Years,* ed. Merle Armitage. New York: Da Capo, 1978 [1937].

———. "Dance Libretto." *Theatre Arts,* September 1942.

"Grandma Was an Activist." Produced by Radio station WBAI. Oral History of the American Left. Tamiment Library, New York University.

Green, Martin. *New York 1913: The Armory Show and the Paterson Strike Pageant.* New York: Collier Books, 1988.

Green, Stanley. *Broadway Musicals of the 30's.* New York: Da Capo Press, 1971.

Greenway, John. *American Folksongs of Protest.* Philadelphia: University of Pennsylvania Press, 1953.

Guthrie, Woody. *Dust Bowl Ballads.* Folkway Records, 1964.

———. "People Dancing." *Dance Observer,* December 1943.

———. "Singing, Dancing and Team-Work." *Dance Observer,* November 1943.

———. "Woody Sez," ed. Josh Dunston. *Mainstream,* August 1963.

Halberstam, David. *The Fifties*. New York: Villard Books, 1993.

Hampton, Wayne. *Guerrilla Minstrels*. Knoxville: University of Tennessee Press, 1986.

Harap, Louis. *Social Roots of the Arts*. New York: International Publishers, 1949.

Heisey, Ruth Ann. "Anna Sokolow—Interview." *Dance Observer*, August–September 1937.

Heretic. Fox Movietone News, 1931. Dance Collection. New York Public Library for the Performing Arts.

Hicks, Granville, Michael Gold, Isador Schneider, Joseph North, Paul Peters, Alan Calmer, eds. *Proletarian Literature in the United States: An Anthology*. New York: International Publishers, 1935.

Higham, John. *Strangers in the Land: Patterns of American Nativism, 1860–1925*. New Brunswick, N.J.: Rutgers University Press, 1955.

Horst, Louis. *Modern Dance Forms in Relation to the Other Modern Arts*. Brooklyn: Dance Horizons. 1967 [1961].

———. *Pre-Classic Dance Forms*. Brooklyn: Dance Horizons, 1968 [1937].

———. "Theatre Dance, Inc." *Dance Observer*, May 1952.

———. "Workers Dance League." *Dance Observer*, March 1935.

Houseman, John. *Run-Through: A Memoir*. New York: Simon and Schuster, 1972.

Humphrey, Doris. *Doris Humphrey: An Artist First*, edited and completed by Selma Jeanne Cohen. Middletown: Wesleyan University Press, 1972.

"Hundreds Sit-In at WPA Theatre." *New York Post*, May 20, 1937.

Jackson, Kenneth T., ed. *The Encyclopedia of New York City*. New Haven: Yale University Press, 1995.

Jackson, Naomi. "Converging Movements: Modern Dance and Jewish Culture at the 92nd St. Y, 1930–1960. Ph.D. diss., New York University, 1996.

Johnson, Oakley. "The Dance." *New Theatre*, February 1934.

Jowitt, Deborah. "A Lifetime of Art on the Left." *Village Voice*, July 6, 1982.

———. *Time and the Dancing Image*. New York: William Morrow, 1988.

Kendall, Elizabeth. *Where She Danced*. Berkeley: University of California Press, 1979.

Kirshenblatt-Gimblett, Barbara. "Authorizing Lives." *Journal of Folklore Research* 26, no. 2 (1989).

Kirstein, Lincoln. *Dance: A Short History of Classic Theatrical Dancing*. Brooklyn: Dance Horizons, 1977 [1935].

———. "Martha Graham at Bennington." *Nation*, September 3, 1938.

———. "Revolutionary Ballet Forms." *New Theatre*, October 1934.

Klehr, Harvey. *The Heyday of American Communism: The Depression Decade*. New York: Basic Books, 1984.

Klein, Joe. *Woody Guthrie: A Life*. New York: Alfred Knopf, 1980.

Kline, Herbert, ed. *New Theatre and Film, 1934 to 1937*. New York: Harcourt Brace Jovanovich, 1985.

Krevitsky, Nik. "American Dance Festival." *Dance Observer*, August–September 1950.

———. "Anna Sokolow and Company." *Dance Observer*, May 1951.

———. "Delakova and Berk." *Dance Observer*, April 1947.

———. "Jewish Dance Guild." *Dance Observer*, January 1948.

———. "New Dance Group Festival." *Dance Observer*, April 1953.

Kriegsman, Sali Ann. *Modern Dance in America: The Bennington Years*. Boston: G. K. Hall, 1981.

Krugman, Roberta. *Folksay*. Dance Notation Score, 1951. Dance Collection. New York Public Library for the Performing Arts.

Lally, Kathleen Ann. "A History of the Federal Dance Theatre of the Works Progress Administration, 1935–1939." Ph.D. diss., Texas Woman's University, Denton, Texas, 1978.

Lange, Dorothea, and Paul Taylor. *An American Exodus.* New Haven, Conn.: Yale University Press, 1969.

Laub, Lili Mann. Interview by Karen Wickre, Teaneck, N.J., May 24, 1978. Library of Congress. Research Center for the Federal Theatre Project. Oral History Program.

"Lenin Memorial Program Ready." *Daily Worker,* January 14, 1928.

Limón, José. "Western Marxism and Folklore: A Critical Introduction." *Journal of American Folklore* 96, no. 379 (1983).

Lippincott, Gertrude. "Freedom and the Arts." *Dance Observer,* April 1948.

———. "No Compromise." *Dance Observer,* November 1948.

Litvinoff, Valentina. "The Use of Stanislavsky for the Teacher of Modern Dance." *Dance Scope.* Fall–Winter 1971–1972.

Lloyd, Margaret. *The Borzoi Book of Modern Dance.* Brooklyn: Dance Horizons, 1974 [1949].

Love, Paul. "Workers Dance League." *Dance Observer,* May 1934.

Manning, Susan. "*American Document* and American Minstrelsy." In *Moving Words: Rewriting Dance,* ed. Gay Morris. London: Routledge, 1996.

———. *Ecstasy and the Demon: Feminism and Nationalism in the Dances of Mary Wigman.* Berkeley: University of California Press, 1993.

———. "From Modernism to Fascism: The Evolution of Wigman's Choreography." *Ballet Review* 14, no. 4 (1986).

Marchowsky, Marie. Interview with Laura Caplan. January 1979. Dance Collection. New York Public Library for the Performing Arts.

Margolis, Barbara. *Are We Winning?: America and the Cold War.* Film produced and directed by Barbara Margolis, 1986.

"Martha Graham and Dance Group." *Dance Observer,* March 1935.

"Martha Graham and Group." *Dance Observer,* January 1937.

Martin, John. "The Dance: Americana." *New York Times,* December 6, 1942.

———. "The Dance: The Far East." *New York Times,* October 15, 1933.

———. "The Dance: Organization." *New York Times,* February 9, 1936.

———. "The Dance: Popularity of Folk Forms." *New York Times,* April 12, 1931.

———. "The Dance: Prize Winner." *New York Times,* July 1, 1934.

———. "The Dance: To the NDL." *New York Times,* June 16, 1935.

———. "The Dance: WPA Theatre." *New York Times,* May 16, 1937.

———. "The Dance: Young Talent." *New York Times,* December 2, 1934.

———. *The Dance in Theory.* Princeton, N.J.: Dance Horizons, 1989 [1965].

———. "Gala Debut." *New York Times,* March 15, 1942.

———. *The Modern Dance.* Brooklyn: Dance Horizons, 1972 [1933].

———. "New Dance League Holds 3rd Festival." *New York Times,* June 10, 1935.

———. "Success Scored by Dance League." *New York Times,* November 26, 1934.

———. "Workers League in Group Dances." *New York Times,* December 24, 1934.

Marx, Karl, and Friedrich Engels. *Basic Writings on Politics and Philosophy,* ed. Lewis S. Feuer. New York: Anchor Books, 1959.

Maslow, Sophie. Interview with Elizabeth Kendall. September 1976. Dance Collection. New York Public Library for the Performing Arts.

———. Interview with Lucile Nathanson. December 1976. Dance Collection. New York Public Library for the Performing Arts.

———. Interview with Ellen Graff. New York City, June 16, 1989.

"Mass Dance in the Soviet Union," *New Theatre*, February 1934.

McConachie, Bruce A., and Daniel Friedman, eds. *Theatre for Working-Class Audiences in the United States, 1830–1980*. Westport, Conn.: Greenwood Press, 1985.

McDermott, Douglas. "Agitprop: Production Practice in the Workers' Theatre, 1932–1942." *Theatre Survey*, December 1966.

———. "The Workers Laboratory Theatre." Bruce A. McConachie and Daniel Friedman, eds., In *Theatre for Working-Class Audiences in the United States, 1830–1980*. Westport, Conn.: Greenwood Press, 1985.

McDonagh, Don. *The Complete Guide to Modern Dance*. New York: Doubleday, 1976.

———. "Conversation with Gertrude Shurr." *Ballet Review* 4, no. 5 (1973).

McElvaine, Robert S. *Down and Out in the Great Depression: Letters from the Forgotten Man*. Chapel Hill: University of North Carolina Press, 1983.

———. *The Great Depression: America, 1929–1941*. New York: Times Books, 1984.

"Meet the Theatre Union." *New Theatre*, February 1934.

Melosh, Barbara. *Engendering Culture: Manhood and Womanhood in New Deal Art and Theatre*. Washington, D.C.: Smithsonian Institution Press, 1991.

Mishler, Paul. "The Littlest Proletariat: American Communists and Their Children, 1922–1950." Ph.D. diss., Boston University, 1988.

Mitchell, Louise. "Note to Mr. Hopkins: Dancers Don't Think with Their Feet." *Daily Worker*, May 21, 1937.

"Modern Dance at the New York World's Fair." *Dance Observer*, May 1938.

"More News from the Martha Graham ANTA Tour." *Dance Observer*, March 1956.

Morgan, Barbara. *Martha Graham: Sixteen Dances in Photographs*. New York, Duell, Sloan and Pearce, 1941.

Nathanson, Lucile. "Making the Dance Scene." Interview with Jane Dudley. Dance Collection. New York Public Library for the Performing Arts.

———. "Making the Dance Today." Interview with Judith Delman. Dance Collection. New York Public Library for the Performing Arts.

Negro Spirituals. Filmed by the William Skipper Corporation, with an introduction by John Martin. 1959. Dance Collection. New York Public Library for the Performing Arts.

Nekola, Charlotte, and Paula Rabinowitz. *Writing Red: An Anthology of American Women Writers, 1930–1940*. New York: Feminist Press, 1987.

"New Dance Group." *New Theatre*, November 1934.

"New Dance Group." *Dance Observer*, February 1937.

"New Dance Group." *Dance Observer*, March 1940.

"New School Series: Nadia Chilkovsky of the Workers' Dance League." *Dance Observer*, August–September 1934.

Nochlin, Linda. "The Paterson Strike Pageant of 1913." In Bruce A. McConachie and Daniel Friedman, eds., *Theatre for Working-Class Audiences in the United States, 1830–1980*. Westport, Conn.: Greenwood Press, 1985.

North, Joseph, ed. *New Masses: An Anthology of the Rebel Thirties*. New York: International Publishers, 1969.

Ocko, Edna. "Artist and Audience." *New Theatre*, March 1937.

————. "The Dance Congress." *New Theatre*, July 1936.

————. (Eve Stebbins). "The Dance in America." *Dance Observer*, May 1936.

————. "The Dance League Recital." *New Theatre*, February 1935.

————. "Dance Reviews." *New Theatre*, December 1934.

————. Interview with Ellen Graff. New York City, June 14, 1989.

————. "Letters." *Dance Observer*, November 1935.

————. "Martha Graham Dances in Two Worlds." *New Theatre*, July 1935.

————. "New Dance Group." *New Theatre*, November 1934.

————. "The Revolutionary Dance Movement." *New Masses*, June 12, 1934.

————. "The Swastika Is Dancing." *New Theatre*, November 1935.

————. *Theatre Arts Committee (TAC)*. October 1938.

————. *Theatre Arts Committee (TAC)*. December 1938.

————. "Three Interviews with Russian Dancers." *Dance Observer*, January 1938.

————. "Whither Martha Graham?" *New Theatre*, April 1934.

O'Conner, John, and Lorraine Brown, eds. *Free, Adult, Uncensored: The Living History of the Federal Theatre Project*. Washington, D.C.: New Republic Books, 1978.

Olgin, Moissaye. "M. Olgin Describes Lenin Pageant." *Daily Worker*, January 26, 1928.

Peiss, Kathy. *Cheap Amusements: Working Women and Leisure in Turn-of-the-Century New York*. Philadelphia: Temple University Press, 1986.

Pells, Richard H. *Radical Visions and American Dreams: Culture and Social Thought in the Depression Years*. New York: Harper and Row, 1963.

Perpener, John. "African American Dance and Sociological Positivism During the 1930s." *Of, By, and For the People: Dancing on the Left in the 1930s*, ed. Lynn Garafola. *Studies in Dance History* 5, no. 1 (Spring 1994): 23–30.

"The Presentation of *Dance Magazine*'s 1957 Awards." *Dance Magazine*, April 1957.

Prickett, Stacey. "Dance and the Workers' Struggle." *Dance Research* 8, no. 1 (Spring 1990).

————. "From Workers' Dance to New Dance." *Dance Research* 7, no. 1 (Spring 1989).

————. "Marxism, Modernism and Realism: Politics and Aesthetics in the Rise of American Modern Dance." Ph.D. diss., Laban Centre for Movement and Dance, 1992.

————. "The People: Issues of Identity Within Revolutionary Dance." *Of, By and For the People: Dancing on the Left in the 1930s*, ed. Lynn Garafola. *Studies in Dance History* 5, no. 1 (Spring 1994): 14–22.

————. "Reviewing on the Left: The Dance Criticism of Edna Ocko." *Of, By and For the People: Dancing on the Left in the 1930s*, ed. Lynn Garafola. *Studies in Dance History* 5, no. 1 (Spring 1994): 65–103.

Rappaport, Roy A. "The Obvious Aspect of Ritual." In *Ecology, Meaning and Religion*. San Francisco: North Atlantic Books, 1979.

Read, Sir Herbert. *The Politics of the Unpolitical*. London: Routledge, 1946 [1943].

Remos, Susanne (Nadel). Interview with Karen Wickre. Laguna Hills, Calif., October 23, 1977. Library of Congress. Research Center for the Federal Theatre Project. Oral History Program.

Reuss, Richard. "Woody Guthrie and His Folk Tradition." *Journal of American Folklore*, July–September 1970.

Rhodes, Willard. "Folk Music Old and New." *Folklore and Society: Essays in Honor of Benj. A. Botkin*, ed. Bruce Jackson. Hatboro, Pa.: Folklore Associates, 1966.

Roberts, Adolphe W. "Tamiris Speaks Her Mind: More About the Concert Dancer's League." *Dance Magazine*, April 1931.

Rudhyar, Dane. "Art and Propaganda." *Dance Observer*, December 1936.

Rukeyser, Muriel. "The Dance Festival." *New Theatre,* July 1935.

Ruyter, Nancy Lee. *Reformers and Visionaries: The Americanization of the Art of Dance.* New York: Dance Horizons, 1979.

Sabin, Robert. "Jane Dudley, Sophie Maslow, William Bales." *Dance Observer,* April 1942.

Sandburg, Carl. *The People, Yes.* New York: Harcourt Brace Jovanovich, 1990 [1936].

Sands, Carl (Charles Seeger). "Workers Audience Applauds Gold's Poem Set to Music." *Daily Worker,* June 26, 1934.

Sayler, Oliver. *Revolt in the Arts.* New York: Brentano, 1930.

Schechner, Richard. *Between Theatre and Anthropology.* Philadelphia: University of Pennsylvania Press, 1985.

Schlundt, Christena. "Tamiris: A Chronicle of Her Dance Career, 1927–1955." *Studies in Dance History* 1, no. 1 (Fall–Winter 1989–1990).

Sears, David. "Breaking Down Harmonica Breakdown." *Ballet Review,* Winter 1984.

Seeger, Charles. "Grass Roots for American Composers." *Modern Music,* March–April 1939.

Segal, Edith. *Be My Friend and Other Poems for Boys and Girls.* New York: Citadel Press, 1952.

———. "Directing the New Dance." *New Theatre,* May 1935.

———. Interview with Leslie Farlow. Dance Collection. New York Public Library for the Performing Arts.

———. Interview with Ellen Graff. New York City, December 4, 1991.

———. Interview with Bob Heisler and Judee Rosenbaum. Kinderland Reunion Journal, n.d. Vertical Files. Tamiment Library, New York University.

———. Interview with Bea Lemisch. Oral History of the American Left. Camp Midland Collection. Tamiment Library, New York University.

———. "Kurt Jooss." *New Theatre,* January 1934.

———. *Poems and Songs for Ethel and Julius Rosenberg.* New York: National Committee to Reopen the Rosenberg Case, 1983.

———. *Take My Hand: Poems and Songs for Lovers and Rebels.* New York: Dialog Publications, 1969.

Selden, Elizabeth. *The Dancer's Quest.* Berkeley: University of California Press, 1935.

Shapiro, David, ed. *Social Realism: Art As a Weapon.* New York: Frederick Ungar, 1973.

Shelley, Mary Jo. "Workers' Dance League." *Dance Observer,* January 1935.

Sherman, Jane. *The Drama of Denishawn Dance.* Middletown, Conn.: Wesleyan University Press, 1979.

Showalter, Elaine. "Critical Cross-Dressing: Male Feminists and the Woman of the Year." *Raritan,* Spring 1983, pp. 130–149.

Siegel, Marcia B. *Days on Earth: The Dance of Doris Humphrey.* New Haven, Conn.: Yale University Press, 1987.

———. *The Shapes of Change: Images of American Dance.* Berkeley: University of California Press, 1979.

Soares, Janet. *Louis Horst: Musician in a Dancer's World.* Durham, N.C.: Duke University Press, 1992.

Sokolow, Anna. Interview with Barbara Newman. February 1974, May 1975. Dance Collection. New York Public Library for the Performing Arts.

Sorell, Walter. *Hanya Holm: Biography of an Artist.* Middletown, Conn.: Wesleyan University Press, 1979 [1969].

Stearns, Marshall, and Jean Stearns. *Jazz Dance: The Story of American Vernacular Dance.* New York: Schirmer Books, 1979 [1964].

Stewart, Virginia. "German Letter." *Dance Observer,* October 1935.

Stewart, Virginia, and Merle Armitage. *Modern Dance.* New York: Dance Horizons, 1970 [1935].

Stodelle, Ernestine. *Deep Song: The Dance of Martha Graham.* New York: Schirmer Books, 1984.

Stott, William. *Documentary Expression and Thirties America.* Chicago: University of Chicago Press, 1986 [1973].

The Strange Funeral in Braddock, performed by Elie Siegmeister and Mordecai Bauman. San Francisco: New Music, c. 1936.

Stratyner, Barbara. "Significant Historical Events . . . Thrilling Dance Sequences: Communist Party Pageants in New York, 1937." *Of, By, and For the People: Dancing on the Left in the 1930s,* ed. Lynn Garafola. *Studies in Dance History* 5, no. 1 (Spring 1994): 31–37.

Strong, Roy. *Art and Power.* Berkeley: University of California Press, 1984.

"Summing Up." *Dance Observer,* June–July 1939.

Susman, Warren I. *Culture as History: The Transformation of American Society in the Twentieth Century.* New York: Pantheon Books, 1984.

Szanto, George. *Theatre and Propaganda.* Austin: University of Texas Press, 1978.

Tamiris, Helen. *Negro Spirituals.* Film produced by the William Skipper Corporation, with an introduction by John Martin. 1959. Dance Collection. New York Public Library for the Performing Arts.

———. "Tamiris in Her Own Voice: Draft of an Autobiography." *Studies in Dance History* 1, no. 1 (Fall–Winter 1989–90).

Taper, Bernard. *Balanchine: A Biography.* New York: Times Books, 1984.

Taylor, Ralph. "Workers Dance League." *Dance Observer,* February 1935.

Tehranchian, Hassan. "Agit-Prop Theatre: Germany and the Soviet Union." Ph.D. diss., New York University, 1982.

Terkel, Studs. *Hard Times: An Oral History of the Great Depression.* New York: Pantheon Books, 1970.

Terry, Walter. *The Dance in America.* New York: Harper and Row, 1971 [1956].

Thatcher, Molly Day. "Stanislavsky's Method of Acting," as arranged from Chekhov's notes. *New Theatre,* December 1934, January 1935.

Tish, Pauline (Bubrick). "Remembering Helen Tamiris." *Dance Chronicle* 17, no. 3 (1994).

Tomko, Linda J. "The Settlement House and the Playhouse: Cultivating Expressive Dance in Early Twentieth-Century New York City." Fifth Hong Kong International Dance Conference, July 15–28, 1990. *Conference Papers,* vol. 2.

Trailblazers of Modern Dance, directed by Emile Ardolino. Dance in America. Public Broadcasting System, 1977.

Verne, Mignon. "Observer or Partisan?" *New Theatre,* November 1934.

Veyne, Paul. *Writing History.* Middletown, Conn.: Wesleyan University Press, 1984 [1971].

Vickery, Catherine. "*American Document* Tours America." *Dance Observer,* April 1939.

Ware, Susan. *Beyond Suffrage: Women in the New Deal.* Cambridge, Mass.: Harvard University Press, 1981.

Warren, Larry. *Anna Sokolow: The Rebellious Spirit.* Princeton, N.J.: Dance Horizons, 1991.

Watkins, Mary. "Concert Dancers Unite in Battle-Array to Combat Lions in the Pathway of the Sunday Recital." *New York Herald Tribune,* March 16, 1930.

Weisstuch, Mark Wolf. "The Theatre Union, 1934–1937: A History." Ph.D. diss., City University of New York, 1982.

"We Visit Martha Graham." *Dynamics,* May 1934.

Whitfield, Stephen J. *The Culture of the Cold War.* Baltimore: Johns Hopkins University Press, 1991.

Wilder, Lucy. "Stage for Dancers." *Dance Observer,* April 1952.

Williams, Jay. *Stage Left.* New York: Charles Scribner's Sons, 1974.

Wirth, Nicholas. "Mary Wigman, Fascist." *New Theatre,* August 1935.

Woloch, Nancy. *Women and the American Experience.* New York: Alfred A. Knopf, 1984.

"Workers' Dance League." *Dance Observer,* March 1935.

"Workers' Dance League." *New Theatre,* January 1934.

"Workers' League in Group Dances." *New York Times,* December 24, 1934.

Worster, Donald. *Dust Bowl: The Southern Plains in the 1930s.* New York: Oxford University Press, 1979.

"WPA and the Arts." *Washington Post,* May 3, 1938.

Wylie, Grace. "Dance Convention." *New Theatre,* July–August 1934.

———. "A Reply from the New Dance Group." *New Theatre,* September–October 1933.

Index

Numbers in italics refer to illustrations. Locations are in New York City unless otherwise indicated.

Ellen Graff is Assistant Professor in the Department of Dance at
Barnard College, Columbia University.

Library of Congress Cataloging-in-Publication Data
Graff, Ellen.
Stepping left : dance and politics in New York City, 1928–1942 /
Ellen Graff.
Includes bibliographical references (p.   ) and index.
ISBN 0-8223-1953-5 (alk. paper). — ISBN 0-8223-1948-9
(pbk. : alk. paper)
1. Dance—Political aspects—New York (State)—New York—
History—20th century.   I. Title.
GV1624.5.N4G73   1997
792.8′09747′109043—dc21   96-50908   CIP